# SEARCHING FOR LEADERSHIP:
# SECRETARIES TO CABINET IN CANADA

Edited by Patrice Dutil

Although the subject of leadership is widely studied and debated, it has never attracted much attention in relation to the public sector. *Searching for Leadership* is the first book to examine the evolving role of the highest-ranking public servant both in Ottawa and in Canada's provinces and territories, namely, the secretary to cabinet or the clerk of the Executive Council.

Arguing that the leadership role of the secretary to cabinet must be appreciated and understood in light of modern management practices and the centralization of administrative procedures, the contributors to this volume study the position from a variety of angles, employing structural approaches, reviews of both historical and recent literature on the topic, and biographical case studies of influential secretaries to cabinet. Analysing the role of secretaries to cabinet in Ottawa as well as in Alberta, Saskatchewan, Quebec, and Ontario, the contributors detail the complex roles, key functions, and political impact of these influential public servants, highlighting the ways in which the leadership skills of secretaries to cabinet have both changed and responded to change.

An important contribution to our understanding of Canadian governance and public management, *Searching for Leadership* is essential reading for scholars and students in political science, history, and public administration and management, as well as for public servants.

PATRICE DUTIL is an associate professor in the Department of Politics and Public Administration at Ryerson University.

**IPAC** The Institute of Public Administration of Canada

**IAPC** L'Institut d'administration publique du Canada

**The Institute of Public Administration of Canada Series in Public Management and Governance**

Editor: Luc Bernier

This series is sponsored by the Institute of Public Administration of Canada as part of its commitment to encourage research on issues in Canadian public administration, public-sector management, and public policy. It also seeks to foster wider knowledge and understanding among practitioners, academics, and the general public.

For a list of books published in the series, see page 251.

EDITED BY PATRICE DUTIL

# Searching for Leadership

## Secretaries to Cabinet in Canada

IPAC IAPC
The Institute of
Public Administration of Canada
L'Institut d'administration
publique du Canada

UNIVERSITY OF TORONTO PRESS
Toronto  Buffalo  London

© University of Toronto Press Incorporated 2008
Toronto Buffalo London
www.utppublishing.com
Printed in Canada

ISBN 978-0-8020-9889-4 (cloth)
ISBN 978-0-8020-9592-3 (paper)

Printed on acid-free paper

---

**Library and Archives Canada Cataloguing in Publication**

Searching for leadership : secretaries to cabinet in Canada / edited
by Patrice Dutil.

(Institute of Public Administration of Canada series in public
management and governance)
ISBN 978-0-8020-9889-4 (bound).   ISBN 978-0-8020-9592-3 (pbk.)

1. Government executives – Canada.   2. Government executives –
Canada – Provinces.   3. Leadership – Canada.   4. Canada. Privy
Council Office – Officials and employees.   5. Executive advisory
bodies – Canada – Provinces – Officials and employees.   I. Dutil,
Patrice A., 1960–   II. Series.

JL93.S43 2008      352.24'322930971      C2008-901780-3

---

Financial support from the Canada School of Public Service for this book is
gratefully acknowledged. The views expressed herein are not necessarily
those of the Canada School of Public Service or of the Government of
Canada.

University of Toronto Press acknowledges the financial assistance to its
publishing program of the Canada Council for the Arts and the Ontario
Arts Council.

University of Toronto Press acknowledges the financial support for its
publishing activities of the Government of Canada through the Book
Publishing Industry Development Program (BPIDP).

*In memory of Joseph Galimberti,*
*Executive Director of the Institute of Public Administration of Canada*
*(1975–2006)*

# Contents

## PART THREE: LEADERS IN ACTION

# Acknowledgments

This book stems from a 'Leadership Lessons of Secretaries to Cabinet' conference held over two days in Toronto in May 2005. It was an unprecedented event, both because of its theme and because ten of the occupants of the position of cabinet secretary at the time were either speakers or participants. The conference attracted close to 250 people from all parts of Canada and many of the papers presented were provocative and insightful. Collectively they pointed not only to the urgent need to understand better the kind of leadership that scholars, politicians, and members of the public sector expect secretaries to cabinet to exercise, but also to the quality of scholarship that can be generated in such a potentially rich area.

In the aftermath of the conference, many who attended recommended that the proceedings be collected in book form. The challenge was taken up and I am indebted to the contributors whose papers are contained in this volume. They were generous with their time and knowledge and showed great patience in seeing this book through to publication. Their essays, I am confident, will help to launch a new field of inquiry.

I am also indebted to members of the Board of Directors of the Institute of Public Administration of Canada (IPAC), who supported without fail my efforts to organize the conference and the book that arose out of it. Among them were Jocelyn Soulière of the government of Saskatchewan, who was president of IPAC in 2005, and Michael Fenn, deputy minister of security in the government of Ontario, who chaired the research committee of IPAC at the time.

My colleagues and friends at IPAC made sure this venture would be accomplished with success and good cheer: Pia Bruni, Doug Dawson,

Gabriella Ciampini, Robin Harrison, Diana Ivancic, George Khoury, Elisabeth Laviolette, Ann Masson, Rosalie McKenzie, Christine Michaty, Jane Serrano, and Marisa Rosati have earned more praise and thanks than I could ever utter. Michael McConkey, the research officer at the time, also played an invaluable role in helping to assemble the manuscript. Thanks go to Gabriel Sekaly, IPAC's CEO, and Wendy Feldman, director of research, for their unequivocal support of the IPAC publishing program and their encouragement as we finalized this volume. Publication of this book was also made possible by a manuscript-preparation grant from Ryerson University. I am grateful to Dr Carla Cassidy, dean of the Faculty of Arts, for this vital support.

The 'Leadership Lessons of Secretaries to Cabinet' conference was Joseph Galimberti's last big event at IPAC before he passed away suddenly in April 2006, ending a thirty-year career as the institute's executive director. Joe was the first person with whom I shared my idea for such a conference and I will always remember his immediate enthusiasm for the project and his help in securing support for it. I had many great conversations with Joe over the six years we worked together and relished our discussion of public administration, politics, and global affairs. I'm sorry he is not around to tease me about the strengths and weaknesses of this book.

A word of thanks to the many friends across the country who helped produce the list of holders of the office of 'clerk' or 'secretary' in our collective past, as well as the anonymous reviewers whose comments strengthened every part of the manuscript, is in order. Finally, my gratitude goes to the University of Toronto Press: to Virgil Duff, executive editor, for his unflagging support of the project; to Anne Laughlin, managing editor, for organizing the production; and to Curtis Fahey, who copy edited nine writers with equal measures of harshness and sensitivity. We are all the better for it.

Patrice Dutil
Toronto
April 2008

# Contributors

**Luc Bernier** is professor at the École nationale d'administration publique, Quebec, and a former president of the Institute of Public Administration of Canada. His publications include (with Guy Lachapelle and Pierre Tremblay, eds.) *Le processus budgétaire au Québec* (Quebec: Presses de l'université du Québec, 1999), *De Paris à Washington: la politique internationale du Québec* (Quebec: Presses de l'université du Québec, 1996), and (with Keith Brownsey and Michael Howlett), *Executive Styles in Canada: Cabinet Structures and Leadership Practices in Canadian Government* (Toronto: University of Toronto Press, 2005).

**Jacques Bourgault** is professor of political science at the Université du Québec à Montréal and adjunct professor at the École nationale d'administration publique. A former president of the Institute of Public Administration of Canada, he is the author of numerous studies. His most recent publications include *Horizontalité et gestion publique* (Quebec: Presses de l'université Laval, 2002) and, with Henry Mintzberg, *Managing Publicly* (Toronto: Institute of Public Administration of Canada, 2000).

**Keith Brownsey** is professor of public policy at Mount Royal College in Calgary. His recent publications include (with Luc Bernier and Michael Howlett) *Executive Styles in Canada: Cabinet Structures and Leadership Practices in Canadian Government* (Toronto: University of Toronto Press, 2005) and (with Michael Howlett) *The Provincial State in Canada* (Peterborough, Ont.: Broadview Press, 2001).

**Patrice Dutil** is associate professor in the Department of Politics and Public Administration at Ryerson University in Toronto. He was director of research at the Institute of Public Administration of Canada from 1999 to 2006. The founder of the *Literary Review of Canada*, he is the author of *The Politics of Liberal Progressivism: Godfroy Langlois and the Liberal Party of Quebec* (Montreal: Robert Davies Publishing, 1995).

**Bryan Evans** is associate professor in the Department of Politics and Public Administration at Ryerson University in Toronto. He is the author of numerous articles and (with John Shields) of *Shrinking the State: Globalization and Public Administration 'Reform'* (Halifax: Fernwood, 1998).

**Ruth Hubbard** is senior research fellow of the Centre on Governance at the University of Ottawa. A senior partner in the consulting firm Invenire, she served as deputy minister in a number of federal government ministries and was president of the Public Service Commission from 1994 to 1999. Recently, she published, with Gilles Paquet, *Gomery's Blinders and Canadian Federalism* (Ottawa: University of Ottawa Press, 2007).

**Gilles Paquet** is professor emeritus at the University of Ottawa, a senior research fellow of its Centre on Governance, and the editor-in-chief of www.optimumonline.ca. His recent publications include (with Ruth Hubbard), *Gomery's Blinders and Canadian Federalism* (Ottawa: University of Ottawa Press, 2007), *The New Neo-Governance: A Baroque Approach* (Ottawa: University of Ottawa Press, 2005), and *Governance through Social Learning* (Ottawa: University of Ottawa Press, 1999).

**Gregory P. Marchildon** is professor in the Johnson-Shoyama Graduate School of Public Policy at the University of Regina and a former deputy minister to the premier and secretary to cabinet in Saskatchewan. He also served as executive director of the Commission on the Future of Health Care in Canada. His publications include *Health Systems in Transition: Canada* (Toronto: University of Toronto Press, 2006) and *Profits and Politics: Beaverbrook and the Gilded Age of Canadian Finance* (Toronto: University of Toronto Press, 1996).

**Ken Rasmussen** is director of the Johnson-Shoyama Graduate School of Public Policy at the Univesity of Regina. He is the author of numerous articles on public-management reform, provincial politics, and public policy. He recently co-edited with David Siegel *Professionalism and Public Service: Essays in Honour of Kenneth Kernaghan* (Toronto: University of Toronto Press, 2008).

SEARCHING FOR LEADERSHIP:
SECRETARIES TO CABINET IN CANADA

# Introduction

PATRICE DUTIL

I first heard about the 'clerk of the Privy Council' as an undergraduate in Jack Granatstein's history class at York University in the early 1980s. At the time, he was knee-deep in writing his biography of Norman Robertson (who was clerk and secretary to cabinet from 1949 to 1952), and it often seemed – listening to Granatstein's memorably enthusiastic lectures – as though everything in Canada seemed to go across the clerk's desk, awaiting his judgment and directives.

Granatstein's chapter on Robertson and his work in documenting the work of various other clerks in *The Ottawa Men: The Civil Service Mandarins, 1935–1957* then constituted, with a few other, much shorter texts, the sum of the public knowledge about clerks and secretaries to cabinet. Meanwhile, the position was changing. If Granatstein succeeded in painting Norman Robertson as a man of influence (even though his tenure as secretary to cabinet was not particularly successful), what could be said of his successors, who held their posts when the offices of prime ministers and provincial premiers began exercising greater power and authority than ever before? Were the secretaries more influential in a new epoch of institutionalized cabinet, or less? How did the job change as powers shifted inexorably to the central agencies with which the secretary is now constantly in contact? More important, in an era that calls for leadership in order to improve performance and help organizations cope with change, have secretaries been allowed to hear the message, and, if they heard it, have they responded?

This book is about the highest-ranking position in Canada's government bureaucracies. It advances the hypothesis that secretaries to cabinet have effectively moved beyond mere 'management' to a position where they exercise 'leadership' and explores the theory and practice of how they have made that transition. Collectively, the articles do not argue that all secretaries to cabinet have been 'great' or even 'good' leaders. We simply do not have the evidence to measure their performance or make that sort of judgment. But, taken as a whole, the articles in this volume point to the increasingly visible role of the secretaries to cabinet and seek to open the debate on how they should lead in the particular Canadian context.

Typically, the individuals holding these positions wear three hats. First, they are called 'secretary to cabinet' or sometimes 'clerk to Privy Council' or 'clerk of the Executive Council.' In all cases, their job is to ensure that cabinet affairs are run smoothly: that agendas are set and supported, that decisions are recorded and followed up, and that cabinet documents are preserved. A second responsibility is to be deputy minister to the prime minister or premier who has named him or her to the position. In this task, the occupant is more than the 'first among equals' among deputy ministers. His or her task is to transmit the directives of the political executive, help orchestrate consensus so that the files keep progressing, and, of course, advise the first minister on a myriad of topics, crises, and issues. Finally, the occupants are also the de facto, if not titular, 'heads' of the public service of their jurisdiction. As such, the occupant is the chief executive officer of an important branch of government, the key spokesperson for the bureaucracy, its chief engineer (especially in leading succession planning for the senior ranks of the bureaucracy), and its champion and guardian before the cabinet.

The job of secretary to cabinet has been transformed since the 1960s. Those holding this position wield significant (if unreported) influence in steering the ship of state, but their position on deck is difficult to interpret. What persuasion they exercise is based upon the conventional authority of the position and the reservoir of trust, respect, and communication skill that they must draw upon – and constantly replenish. It is undeniably related to the personality and ambitions of the prime minister or premier whom they represent. And here a hard question must be asked: Are secretaries merely highly efficient agents of the political principals or are they in a genuine position of 'leadership'? It is a complex and demanding position, and each secretary inevitably shapes the job according to his or her own personalities, interests, and circumstances.

Besides analysing the position of secretary to cabinet, this volume aims to contribute to a more general discourse on leadership in the public sector in Canada, an area that has been the object of some rhetoric but precious little research. This lack of attention is consistent with the experience of other Westminster jurisdictions, and glaringly contrasts with the importance given to leadership in business and in studies of political figures.

Leadership studies have evolved dramatically in the last decade from the three main schools of thought on the matter. For centuries (arguably), leadership was mostly understood as a personality trait. Sometimes boiled down to a 'great man' theory that placed individuals and their decisions at the root of policy and political change, this school of thought still has traction. Books examining the psychology, intelligence, and ethics of particular leaders have abounded and remain endlessly fascinating. Even Chester Barnard, when breaking new ground with his *Functions of the Executive* in the 1930s, emphasized the 'moral' characteristics that distinguished private-sector leaders at the time.[1] Little interested in empirical evidence, Barnard was nonetheless an astute interpreter of leadership and many of his observations on what would be today considered 'values' as well as his emphasis on 'communication' are still valid. In this regard, Barnard's work resonates with some who insist that the particular values of the public service are what distinguishes it most from the private sector. The impact of such studies is echoed in all sorts of formal and informal 'leadership' programs that often start with 'know yourself' exercises of personality self-discovery as a first step in understanding how one's abilities can best be deployed in a position of command.

The search for heroic leaders had a distorting effect in that it did not shed light on the effective leadership displayed by others who were unknown to history textbooks. Nevertheless, Barnard's work did make a leap between understanding the traits of great leaders and examining how they actually behaved. So was born the second school, of which Barnard was also a member. Focusing on behavioural traits, this school was less inward-looking than its predecessor and instead examined leadership in its lived environment. The study of context, consequently, became all the more important. Any book with the 'life and times' subtitle offered a clue to its fundamental premise that, while personality mattered, the conjunction of personality with circumstance mattered equally: in other words, in addition to answering the 'who' of leadership, it also answered the 'why.' If some leaders, to play with the old adage, were *born* great, others were *called* to be great by particular events and conjunctions. Writing his influential *Leadership in Administration* in the 1950s, Philip Selznick (borrowing a good deal from Plato's *Politics*), emphasized the 'statesman' qualities of leaders that distinguished their behaviour from that of merely efficient managers. He argued that the qualities of the statesman could be learned and indeed had to be absorbed by all executives if they were to lead their organizations in adapting to changing environments.[2] Selznik's perspective also had a deep impact on the interpretation of public-sector leadership. Thirty years after Selznik, James Q. Wilson's *Bureaucracy* applied Selznik's idea of leadership to the public service because it described so well the work of institutional (as opposed to business) executives.[3]

In a larger context, leadership studies changed dramatically as technological change and global competition emerged as real factors in the 1960s. The voluminous leadership literature today still applies approaches that emphasize personality traits and behaviours with varying degrees, but it also has accented a new element: the climate in which leadership is incubated and fostered. Most typical of the thinking of this third school is Peter Drucker's interpretation of leadership as something far more than the role of a figurehead or protector of values: it is also, as he puts it bluntly in *The Effective Executive*, about 'doing things.'[4] In his *oeuvre*, the job of a leader is to ensure that competition and changing environments do not kill the business – to find the necessary tools to remain competitive and aggressive and to make the right decisions at the right time for the right reasons. In other words, to be a leader is less about conserving values and protecting a status quo than about asserting new values and applying older ones to new contexts. Drucker made room for discussions about values, cultures, and traditions, but his main contribution was to remind business leaders that their task is to ensure that their corporations are innovative, productive, and profitable. And so, if there has been a slight change in leadership theory over the years, it has been in asking the question of 'how' individuals lead, instead of the 'who' and the 'why.'

Drucker was the most influential, if indirect, figure in this third school on leadership, which focused more on the leader-follower exchange in order to understand better how leaders are (or, just as important, are not) 'effective.' Known for their 'situational' approach, observers of leadership who practise this method analyse the quality of the relationship that exists between leaders and their colleagues and subordinates. Chief among their intellectual contributions are the variants of the 'contingency theory' of leadership that emerged in the late 1960s to capture the fine detail of how it is that some individuals are more successful in leadership than others. The key theorist in this area was Fred Fiedler, who argued that particular situations are likely to affect a leader's effectiveness. Like many others, he maintained that the position of a leader matters. In other words, if a leader occupies the highest reaches of a bureaucracy, the dynamics of authority, power, and influence he exercises will be very different from those of a manager. Fiedler was particularly innovative in seeking to understand more fully the relationship between subordinates and leaders. He also looked at work relations and argued that the routine or non-routine tasks the subordinates had to perform would have an effect on their loyalty to the leader.[5]

Studies of leadership are not limited to organization and business theorists, however. One thinker in particular, James MacGregor Burns, has played an important role in shaping ideas on the subject by establishing a demanding test of leaders. In various books, but notably in *Leadership* (1978) and *Transforming Leadership* (2003), he theorizes that leaders can be classified in two broad categories, transactional or transformational. In the transactional category, Burns includes the vast majority of individuals who occupy leadership positions: people who use their positions to pursue the goals of their predecessors in a manner that is also very similar to theirs. Transformational leaders, in contrast, are ones who change the institutions, circumstances, and people they lead. Burns's theories have had a great impact. Following the parameters he set out, Bernard Bass and Noel Tichy have deepened the understanding of transformational leadership and sought to explain its manifestations as well as the conditions that allow it to thrive.[6]

The essays in this book apply various approaches to the study of the leadership of secretaries to cabinet and test the theories about institutional leadership. In Part One, the essays by Patrice Dutil and Jacques Bourgault explore the modern concepts of leadership and paint a broad canvas featuring the evolving functions of secretaries to cabinet and their multifaceted challenges. Dutil ranges through the literature of the last decade in search of clues to the personal and behavioural qualities that are typical of successful secretaries in the era of the 'New Public Management.' Bourgault focuses more on the microphysics of leadership situations faced by secretaries across a full spectrum of Canadian jurisdictions, but particularly at the federal level.

The three chapters in Part Two provide a longitudinal perspective on the institution of the 'clerk' as it has been transformed in three very different jurisdictions. Ruth Hubbard and Gilles Paquet offer a provocative examination of the complex intersections at which, historically, the clerk/secretary has had to operate in the government of Canada. Drawing upon the historical record, their essay nevertheless looks ahead: it speculates on the implications of the lessons that can be read into the unfolding of the future 'polycentric-networked' governance towards which Canada seems to be moving. Bryan Evans examines the evolution of the role of the secretary to cabinet in Ontario as complex problems of governance are increasingly managed from the centre. It is worth noting in this context that the evolution of the post of secretary to cabinet in the Canadian and Ontario governments has been fairly similar to that in the United Kingdom and in Australia. In other parts of the Commonwealth (New Zealand, notably) and in Saskatchewan, the position has sometimes been dismembered. The 'secretary to cabinet' in those jurisdictions is typically a mid-level functionary who performs the routine duties of keeping cabinet affairs running smoothly. The occupant is not the 'head of the public service' or 'deputy minister to the premier.' In the final chapter of Part Two, Gregory Marchildon, who himself occupied the position of deputy minister to the premier of Saskatchewan for six years, offers an examination of the particular circumstances of public-service leadership of his province. He makes clear that, while the Saskatchewan experience is unique, the person who holds the post of deputy to the premier plays the same critical role that the 'secretary' plays elsewhere.

In Part Three, the concluding section of the book, three essays look beyond structures to capture leadership as it was personified in the concrete *transformation* of the secretary's role. Keith Brownsey examines the part played by Harry Hobbs in reshaping the position in Alberta under the Peter Lougheed government; Ken Rasmussen describes the work of Wes Bolstad in Saskatchewan; and Luc Bernier studies the leadership of Guy Coulombe in Quebec. The three individuals were very different and the experience of each illuminates the political circumstances and administrative structures in which they evolved. All three remade the function of secretary to cabinet in the 1970s and applied their skills to transforming cabinet operations and assuming the leadership of their public services. This was a heady time in provincial affairs. Bureaucracies were growing and government expenses were mounting at the same time as economic problems of high unemployment and high inflation were proving impossible to master. In all cases, the premiers called on these individuals to help change the way cabinet government – and the public services that reported to it – could make decisions and enforce its will.

Context mattered in this regard, and Harry Hobbs, Wes Bolstad, and Guy Coulombe can all be seen as leaders whose conduct was shaped by their particular circumstances. They reported to premiers who were keen to build their provinces economically and socially and to affirm their jurisdictions in the presence of the threatening aspects of Trudeau federalism. In the case of Guy Coulombe, the election of the Parti Québécois (PQ) in November 1976 was especially challenging for the bureaucracy. Coulombe drew on traditions of non-partisanship and efficiency to ensure that the transition from a Liberal administration to a PQ one went smoothly and the new government of Quebec could function with aplomb.[7] The structures he installed in those critical days are recognizable thirty years later. Wes Bolstad was in a slightly different position, having served many years in the Saskatchewan public service before becoming deputy to Premier Allan Blakeney.[8] Working in close collaboration with the premier (who also boasted a long experience in public service and in Saskatchewan politics), Bolstad ushered in a modernization of the state apparatus that has survived the test of time. Finally, unlike Bolstad and Coulombe, who were drawn from the public service of their provinces, Harry Hobbs was an outsider: a businessman and trusted friend of the premier who had had no experience in government. Alberta was in the middle of an oil-industry shockwave that roiled every aspect of business and government in the province. Hobbs's leadership was cemented by the authority of the premier and, more important, by his quick mastery of other tasks proper to high leadership of institutions. He applied himself to understanding the traditions of the Alberta public service and used his personal influence to engineer a smooth relationship between a new Conservative political class and a bureaucracy that had worked for almost thirty years for Social Credit governments. Hobbs, Coulombe, and Bolstad proved that leadership mattered.

In interviews, past secretaries to cabinet have consistently defended their roles and also argued that their distinctive approaches to problems and opportunities demonstrated that their leadership functions were as undeniable as they were effective. Still, there are unanswered questions. It is hoped that the essays in this book will help shed some light on the phenomenon of public-service leadership, as well as on the more general issue of how the concept of leadership can be applied to the particular nature of the Canadian public sector.

NOTES

1  Chester Barnard, *The Functions of the Executive* (1938) (Cambridge, Mass.: Harvard University Press, 1964); Edward Boland Smith, 'Chester Barnard's Concept of Leadership,' *Educational Administration Quarterly*, 11, no. 3 (1975):

37–48. See also Larry D. Terry and Maxine G. Levin, 'Organizational Scepticism: The Modern Conception of Leadership and the Obsession with the New,' *Journal of Management History*, 4, no. 4 (1998): 303–17.

2  Philip Selznick, *Leadership in Administration: A Sociological Interpretation* (New York: Harper and Row, 1957).

3  James Q. Wilson, *Bureaucracy: What Government Agencies Do and Why They Do It* (New York: Basic Books, 1989).

4  Peter F. Drucker, *The Effective Executive* (New York: Harper and Row, 1966).

5  See Fred Fiedler, *A Theory of Leadership Effectiveness* (New York: McGraw-Hill, 1967), and Fred Fiedler and Joseph Garcia, *New Approaches to Effective Leadership: Cognitive Resources and Organizational Performance* (New York: John Wiley, 1987).

6  See B.M. Bass, *Leadership and Performance beyond Expectations* (New York : Free Press, 1985); *Bass & Stogdill's Handbook of Leadership: Theory, Research, Managerial Applications, 3rd Edition* (New York: Free Press, 1990); and B.M. Bass, Transformational Leadership: Industrial, Military, and Educational Impact (London: Lawrence Erlbaum Associates, 1998). See also, more recently: B.M. Bass, 'Two Decades of Research and Development in Transformational Leadership,' *European Journal of Work and Organizational Psychology*, 8, no. 1 (1999): 9–32; B.M. Bass et al., 'Predicting Unit Performance by Assessing Transformational and Transactional Leadership,' *Journal of Applied Psychology*, 88, no. 2 (2003): 207–18; Noel Tichy, *The Transformational Leader* (New York: Wiley, 1986); and Micha Popper, *Leaders Who Transform Society: What Drives Them and Why We Are Attracted* (Westport, Conn.: Praeger, 2005).

7  See Martine Tremblay, *Derrière les portes closes* (Montréal: Québec-Amérique, 2006), 70–1.

8  Allan Blakeney and Sandford Borins, *Political Management in Canada* (Toronto: McGraw-Hill Ryerson, 1992), chapter 3 and 103–4.

# PART ONE

## Leadership in Question

# 1 Searching for Leadership

PATRICE DUTIL

> You shall command more with years than with your weapons.
> – William Shakespeare, *Othello*, Act 1, Scene 2

The concept of leadership is not often associated with executives in the public service of Canada. No books focus on the topic; a survey of the key textbooks in public administration shows that their authors have likewise avoided it; and, as evidenced in the scholarly quarterlies, research in the area is sparse. The public service has not done much better. While many senior executives give ample lip service to the idea that 'leadership' is an idea that needs to be promoted (and in some cases have actually created offices dedicated to 'leadership'), their efforts have done little more than puzzle observers both inside and outside government.

One could argue that even the basic vocabulary of leadership is missing in public-service parlance. Distinct concepts of 'executives,' 'management,' 'entrepreneurship,' and 'leadership' are jumbled together, leaving concrete examples wanting. If leadership is everywhere, then it is nowhere. The clerks of Executive Council, or the secretaries to cabinet, the de facto chief executives of the public service, meanwhile work in obscurity, sheltered from assessment and study.

This is not unique to Canada. Few scholars in other Westminster-style governments have ever examined the position of the secretary to cabinet in terms of its leadership qualities.[1] The historian J.L. Granatstein examined the influence of two secretaries to cabinet in particular, Norman Robertson and Robert Bryce, but never used the word 'leadership' to describe their work.[2] Even occupants of the position have proven remarkably timid in describing their tasks and, more important, their influence. Gordon Robertson, who has written an admirable memoir of his distinguished career, devotes only a few pages to the tasks of the clerk of the Privy Council/secretary to cabinet, a post he occupied for no less than twelve years (1963–75), and even he shies away from describing 'leadership.'[3] Donald Savoie's influential studies on the central agencies of government have focused in part on the functions of the Privy Council and discussed the transformation of the role of the secretary to cabinet. In *Governing from the Centre*, he cites an interview with Mitchell Sharp, who had worked as a deputy minister before joining the Liberal Party and then served in the Pearson and Trudeau governments. 'I am not sure that we bothered too much with PCO [Privy Council Office],' Mitchell told Savoie. 'Putting aside [Jack] Pickersgill [who held the position in 1952–3 and who would soon become a key figure in the Liberal Party], secretaries to the cabinet were rather low-profile people and they didn't much bother you.'[4] Savoie interprets the role of the secretary to cabinet more in terms of an all-round 'fixer.'

In her study of the clerk of the Privy Council for the Commission of Inquiry into the Sponsorship Program and Advertising Activities (the Gomery Commission), Sharon Sutherland invokes the image of a critical 'mediator' and 'important problem solver' to describe the role of the secretary to cabinet.[5] 'Given the frequency of the Clerk's contacts with the Prime Minister, with the political staff in the Prime Minister's Office who support the Prime Minister in his or her political responsibilities, and with senior public service colleagues,' she writes, 'the Clerk is the centre of the most urgent and perhaps the single broadest information flow in Government.'[6] The Gomery Commission, however, recommended in its final report that the role of the secretary to cabinet be redefined by eliminating its 'head of the public service' and 'deputy minister to the prime minister' designations, a move that would effectively undercut the post's leadership potential.[7]

Neither Savoie nor Sutherland, both sharp observers of the clerk, ever use the word 'leadership' to define the work of the secretary to cabinet. This may not be surprising: government bureaucracies have always incubated strong consensus builders. It may be inevitable that the individuals who were chosen to fill the role were better known as quiet artisans of agreement, not as entrepreneurial decision makers who could establish visions, convince bureaucracies to make sacrifices, and, as many observers of leadership have put it, 'lead people where they don't want to go.' Based on an exhaustive study of 'receptivity' to leadership, B.S. Pawar and K.G. Eastman argue that organizations that are focused on efficiency, particularly technical predictability, and that have a highly bureaucratized form of governance are likely to resist any leadership that breaks with traditions.[8] Perhaps, as the noted leadership observer Jay Conger says, 'many organizations are simply not prepared for leadership. Conformity is more important to them than vision and risk taking.'[9]

## Parameters of Public-Sector Leadership

In Canada, at both the federal and provincial levels, secretaries to cabinet are undeniably the most powerful officials in government. They have all the hallmarks of leadership: they wield the influence and the authority necessary to affect how the bureaucracy chooses its priorities, builds its capacity, organizes itself for emergencies and longer-term issues, responds to political directives, and accounts for its progress in meeting them. At the same time, secretaries know that they evolve in a particularly limiting situation: they are the first servants of the state. Indeed, their role incarnates the conventional understanding that has been struck between the political and administrative spheres of governments in Canada: that the bureaucracy's mandate is to advise cabinet but, above all, execute its will. It is the secretary to cabinet's job to absorb the cabinet's wishes and determine how that body's hunches, impressions, and outright directives will be acted upon.

Secretaries to cabinet therefore have an enormous amount of discretion in carrying out their duties, and that level of freedom is calibrated in terms of their leadership abilities. A secretary to cabinet leads the bureaucracy in offering advice to the cabinet. He or she will time the counsel, measure its dosage, and sometimes withhold it. At the same time, he or she will instruct the bureaucracy on the priorities of cabinet, again quietly advising particular deputies to take a lead on an issue or indeed to limit their involvement. They themselves will take the lead in acting when legislation does not exist or is deficient. To be the secretary to cabinet is surely to undertake gate-keeping duties: to be clear, forthright, and endlessly open to advice and feedback. Should it be recognized as more than that? Do secretaries to cabinet exercise more than transactional functions and actually lead in the sense of transforming government? The position seems on the very cusp of the discussions and debates that have taken place in Canada and elsewhere on the nature of leadership, management, modernization, and accountability of the bureaucracy.

Many scholars have tried to understand leadership by placing its various manifestations on a continuum ranging from merely 'transactional' to 'transformational.'[10] The leadership of secretaries to cabinet – most of whom officially carry the title of 'head of the public service' and are the de facto chief executives of the administration – can undoubtedly be put to the same test if observers will indeed consider them as 'leaders.' Their role is to transmit faithfully the wishes of the prime minister and of the cabinet and to ensure that the decision-making apparatus is sensitive and responsive to the political will. They themselves should not be deemed to be 'responsible.' The task of the secretary to cabinet is not to assume responsibility; it is to act responsibly on the decisions of cabinet.

Leadership must be the test for secretaries to cabinet, yet the office may not be equipped with the necessary tools to exercise this function. Unlike private-sector CEOs, secretaries have only limited inducements to offer in exchange for dynamic, extraordinary commitment to improving government performance. They have few financial rewards to transmit, and inspiring words of recognition go only so far. They have the power to promote and demote but exercise this discretion among a group of tenured senior executive peers. Moreover, they must convince the members of this group to streamline their operations, improve their corporate performance, fight complacency, manage risk and innovation, and maintain a consensus that will withstand crisis and political meddling. Based on their expertise and their experience, they must make a visible contribution towards defining the synthesis of what the government wants.

To perform all these roles, secretaries to cabinet must exercise another defining quality: they must *search* for leadership. Leaders themselves, they cannot be content with securing followers only. They must encourage leadership within the public sector that they lead, constantly looking there for leaders who, with little incentive, will help define and transmit what the state wishes and build within their offices and administration an effective commitment to the secretary's work and mission. At the same time, they must interpret the clear signals given by the prime minister (or his office) and cabinet members and communicate these signals to peers in the senior ranks of the bureaucracy. Only by doing all of this can they then implement the real agenda of a government.

Observers have seen the secretaries as a pinnacle expression of any government manager's functions, an interpretation anchored in traditional perspectives of public administration. According to this view, they are merely the most senior administrators of a chain of command that executes particular tasks. In the words of management scholars like Henri Fayol, who first identified and articulated the functions of managers, their job is to forecast, organize, coordinate, command, and control (tasks summarized affectionately as FORCC) the routine work of a cabinet office. In the 1930s and 1940s, senior managers were seen as having a few more roles. Luther Gulick and Lyndall Urwich popularized their tasks with the acronym POSDCORB (planning, organizing, staffing, directing, coordinating, reporting, and budgeting). The control of the unit was increasingly done through the exercise of formal authority, something the historians of the period have confirmed as the state, particularly the government of Canada, assumed more duties, responsibilities, and services in the creation of social-welfare infrastructure.

If the position was, for a long time, a seemingly passive, administrative one, it has become over the past thirty years more assertive. Yet the leadership label seems to be resisted.[11] James McGregor Burns's comment that 'leadership is the most observed and least understood phenomena on earth' would seem to apply to the Canadian situation.[12] One of the most insightful students of public-sector leadership, Robert D. Bhen of the John F. Kennedy School of Government at Harvard University, notes that 'the leadership question is not ... the question about government performance that is usually asked.' He continues: 'Traditionally, we have asked the systems question. Rather than develop public managers with the leadership capacity to improve the performance of their agencies, we have sought to create performance systems that will impose such improvements. We have sought to create government-wide schemes that will somehow require performance from all departments, agencies and bureaus. Thus we have tended (if only implicitly) to ignore the leadership question.'[13]

As government operations become more complex and as turnover in Parliament accelerates to the point where cabinets often assume power with few individuals having first-hand experience of the operations of a modern state bureaucracy, the role of secretaries to cabinet must be defined and its *leadership* dimension reappraised urgently both in theory and in practice.

Over the past two decades, a number of scholars have written incisively about the nature of leadership in the public sector and about the need to understand it. Robert Behn has been among the most eloquent, advocating that public managers have an 'obligation' to lead if only to compensate for the imperfections of the checks and balances of the American system. He argues that public managers have 'expertise, and we should not ask them to wait quietly and politely until they are formally asked for their judgments. Rather, it should be an explicit part of the public manager's job to exercise leadership.'[14]

In her study for the Gomery Commission, however, Sharon Sutherland observes that even in their role as head of the public service, 'it seems clear from the brevity of the establishing clause and from the lack of duties and resources attached to the role that it was never intended to be an executive function.'[15]

Is it possible to define the role of the office of secretary to cabinet so that it actually resembles what its occupants do on a daily basis, and, in the process, recognize that this official invariably plays a leadership role as 'head of the public service'? I believe that it is, but first the leadership of secretaries to cabinet must be put into context. While leadership certainly is not new, the understanding of leadership in public bureaucracies is only in its infancy. Armies have been led into battle since the dawn of humanity, and history is dotted with telling examples of individuals who have led family, friends, and nations into new ways of thinking, doing, communicating, and governing. What makes leadership so much more interesting today is that it is easily contested and therefore much more difficult to sustain. Given the shelf load of books that is produced every month on leadership, it is clear that insights into this phenomenon is earnestly sought, and not necessarily among executives only.[16] Indeed, 'administration' and 'management' seem to have almost completely surrendered to the concept of 'leadership' as it becomes less of a description of authority and more of a 'skill.' A survey of 522 mostly private-sector Canadian human-resource managers in 2003 found that 31 per cent of respondents identified leadership as the most important 'skill' required of employees. When asked to project the importance of that skill to the year 2013, 39 per cent indicated that leadership would be the top skill.[17]

The literature on leadership is vast and endlessly varied, but it is possible to boil down the *skills* of leadership to six broad categories that apply to the work of the top executives working in Canada's public sector.

## Public-Sector Leadership Skills

*Understanding Issues*

Although there is often a dispute as to the degree of knowledge that executives should possess (in comparison, say, with an ability to manage processes), there is little doubt that executives with little knowledge of their business are not likely to sustain good performance. Leadership is tested in this regard as issues become more and more complex, both in terms of technologies and in terms of the political ramifications of new methods. Leaders must understand product but also public relations, policy issues, and accountability. Moreover, they must have the ability to acquire new knowledge on the run, keep pace with the brisk rate of change, and be able to absorb information from a wide variety of sources, ranging from scholarly analyses to water-cooler conversations. As well, the ability to communicate this understanding – to exercise in the public sector what W. Chan Kim and Renée Mauborgne call 'tipping point leadership' by putting 'key managers face-to-face with the operational problems so that the managers cannot evade reality' – is also critical.[18]

Larry D. Terry has introduced an interesting dimension of leadership in public bureaucracies that is rooted in a deep understanding of 'issues': that of administrator as 'conservator.' 'The primary function of bureaucratic leaders,' he argues, 'is to protect and maintain administrative institutions in a manner that promotes or is consistent with constitutional processes, values and beliefs.'[19] He outlines a continuum of leadership roles performed by administrative conservators as well as their three primary functions: conserving mission, conserving values, and conserving support. Among these functions, he sees the 'conserving mission' as central and even as a form of 'statesmanship'[20]: leaders are 'entrusted with the responsibility of preserving and nurturing authority embodied in legal mandates that determine the mission of public bureaucracies.' Preserving core values, however, is self-descriptive. By conserving support, both internal and external, leaders must, Terry says, devote themselves to building and maintaining commitment among internal interest groups. At the same time, Terry is careful to point to the dangers of 'administrative conservatorship,' warning that missions can be 'distorted and abused' by managers who prefer to avoid change and thus impair the bureaucracy's ability to respond to newly emerging problems and conditions.[21]

Not so long ago, the success of public administrators would be measured by the development of a solution, their leadership being focused on the examination of social and economic needs and financial analysis. But now the knowledge base of governments is changing. The 'New Public Management' added consumers' concerns to the factors requiring consideration and made use of ethnography to learn more about such concerns. Today, public administrators must develop services with features that might potentially appeal to deciders and citizens alike. The process takes time, expertise, and a well-rounded approach that will respond to a broad range of demands. Governments are called to adopt a new model of thinking to promote innovation and open up opportunities.

Justin Menkes, in his recent book *Executive Intelligence: What All Great Leaders Have*,[22] cites a range of private-sector leaders who thrived because they were great critical thinkers possessed of superior reasoning and problem-solving skills. It was this ability to create solutions tailored to suit each situation that made them different. Menkes defines more than a dozen critical skills, including the capacity to distinguish between primary and secondary goals, anticipate probable outcomes as well as unintended consequences, and detect the underlying agendas of others. These are easily recognizable in the work of senior executives in the public sector.

Much along the same lines, but this time in an applied public-sector context, Alex Matheson and Hae-Sang Kwon argue that 'if governments are to adapt successfully to the changing needs of their society, they require better analytical and empirical tools, and more sophisticated strategies than [they] have generally had to date.'[23] Claiming that many government 'reforms' had more to do with sloganeering than with concrete actions, they point to the levers that leaders had to pull in order to bring about the transformations of public bureaucracies that would make them responsive to emerging challenges. All these cases involved functions of central agencies where secretaries to cabinet play decisive roles. The first was a call for major changes to the budgeting and financial-management processes that would enhance their accuracy, clearly describe risk and response to risk, and bring clarity in reporting. The second lever involved effecting major changes to the civil service in terms of its organization and flexibility. Matheson and Kwon state that the creation and closure of organizations was slow, frequently poorly conceived, and too often untied to concrete performance objectives. Part of the challenge here is to rethink the powers of departments vis-à-vis the central agencies and commit to the complicated task of devolving decision-making power instead of consistently centralizing it.

These levers need to be operated judiciously with a clear sense of the problem being addressed and an understanding of its long-term dynamic. Unless reform uses one or more of these levers, it is most likely to be incapable of systemic change. Instruments like strategic

planning, evaluation, information technology, performance management, management information, performance pay, and statements of
missions and values can be useful only if they are used in support of the
systemic levers named above.

Public-sector leaders are therefore not much different in this regard
from their private-sector counterparts. Governments must provide low-
cost, high-quality, innovative services. That driving need makes innovative thinking necessary. If engineering, control, and technology were
once the central tenets of public-sector culture, then anthropology, creativity, and obsession with unmet needs will inform the future.

*Creating Visions and Setting Priorities*

The ability to 'create a vision' for the organization and to identify both
the opportunities and the threats that await it are critical for leaders.
Indeed, the literature confirms that this is the sine qua non of leadership.
Leaders distinguish themselves in their ability to anticipate changes in
the environment of the organization and adopt ways to accommodate
them, and no less critical is the ability to communicate the organization's vision. This is especially true for organizations in trouble and in
need of transformation.[24]

In an insightful essay, Allen Schick emphasizes the need for effective,
visionary leadership in the reform of public management. 'Successful
reform does not just happen by itself; it depends on leaders who exploit
opening and give impetus and direction to change,' he writes. Effective
leaders make opportunities happen by shaping public opinion, creating mechanisms that will bring innovative new talent into government,
and reaching beyond the 'safe and traditional constituencies' to create
networks that will support change and take the managerial risks that
will broaden the 'possibility of change.'[25]

*Managing Competency*

How is visionary leadership recognized? Since the 1990s, Jim Collins
has argued that the best approach to leadership is one based on performance results. He attaches the 'Level 5' label to the highest reaches in
the hierarchy of executive capabilities. Leaders at the other four levels
can produce high levels of success but not enough to elevate their organizations from mediocrity to sustained excellence. Collins identifies the
creation of a 'culture of discipline' as a particularly significant accom-

plishment. Leadership, however, is the critical factor, especially when it comes to improving the performance of an organization. 'Good-to-great transformations don't happen without Level 5 leaders at the helm,' he writes. 'They just don't.'[26]

In a study of department secretaries in a variety of Westminster systems, R.A.W. Rhodes and P. Weller conclude that they 'managed' a lot more than they used to, although they admit that the meaning of the phrase 'is less clear.'[27] 'Departmental secretaries,' they argue, 'must now account for how well their departments are doing. Client focus, greater emphasis on outcomes, responsibility to meet targets, performance outcomes, all need a degree of management attention ... The department secretaries must ensure the department "delivers."'[28]

This theme has attracted the attention of some of the most important theorists of leadership. One of the most influential is John P. Kotter. In his landmark piece 'What Leaders Really Do,' he argues that leaders indeed do manage critical issues such as planning and budgeting, but that what distinguishes them is their ability to prepare their organizations for change and to guide them through it. Kotter goes further by identifying one particular task: aligning people. By this he means ensuring that the right people are promoted to the right positions, and also that they are consistently motivated by a compelling vision of an organization facing change. Kotter insists that what makes leaders different is ultimately their ability to sustain a culture of leadership across all ranks.[29] Similarly, Peter Drucker defines leadership as the task of setting priorities and – more important – 'sticking' to them, across the ranks: 'For [a private-sector] CEO, the priority task might be redefining the company's mission. For a unit head, it might be redefining the unit's relationship with headquarters ... After completing the original top-priority task, the executive resets priorities rather than moving on to number two from original lists. He asks, "What must be done now?" This generally results in new and different priorities.'[30] Drucker assigns a number of key priorities to these executives: taking responsibility for decisions, taking responsibility for communicating, and focusing on opportunities.

In a discussion of public-sector leadership that uses the case of U.S. General Colin Powell, Oren Harari describes Powell's techniques in making individuals perform and his ability to articulate vivid goals and values. He talks about changing before being forced to, putting people over plans, credibility of leadership, integrity of organization, and victory in performance.[31] W. Chan Kin and Renée Mauborgne point to the same skills in their discussion of Bill Bratton's successive transformations of no less than six police forces in the United States.[32]

Leaders invariably have an ability to manage the processes that will bring the results anticipated, mainly by their sound reading of the evolving environment and the objectives set by their organization. The capacity to organize to respond to crisis, organizational awareness, promotion of teamwork and partnering, building institutional resources to deal with emerging situations – all are critical skills. Inevitably, too, leadership means managing a team.

Leaders display their effectiveness when they noticeably spark passion in the work performed by their supervisors, colleagues, and subordinates. They have a knack for getting commitment and cooperation from those who work around them. They make themselves available and visible and devote a good portion of their time to developing and mentoring their staffs. They are trusted. A key characteristic of leaders seems to be an obsession for aligning talent with tasks and succession planning.[33] It goes without saying that leaders tend to excel in managing projects and choosing priorities. They typically have superior communication skills and are quick to identify the causes of poor performance in their organization.

Many observers of modern management have argued that managing competence must be the constant task of leaders, and that leaders will distinguish themselves by ensuring that their organizations are constantly learning. Certainly, there seems to be agreement in the Anglo-American world on the need for a particular brand of education that will sustain leadership in the public sector. In Canada, two senior members of the Office of the Auditor General have argued that public-sector organizations can learn but only if effective leadership allows it to happen.[34] Brian J. Cook, writing in an American context, points to the need for better political education for senior public managers so as to improve their ability to lead.[35] Don Dunoon, an Australian writer, has argued that only learning strategies for developing collective leadership will enable public-service organizations 'to strike and maintain a suitable balance between management for ongoing operations and leadership for deep-reaching changes.'[36]

In *Managing Publicly*, Henry Mintzberg addresses the subject of public-sector leadership in Canada by focusing on the qualities and functions of deputy ministers. He identifies three models of public management: the 'managing on the edges' model (essentially managing up, down, and sideways), the 'cultural management model,' and the policy management model. The cultural management model gives the creation and introduction of an organizational culture priority over the other management roles. Mintzberg puts the emphasis on ethics, the creation of an integrated system of socialization, management by principles, and shared responsibility. Indeed, Mintzberg sees 'communicating' as a central feature of managing publicly, both to impart and receive information and to exercise control. This is independently confirmed in the Canadian context by Jacques Bourgault, who found that senior mangers in government spent most of their time in various meeting in order to 'fulfill this role of nerve centre or "market place" of numerous organizations subsystems – the minister, the department, the management team, colleagues, clients.'[37] On average, deputy ministers spent 5 per cent of their time with ministers, 10 per cent with colleagues, 40 per cent with their assistants, and 40 per cent with external players, the remaining 5 per cent being spent working alone in their offices.[38]

*Building Networks*

Leaders are distinguished by their ability to create bridges creatively and effectively with a wide variety of stakeholders. The use of lateral influence and networks (across services, departments, and organizations, drawing in appropriate partners according to contribution rather than position) is different from the vertical, hierarchical relationships that are fostered in structured organizations which provide services on a large scale.[39]

Does the individual executive make a difference in network building? A study of modernization and improvement of public services in the United Kingdom at the local level firmly concluded that leadership was 'clearly crucial': 'We found that they do not always lead from the front but that some empower nominated others to foster and promote change in the organization. They also create a climate of innovation. Innovation is nurtured rather than mandated. Leadership which "grows" development, rather than "pulls levers," was commented on among those we interviewed. This is either a different kind of leadership or a different dimension of leadership than is sometimes assumed from the debates about "strong" leadership, which often imply more of a command and control approach to leading organizations.'[40]

More than managing bureaucracies, according to R.A.W. Rhodes and Patrick Weller, public-sector executives must also manage networks.

They see the 'fragmentation of service delivery and the proliferation not of markets, but of networks' as the most 'significant unintended consequence of public sector reform.' This has entailed a transformation of the leadership role:

> Of their [networks'] characteristics, trust is central because it is the basis of network coordination in the same way that commands and price competition are the key mechanisms for bureaucracies and markets respectively ... As a working axiom, networks are high on trust and contracts are low on trust ... with the spread of networks, there has been a recurrent tension between contracts on the one hand, with their stress on competition to get the best price, and networks on the other, with their stress on cooperative behaviour ... The diplomatic skills required – for managing networks, for sitting where the other person is sat [sic], and for eliciting cooperative behaviour through negotiation – are not new but they are now at a premium ... They chase the holy grail of coordination. Public sector reform created a greater need for coordination while reducing governmental ability to coordinate.[41]

In networked management, it is clear that even senior managers such as secretaries to cabinet will need a much greater tolerance for ambiguity. Working in a networked context will entail a willingness to take risks and to manage a myriad of different professional cultures in the search for cooperation between the constituent elements of the network. As Rhodes and Weller put it, 'they will need to be expert brokers of contracts and builders of trusts. This will require them to be diplomats and mediators. Unless public sector organizations and their managers are prepared to embrace these changes enthusiastically, social order as we have known in the 20th century is likely to decay in the next.'[42]

*Relating to People*

The adoption and display of interpersonal skills by leaders – an ability to empathize and sympathize, behave courteously, and communicate effectively – has become critical to the success or failure of organizations. Being able to work with, understand, and motivate individuals and groups now is considered as important as having technical skills.

There seems to be a consensus that the most defining feature of effec-

tive leaders is the ability to communicate with a wide variety of people
and stakeholders in a manner that will foster trust and candour. In a
study of public-sector managers, Andrew Kakabadse and his team
concluded that 'fundamental to effectively leading an organization is
to ensure a high quality dialogue among the members of the senior
management team.'[43] They identified key strategies in facing the challenge of both vertical-management and horizontal-management problems and proposed an emphasis on dialogue to reduce the leadership
gap. Their study led them to the view that the essential quality of public-sector executives was an ability to sustain a positive conversation
with their peers on issues of public good and the promotion of cabinet
responsibility, not on matters relating to 'territory.' These executives
also promoted the qualities of leadership: they had an ability to invite,
receive, and handle feedback, and they studied their management
structures to get the interpersonal connections and dialogue 'right.' At
the core of their emphasis on dialogue was a deeply felt and expressed
commitment to learning, both collective and personal. Indeed, another
Canadian public-sector study showed that the instrument of choice
in exercising influence was dialogue/reasoning (pressuring came in
second!).[44]

As critical nodes in a variety of networks, secretaries to cabinet play
an important role in defining policy and in orchestrating government
so that cabinet decisions are carried out with appropriate dispatch and
intensity. They are in the best position to read the cabinet's collective
mood and in interpreting the will of the prime minister and premier.
The inverse should also be true. The secretaries must know intimately
the strengths and weaknesses of various departments. Their say in
building capacity, or in weakening mandates, is influential, but they
can achieve their goals only through a collegial, peer leadership which
is typical of any organization that employs highly knowledgeable and
creative individuals. Peer leaders, as such, may have some official
authority to 'command and control,' but they can sustain it only if they
lead through respect, knowledge, charisma, and rapport. Peer leadership is increasingly important in today's informal, fluid organizations.

In *Leading Leaders*, Jeswald Salacuse argues that most leadership concepts do not apply to situations where a leader must lead peers and that
calls to support 'cabinet responsibility' may not always be successful.
His description of leaders leading other leaders certainly would apply
to any secretary to cabinet. First, the people who report to the secretary
to cabinet have intelligence, talents, wealth (likely near their pension),

and power. Often they may have options outside government and those options give them a strong sense of independence from both the organization and its leader. Most have a formal or informal proprietary interest in the institution where they work and often have played a role in choosing their leader. Consequently, as Salacuse puts it, 'they often believe that the leader is beholden to them and not the other way around.'

Salacuse notes that peers have their own followers and constituencies, whose loyalties and respect they value and on whom they depend in order to hold on to their positions as elites, and inevitably their networks reach outside their organizations. But perhaps most of all, they do not see themselves as followers. They see themselves as leaders and want to be seen as such. They are therefore quick to challenge anything that suggests they are being led. 'Traditional symbols of leadership such as stirring speeches, emotional appeals to action, and directives from the top are likely to fall on deaf ears or, worse yet, become the subject of ridicule,' Salacuse observes.[45] Ultimately, secretaries to cabinet must lead their peers based on the interests of the latter. Deputy ministers, associate deputy ministers, and public-sector executives will follow and participate in the policy-planning process because it is in their interest to do so.

### The Sixth Skill: Searching for Leadership

In his discussion of the Privy Council Office, Donald Savoie cites one of his interlocutors, a former deputy minister in the government of Canada: '"If PCO ... were ever asked to ice a hockey team, they would put six goaltenders on the ice."'[46] Savoie notes that secretaries have grown more influential as a result of also acting as the prime minister's deputy minister. He gives a few examples where the PCO will be asked to take charge of files in order to 'make things happen.'[47] Inevitably, secretaries to cabinet have been creative in putting a better combination of players on the ice. This has become the critical and most distinctive skill of secretaries to cabinet: finding the right mix of players from a bench whose members they did not select. To make the challenge even greater, the players are limited in number, too often use the same skills in the same way, and are frequently ill at ease in passing the puck.

In the past, the focus of the work of secretaries to cabinet was on the process aspects of management, such as planning, managing central agencies, and budgeting. Naturally, they saw government work as resembling their own. Employment trends in government, however, have changed dramatically in the past twenty years and have led to a greater need to be familiar with and to understand employees who are of different generations, who come from different backgrounds and cultures, and who, perhaps, also have different sets of values. The tighter labour market in a number of jurisdictions, coupled with a drive for effectiveness and efficiency, has moved public-sector leadership to make an effort to seek out and try to retain top performers. Secretaries to cabinet will have to perform the five tasks outlined above: understanding issues, creating visions and setting priorities, managing competency, building networks, and relating to people. But they will also have to add a sixth discipline: searching for – and finding – leadership.

Many governments in Canada have created offices to examine the issue and to make recommendations on how a new generation can learn 'leadership' skills. The governments of Canada and Ontario have even created 'leadership' networks and offices. While these are laudable initiatives, the task of searching for leadership is much more than trying to ensure that governments adopt a succession plan. The search for leadership, in this case, is a daily activity that is framed by a sense of policy and administration and the need to plan for as many contingencies as possible. A study performed by the AT Kearney company and the Public Policy Group of the London School of Economics and Political Science recently made the case that 'clear leadership' and its concomitant 'skilled and motivated staff' are the two most important characteristics of an 'agile' government agency. Agility was measured in terms of productivity, employee satisfaction, and customer satisfaction. The study ranked leadership as the most important aspect of agility, but also as the biggest obstacle. It noted that 'many of our respondents said their biggest impediments to agility were a lack of a clear strategy and little (or no) commitment to change from the senior levels of the organization. All agree that senior-level commitment is essential and will *always* mean the difference between success and failure.'[48]

Paul Tellier demonstrated this 'search for leadership' clearly when, as clerk of the Privy Council, he publicly called on executives in the government of Canada bureaucracy in the late 1980s to 'create a culture of responsible risk-taking in the public service.'[49] He introduced new community-building practices among deputy ministers in order to get to know their personalities and abilities better, and also spearheaded a renewal initiative known as *Public Service 2000*. Weekly breakfasts proved to be an enduring success, but he was the first to admit that the corporate initiative had been a failure, largely because it was never a priority of government. Some years later, in 2000, a permanent secretary in the Department of Education and Employment in the United Kingdom wrote:

> A fast moving uncertain environment demands a fast-moving creative public sector and that is the 21st century challenge to effective people management in the not-for-profit sector – enhancing, releasing, and harnessing the creativity of our people. For public services, that will be the difference between success and failure in the new millennium. Now, the British have some odd ideas about creativity. Some – maybe the civil service – believe that intellect equals creativity in the sense that, if you are clever, then you must be creative. Not so ... The worrying thing is that each of these perceptions suggest that there is nothing much you can do to enhance creativity, so there is not much point in hard-pressed public managers trying. You just make the most of the hand you are dealt.[50]

The constant search for leadership will determine whether secretaries to cabinet succeed or fail. In some cases, because the office's occupants have not demonstrated familiarity with the structures of power inside the bureaucracy, the office has been challenged from the outside. In many jurisdictions in Canada, the position has been filled not by career public servants but by political appointees with little experience in the public sector who come and go depending on political whim. Political appointees, however, do seem to have an advantage in some minds: they are better 'connected' with the outside, be it the political or the broader social and intellectual environment. The appointment of political partisans to the top position of the public sector can have a far-reaching, rippling influence. In their conclusion to a book on bureaucratic elites in Western European states, Edward Page and Vincent Wright observe that the trend of politicizing top administrative jobs 'has produced limitations on the political discretion of civil servants that has also itself produced a greater sensitivity to their political environment – political craft among civil servants becomes helpful to career prospects.'[51]

The search for leadership is an activity that must yield a 'find' and thus poses a particular challenge for secretaries to cabinet. They must use their leadership skills to breed more leadership, by which is meant an ability to cede autonomy to departments and individuals so as to lay the groundwork for innovation and experimentation. The modernization of the state has changed the role of the secretary to cabinet, and occupants of the position are now called upon to do more than 'administer' or 'manage.' Some have started behaving in ways that are typical of leaders, but change has been slow. Many occupants, and this observation can be more broadly attributed to many strata of the public-sector executive, are too concerned with immediate results to be worried about anything except 'followership.' Certainly, their latitude in exercising leadership remains constrained because they themselves exercise a deferred leadership. Their authority is derived from a decision by an individual (the prime minister or premier) to install them in their post. This is not the decision of a board or of a nominating committee, or the result of an election, but rather the product of a mix of personal instinct, emotion, logic, and trust on the part of the prime minister/premier. In many cases, individuals have won the authority conferred on them by decades of hard work and dedication. In many others, individuals have been named 'secretary' because of a personal or political link with the chief elected official.

Regardless, secretaries to cabinet have become influential, powerful individuals who can actively 'search' for leadership. They head central agencies that have grown to become critical to modern governance and can exercise leadership using the variety of methods and tools at their disposal. They must persuade, cajole, and offer incentives to comply and perform. In jurisdictions where the functions of the secretary to cabinet are manifestly very political, they play an important role in shaping coalitions in cabinet that will support the directions of the prime minister or premier. They can also threaten: they are both messengers and authorities in their own right. As such, they wield a leadership that is unique in its features and in its expression. How they use that leadership is critical to the future of the public service and its role in modern governance.

Students of the United Kingdom's public service have been explicit in their recognition of this reality. In his report to the British prime minister in December 1999, Sir Richard Wilson, the cabinet secretary, stated that leadership was critical to achieving change and called for transformational leaders throughout departments and agencies.[52] A keen observer of the Whitehall scene noted later that 'leadership has emerged as a key element of innovation, particularly of process development. It is the translation of policy into the instruments of the organization and the clarification of the responsibility for ensuring the process development is appropriate for the innovation which has often been weak in the public sector.'[53] The Performance and Innovation Unit of the U.K. Cabinet Office produced a remarkably frank document on Whitehall's capacities in 2001. It concluded that the British system was experiencing real trouble in attracting and keeping the 'best leaders' and that there was 'little shared understanding in the system of the qualities required for effective leadership in today's public services.'[54]

Poor leadership was held to blame in a McKinsey and Company study of public-sector productivity in 2006.[55] Shortly afterwards, the British Institute for Public Policy Research found that senior civil servants were resistant to modern management methods largely because 'leadership was lacking.' Pointing to efforts to bring in outside expertise, it concluded that mobility both in and out of the services remained 'limited.' The consequence was a public service often caught unaware of new trends and ill-equipped to converse with many sectors of British society. 'Amateurism still too often prevails,' wrote the authors of the study, 'reflecting a skills gene pool that is too narrow ... management and delivery expertise, in particular, are still lacking ... Whitehall is poor at reflecting on its purpose, strategic thinking, dealing with inadequate performance, managing change effectively, learning from mistakes or working across departments.'[56] The report called for an overhaul of the way the civil service is run, with the creation of a powerful new head of the service able to dismiss senior officials who are not performing up to expectations: 'It [the civil service] lacks a strong centre able to think strategically, manage civil-service change or drive standards up. Performance is poorly managed, and poor performance too often goes unchecked.' At the root of the problem, the report said, are the 'anachronistic and severely inadequate constitutional conventions governing relations between the civil service, ministers, Parliament and the public. They have become a recipe for ambiguity, confusion, weak leadership, and buck-passing.'[57] The report circled the reporting arrows on the British public service's organization chart and observed that 'the relations between Permanent Secretaries (the DMs, or heads of departments) and the Cabinet Secretary (nominally the head of the civil service) were ill-defined. Permanent secretaries were said to answer to their ministers, and, in their role accounting officers, to Parliament. At the same time, the centre, in the form of the Cabinet secretary, Prime Minister and Treasury, make increasing demands on them, and exercise a growing, if mainly informal, authority offer them. Too often, responsibility and accountability falls between the gaps in this arrangement.'[58]

Even a turn to the bureaucracy can prove difficult in the search for leadership. A 2006 survey of government of Ontario employees, for instance, showed that while people were fairly satisfied and 'reasonably' engaged with their jobs, most found that the leadership of their organization was seriously wanting. No less than 68 per cent of respondents said they had lost confidence in senior leadership, and 78 per cent believed that senior managers did not provide clear leadership. More startling was the revelation that 75 per cent of respondents believed that senior leadership was not interested in the well-being of their employees. Only 24 per cent considered the hiring and promotions process fair and free of favouritism.[59] According to the consultant responsible for the survey, 'leadership practices' and 'organizational communication' had to become key priorities for improvement.

**The Way Forward**

The secretary to cabinet is inevitably going to be subjected to pressures to be more visible, present, and engaged in the lives of employees. As in the private sector, executives in the public sector are dealing with more critical challenges than those faced by their predecessors. In the private sector, leadership experts declare that 'the venerated reciprocity between company and employee (especially white-collar, managerial employee) ... crumbled in the 1980s.'[60] Donald Savoie, for his part, makes the same point regarding the traditional understanding of accountability between the bureaucracy and the elected government on their respective roles. 'The traditional bargain between politicians and public servants is coming unglued,' he writes, 'and the space that was once established to determine who is responsible for what is no longer clear.'[61]

Gone are the days when one could assume that government employees 'bought into' a particular service ethos or public-service mission. In the future, secretaries will have to make a significant effort to 'sell' the message of public service to their staff. They will have to make the government's goals clear and measurable. They will have to work to align those goals with talent and with suitable compensation systems. They will have to devote serious attention to employee engagement and make public service an interesting and creative pursuit. Above all – and this will be a mark of their leadership – they will have to act fast. They will also have to weather more criticism. As whistleblower provisions are gradually adopted by most governments, the role of the secretary to cabinet will inevitably come under closer scrutiny, both as an executive authority ultimately responsible for misdeeds and in investigations designed to uncover and correct malfeasance. It is too early to tell what the impact will be, but there is no denying that this will change dramatically the landscape in which the secretary, as 'head of the civil service,' operates.

In a comparison of the values and commitment of 'knowledge workers' in the private sector and public-sector and para-public-sector employees, researchers found that while Canadian public servants did value intellectual stimulation and challenging work more than other employees, they were less committed to their organizations than were private-sector employees. [62] The study also found that there is no fundamental value predisposition that guides people into a career in one sector or the other. Public-sector employees are no more altruistic and no less self-interested than employees in the private sector. Indeed, the study showed that there was no significant difference in the importance of job security between public- and private-sector employees.[63]

The secretary to cabinet's critical influence in the management of the most senior executives of government is matched only by his/her role in policy making. As leaders, they will have to invest more of their time in evaluating creative solutions to policy and – it must be said – political issues. In this vein, a crucial test of their leadership will be their ability to cultivate a succession plan that will encourage the bureaucracy to be more creative and effective in anticipating and responding to complex policy issues.

For secretaries to cabinet, the biggest challenge will be making the leap to new ways both of thinking and of communicating with executives and employees. Already, the private sector is experimenting with new sets of values and organizational principles and leading-edge companies are implementing strategies that will help them adapt to rapidly changing realities. Gone are the acronyms FORCC and POSDCORB. Large private-sector firms are putting 'design strategies' into place to apply the best of their knowledge. The new acronym is CENCOR (calibrate, explore, create, organize, realize). Can the public sector avoid a similar transformation? In the face of the ill-defined, novel, and complex problems facing governments, it is difficult to imagine how public-sector executives can maintain ancient habits. Already, various agencies of the government of the United States have identified five core competencies for leaders: leading change, leading people, results-driven, business acumen, and building coalitions and communicating.[64] Together, they constitute what is becoming increasingly known as 'cross-leadership': a complex practice of management essential to the success of every organization operating in a rapidly changing environment.

In many jurisdictions, secretaries to cabinet have assumed leadership roles to articulate a vision for their respective bureaucracies. Many now issue annual reports, communicate to staff on a government-wide basis, and convene meetings with employees of all ranks. Many have championed effective employee-recognition programs and have taken advantage of opportunities to express publicly their thanks to employees and to provide senior leaders with more freedom in determining how the work gets done. One of their challenges going forward will be to recognize the middle managers who most often are the most innovative members of the public sector. Secretaries to cabinet will need to understand that commanding respect starts with showing respect. Since the research leaves no doubt that peak performers want their work to be recognized regularly and repeatedly, secretaries to cabinet must surely be alert to opportunities to offer recognition on a daily or weekly basis.[65]

The transformation will not be easy. Unlike big business, governments cannot suddenly decide to hire thousands of individuals who can combine to transform the public sector to make it more innovative and creative. They need to go beyond these sources of leadership and draw on the well that has been given to them. Secretaries to cabinet will have to devote themselves to the search for leadership, something that goes far beyond succession planning. Governments have great difficulty in absorbing creative talent from private or non-profit sectors.[66] In most cases, the effect has been to discourage candour and challenges to the conventional wisdom. Risk is anathema. Partnerships are seen as suspect and involving a potential loss of power. The walls of the silos remain remarkably strong. To borrow an elegant phrase from Gilles Paquet, the secretaries to cabinet will have to lead the search for wisdom and connoisseurship[67] and manage with expertise the creative people who can bring innovation to bear on policy and program development.[68]

In their own search for leadership, secretaries to cabinet will have to go far and wide: to the PMO, to the cabinet, to their own secretariat, to their colleagues at the deputy-minister level, and to the senior levels of bureaucracy. As Henry Mintzberg notes, different scholars identify different traits as the defining characteristics of outstanding public-sector executives: 'controlling' (Henri Fayol), 'doing' (Tom Peters), 'conceiving' (Michael Porter), and 'leading' (Warren Bennis). Secretaries to cabinet in Canada will have to perform all these tasks and find the resources necessary to do so according to a standard acceptable to Canadians. Above all, they will distinguish themselves by how they exercise the sixth skill that is particularly relevant to their job: how they search for – and find – leadership. 'Stars keep not their motion in one sphere,' Shakespeare's Henry, Prince of Wales, observes in the fifth act of *Henry IV.* The job of the secretary to cabinet will be to bend the laws of physics and make sure that the stars of the public service share the same orbit.

NOTES

1 See Peter Hennessy, *Whitehall* (London: Secker and Warburg, 1999).
2 See *The Ottawa Men: The Civil Service Mandarins, 1935–1957* (Toronto: Oxford University Press, 1982); and *A Man of Influence: Norman Robertson* (Ottawa: Deneau Publishing, 1981).
3 Gordon Robertson, *Memoirs of a Very Civil Servant: Mackenzie King to Pierre Trudeau* (University of Toronto Press, 2000), 302–17.
4 Cited in Donald Savoie, *Governing from the Centre* (Toronto: University of Toronto Press, 1999), 302.
5 Sharon Sutherland, 'The Role of the Clerk of the Privy Council,' in *Commission of Inquiry into the Sponsorship Program and Advertising Activities, Phase 2, Restoring Accountability, Research Studies, Volume 3* (Ottawa: Government of Canada, 2006), 24, 64–8.
6 Ibid., 23.
7 Justice Gomery recommended that the secretary of Treasury Board 'assume the title and function of Head of the Public Service' and that the role of 'deputy minister to the prime minister' be removed and not reassigned. This model has long been in place in New Zealand. See 'Restoring Accountability: Recommendations,' in *Commission of Inquiry into the Sponsorship Program and Advertising Activities, Phase 2, Restoring Accountability, Volume 2,* 202. The suspicion of 'leadership' is articulated in Larry Terry, 'Administrative Leadership, Neo-Managerialism and the Public Management Movement,' *Public Administration Review,* 58, no. 3 (1998): 194–200.
8 B.S. Pawar and K.G. Eastman, 'The Nature and Implications of Contextual Influences on Transformational Leadership: A Conceptual Examination,' *Academy of Management Review,* 2 (1997): 80–109.
9 Jay Conger and Beth Benjamin, *Building Leaders: How Successful Companies Develop the Next Generation* (San Francisco: Jossey-Bass, 1999), 180.

10  On the Canadian situation, see Mansour Javidan and David Waldman, 'Exploring Charismatic Leadership in the Public Sector: Measurement and Consequences,' *Public Administration Review*, 63, no 2 (2003): 229–42; Sandford Borins, 'Leadership and Innovation in the Public Sector,' *Leadership and Organizational Development Journal*, 23, no. 8 (2002): 467–76.
11  Montgomery Van Wart, 'Public-Sector Leadership Theory: An Assessment,' *Public Administration Review*, 63, no. 2 (2003): 214–28.
12  James McGregor Burns, *Leadership* (New York: Harper and Row, 1978).
13  Robert D. Behn, 'Performance Leadership: 11 Better Practices That Can Ratchet up Performance,' IBM Center for the Business of Government, May 2004, 5.
14  Robert D. Behn, 'What Right Do Public Managers Have to Lead?' *Public Administration Review*, 58, no. 3 (1998): 221. See also his 'Leadership Counts' in *Journal of Policy Analysis and Management*, 8, no. 3 (1989): 494–500; and *Leadership Counts: Lessons for Public Managers* (Cambridge, Mass.: Harvard University Press, 1991).
15  Sutherland, 'The Role of the Clerk of the Privy Council,' 34. Sutherland argues that, in the case of the clerk of the Privy Council, the role should be stripped of its designations as head of the public service and deputy minister to the prime minister, so as to be limited to strictly the job of handling cabinet affairs.
16  To name only some of the most influential books: Thomas Peters and Robert Waterman, *In Search of Excellence: Lessons from America's Best-Run Companies* (New York: Warner Books, 1982); Rosabeth Moss Kanter, *The Change Masters* (New York: Free Press, 1985); Warren Bennis and Burt Nanus, *Leaders: Strategies for Taking Charge* (New York: HarperCollins, 1985); John Kotter, *A Force for Change: How Leadership Differs from Management* (New York: Free Press, 1990); Noel Tichy, *The Leadership Engine: How Winning Companies Build Leaders at Every Level* (New York: HarperCollins, 1997); Michael Porter, *Competitive Advantage: Creating and Sustaining Superior Performance* (New York: Free Press, 1998); and Conger and Benjamin, *Building Leaders*. In a blazingly original study of 'bad leadership,' Barbara Kellerman has argued that mediocre leadership is so common that it begs a typology of at least seven types – incompetent, rigid, intemperate, callous, corrupt, insular, and evil. See Barbara Kellerman, *Bad Leadership: What It Is, How It Happens, Why It Matters* (Boston: Harvard Business School Press, 2004).
17  Drake Beam Morin-Canada, 2003.
18  W. Chan Kin and Renée Mauborgne, 'Tipping Point Leadership,' *Harvard Business Review*, April 2003, 61–9.
19  Terry, 'Administrative Leadership,' 24.

20  Ibid., 29.

21  Ibid., xxi.

22  New York: HarperCollins, 2005. More technical aspects of leadership skills
    are discussed in a special issue of *Leadership Quarterly*, 11, no. 1 (2000).

23  Alex Matheson and Hae-Sang Kwon, 'Public Sector Modernisation: A New
    Agenda,' *OECD Journal on Budgeting*, vol. 3, no. 1 (2003): 8.

24  Warren Bennis called this the 'Management of Attention' and the 'Manage-
    ment of Meaning' in his *An Invented Life: Reflections on Leadership and Change*
    (Reading, Mass.: Addison-Wesley, 1993), 75–83; Frances Westley and Henry
    Mintzberg, 'Visionary Leadership and Strategic Management,' *Strategic
    Management Journal*, 10 (1989): 17–32.

25  Allen Schick, 'Opportunity, Strategy and Tactics in Reforming Public Man-
    agement,' *OECD Journal on Budgeting*, 2, no. 3 (2002): 7–34 (10).

26  Jim Collins, 'Level 5 Leadership: The Triumph of Humility and Fierce
    Resolve,' *Harvard Business Review*, July-August 2005, 138. Of interest in
    identifying the singular role of one leader in a public-sector 'turnaround' is
    Paul Joyce, 'The Role of Leadership in the Turnaround of a Local Author-
    ity,' *Public Money and Management*, August 2004, 235–42.

27  R.A.W. Rhodes and Patrick Weller, 'Conclusion,' in Rhodes and Weller,
    eds., *The Changing World of Top Officials: Mandarins or Valets?* (Buckingham,
    U.K.: Open University Press, 2001), 239.

28  Ibid., 240.

29  John P. Kotter, 'What Leaders Really Do,' *Harvard Business Review*, Decem-
    ber 2001, 8596. This article was first published in the *Harvard Business
    Review* in 1990.

30  Peter F. Drucker, 'What Makes an Effective Executive?' *Harvard Business
    Review*, June 2004, 59.

31  Oren Harari, *Leadership Secrets of Colin Powell* (New York: McGraw-Hill,
    2002).

32  Kin and Mauborgne, 'Tipping Point Leadership,' 61–9. See also William
    Bratton and Peter Kobler, *Turnaround: How America's Top Cop Reversed the
    Crime Epidemic* (Westminster, Md.: Random House, 1998).

33  Ellen Schall, 'Public Sector Succession: A Strategic Approach to Sustaining
    Innovation,' *Public Administration Review*, 57, no. 1 (1997): 4–10.

34  Maria Barrados and John Mayne, 'Can Public Sector Organisations Learn?'
    *OECD Journal on Budgeting*, 3, no. 3 (2003).

35  Brian J. Cook, 'Politics, Political Leadership and Public Management,' *Pub-
    lic Administration Review*, 58, no. 3 (1998): 225–30.

36  Don Dunoon, 'Rethinking Leadership for the Public Sector,' *Australian Jour-
    nal of Public Administration*, 61, no. 3 (2002): 3–18.

37  Jacques Bourgault, 'The Mintzberg Model and Some Empirical Evidence: Putting It to the Test,' in Henry Mintzberg and Jacques Bourgault, eds., *Managing Publicly* (Toronto: Institute of Public Administration of Canada, 2000) 162.

38  See Jacques Bourgault, 'De Kafka au Net: la lutte de tous les instants pour le contrôle de l'agenda chez les sous-ministres canadiens,' *Gestion*, 22, no. 2 (1997).

39  Jean Hartley and Maria Allison, 'The Role of Leadership in the Modernization and Improvement of Public Services,' *Public Money and Management*, April-June 2000, 38.

40  Ibid., 35–40.

41  Rhodes and Weller, *The Changing World of Top Officials*, 242.

42  P.M. Jackson and L. Stainsby, 'Managing Public Sector Networked Organizations,' *Public Money and Management*, January-March 2000, 11–16 (15).

43  Andrew Korac Kakabadse et al., 'Leadership and the Public Sector: An Internationally Comparative Benchmarking Analysis,' *Public Administration and Development*, 16, no. 4 (1996): 377–96.

44  Germain Julien, 'Tactiques d'influence des cadres supérieurs dans la fonction publique québécoise,' *Canadian Public Administration*, 37, no. 4 (1994): 631–43.

45  Jeswald Salacuse, *Leading Leaders* (New York: Amacom, 2006), 5–6.

46  Savoie, *Governing from the Centre*, 122.

47  Ibid., 134.

48  AT Kearney and London School of Economics, *Improving Performance in the Public Sector* (Chicago: AT Kearney, 2003), 9.

49  Ian D. Clark, 'Encouraging Innovation in a Government Department,' *Optimum*, 20, no. 2 (1989–90): 61.

50  Michael Bichard, 'Creativity, Leadership and Change,' *Public Money and Management*, April-June 2000, 41–6.

51  Edward C. Page and Vincent Wright, eds., *Bureaucratic Elites in Western European States: A Comparative Analysis of Top Officials* (Oxford: Oxford University Press, 1999), 266, 278.

52  *Civil Service Reform: Report to the Prime Minister from Sir Richard Wilson, Head of the Home Civil Service* (December 1999). Available at: http://www.civilservice.gov.uk/archive/civil_service_reform/docum ents/cs_reform_report.pdf

53  Chris Yapp, 'Innovation, Futures Thinking and Leadership,' *Public Money and Management*, January 2005, 57–60; Joe Wallis and Brian Dollery, 'An Evaluation of Leadership as a Response to Agency Failure in the Public Sector,' *Canadian Public Administration*, 75 (summer 1997): 247–65.

54 Performance and Innovation Unit, *Strengthening Leadership in the Public Sector* (U.K. Cabinet Office, March 2001), 4.

55 Tony Danker et al., 'How Can American Government Meet Its Accountability Challenge?' McKinsey and Company, 2006, www.mckinset.com.

56 Guy Lodge and Ben Rogers, 'Whitehall's Black Box: Accountability and Performance in the Senior Civil Service' (London: Institute for Public Policy Research, 2006), 4.

57 Ibid.

58 Ibid., 8.

59 Ipsos-Reid, *2006 OPS Employees Survey*, September 2006.

60 Bennis and Nanus, *Leaders*, 69.

61 Donald J. Savoie, *Breaking the Bargain: Public Servants, Ministers and Parliament* (Toronto: University of Toronto Press, 2003), 7. Louis Bernard, secretary to cabinet of the government of Quebec from 1978 to 1986, denounced this trend and called for a fundamental rethinking of accountability, arguing that it was simply unfair to hold ministers responsible for administrative foul-ups. See his 'Des gestionnaires en liberté surveillée,' *Canadian Public Administration*, 33, no. 2 (summer 1990): 229–33.

62 Sean T. Lyons, Linda Duxbury, and Christopher Higgins, 'A Comparison of the Values and Commitment of Private Sector, Public Sector and Parapublic Sector Employees,' *Public Administration Review*, 86, no. 4 (2006): 605–18; Carole Jurkiewicz et al., 'Motivation in Public and Private Organizations: A Comparative Study,' in *Public Productivity and Management Review*, 21, no. 3 (1998): 230–50. See also Monica Belcourt and Simon Taggart, *Making Government the Best Place to Work: Building Commitment* (Toronto: Institute of Public Administration of Canada, 2002).

63 See Ken Kernaghan, 'The Post-Bureaucratic Organization and Public Service Values,' *International Review of Administrative Sciences* 66, no. 1 (2000): 91–104.

64 Patricia Wallace Ingraham and Heather G. Taylor, 'Leadership in the Public Sector: Models and Assumptions for Leadership Development in the Federal Government.' Paper presented to the Midwest Political Science Association National Conference, April 2003.

65 A good example is Cindy Ventrice, *Make Their Day: Employee Recognition That Works* (San Francisco: Berret-Koehler, 2003).

66 Arthur Kroeger and Jeff Heynen, *Making Transitions Work: Integrating External Executives into the Federal Public Service* (Ottawa: Canada School of Public Service, 2003).

67 See Gilles Paquet, 'The Burden of Office, Ethics and Connoisseurship,' *Canadian Public Administration*, 40, no. 1 (1997): 55–71.

68  See Michael D. Mumford et al., 'Leading Creative People: Orchestrating
    Expertise and Relationships,' *Leadership Quarterly,* 13 (2002): 705–50; and
    Richard Florida and Jim Goodnight, 'Managing for Creativity,' *Harvard
    Business Review,* July-August 2005, 125–46.

# 2 Clerks and Secretaries to Cabinet: Anatomy of Leadership*

JACQUES BOURGAULT

Examining the leadership of the clerk of the Privy Council and secretary to cabinet either in the government of Canada or in the provinces is a daunting task. This is so, in part, because of the breadth and complexity of the role of the highest-ranking executive in the government. It is also because of the wide variety of circumstances each clerk or secretary faces. Michel Vastel captures the mystery of the position when he nicknames its holder the 'mandarin of mandarins.'[1] This chapter examines the evolution of the responsibilities of the clerk, the organization of their office, their role as leaders, and finally the nature of their leadership. The organization of their functions varies in accordance with the history of the jurisdictions in which they have evolved and according to eras.[2] The practice of leadership also varies with those functions and according to the personality of each secretary. Finally, since they serve the prime ministers (PMs) and premiers, the personality and expectations of those figures will inevitably affect the manner in which clerks and secretaries will deploy their leadership skills.

## Sources and Methods

This study draws on a number of sources, including legislation, scholarly examinations of the history and functions of the institution, memoirs of former clerks, and the websites of thirteen governments. Eight former clerks and deputy ministers (DMs) were also interviewed, both at the federal and provincial levels. A number of critically documented cases studies (such as the Al-Mashat affair and the sponsorship scandal) were plumbed for the lessons they yield. The writing was done as interviews progressed and in light of the revelations of the 'Leadership

Lessons of Secretaries to Cabinet' conference organized by the Institute of Public Administration of Canada in May 2005. My interviews with clerks have yielded rich insights but I chose not to identify their personal comments or to refer to private comments made on them by their colleagues. In return for access, anonymity and confidentiality was guaranteed to them. Therefore, no judgment is passed on the performances of the recent clerks – Gordon Robertson, Gordon Osbaldeston, Paul Tellier, Glen Shortliffe, Jocelyne Bourgon, Mel Cappe, Alex Himmelfarb, and Kevin Lynch – simply because there is little objective documentation on which to base an evaluation. This task will have to taken up by future scholars.

The objective is to draw out the leadership commonalities of each role and does not offer a legalistic comparison of the various functions in Ottawa or in provincial capitals. I focused on the Ottawa experience because it pioneered the evolution of the position, has been a reference for other jurisdictions, and has been both vaster and more complex in the way it has interpreted the role of the clerk. Incidentally, the term 'clerk' is used as a generic reference to the position unless the particular context of the discussion requires a more specific term; indeed, of the thirteen jurisdictions in Canada, there are no less than ten distinct models of organization and designation of functions (see appendix 1). Also, for ease of readability, I have opted to use the masculine pronoun 'he' when discussing leaders in general and clerks in particular, even though some who have occupied the position of clerk in Canada have been women.

## Preliminaries

The federal position itself holds no less than four titles – clerk, secretary to cabinet, deputy minister to the prime minister, head of the public service – and its holder also is known as the official 'responsible' for the administrative functioning of the Privy Council Office (PCO). In the provinces, one 'clerk' has four titles; five have three titles (not all the same), three have two titles, and three have only one title. In three of the provincial cases, the leadership of the public service is shared between two individuals who share titles. It is clear that, in one particular case, the clerk plays a lesser role, limited to convening cabinet and to recording minutes.

Among the titles used, 'clerk' is used eight times, 'secretary to cabinet' eleven times. On two occasions, the persons holding the post are re-ferred to as secretaries of the Office of the Executive Council, once as secretary to the Executive Council, and twice as deputy ministers of the Executive Council. Three jurisdictions have designated them as heads of the public service, and five have identified them explicitly as deputy minister to the prime minister, including twice where these responsibilities are shared between two people. (See appendix 1, p. 75.)

The government of Canada website is most explicit in describing the functions of the clerk:

ABOUT THE CLERK

The Clerk of the Privy Council is the most senior non-political official in the Government of Canada, and provides professional, non-partisan support to the Prime Minister on all policy and operational issues that may affect the government. The Clerk of the Privy Council and Secretary to the Cabinet also has particular responsibilities with respect to:

- ensuring the continuity of government between successive administrations;
- keeping custody of the records of previous administrations; and
- enabling the government of the day to understand and recognize the established conventions of Canada's constitutional monarchy.

The first Clerk of the Privy Council was appointed in 1867. A second title, Secretary to the Cabinet, was added in 1940. Changes to the Public Service Employment Act in 1992 brought a third title, Head of the Public Service, and responsibility for setting the strategic directions for the Public Service of Canada.[3]

Notwithstanding these definitions, it is clear that the clerk plays a much larger role than that of ensuring the cohesion of the offices he leads, be it the PCO in the government of Canada or, in the case of the provinces, the Office of the Executive Council or the Ministry of the Executive Council. A number of provincial clerks also have additional responsibilities such as communications, protocol, francophone affairs, and intergovernmental affairs.

## The Portmanteau Concept of Leadership

The term 'leadership' holds many meanings and easily lends itself to confusion. For many, it is a word that refers to the exercise of power. The fourteen competencies of leadership used by the Canadian public service reflect this approach.[4] The second meaning reflects the responsibility exercised by a person who is held responsible for the results of an organization during a specific time frame. On can say that 'under the leadership of "X" such and such a thing happened and it was good (or bad).' Jack Welch, the former CEO of General Electric, has popularized a third meaning of leadership that draws on a long-established literature. He describes leadership as a particular style of management, the refinement of a vision, the incarnation of a certain direction, and the responsibility to inspire, to give an example, to motivate, and to preserve and promote a team approach to management.

It is necessary to distinguish forms of leadership from power and authority for a simple reason: it is possible to exercise authority (hence power) without ever having shown abilities of leadership. A public-sector position does confer, by the strength of law, a formal authority: the power to decide, to act in a certain manner, to hire or fire, to approve expenses, or to delegate authority. The formal authority conferred on a position gives power to the holder of that position. It also confers power in the context in which the officeholder wields authority. Being close to decision makers, with the responsibility to advise intimately, to hold discretionary information, and to offer the last word of guidance, the clerk enjoys opportunities and resources to influence decision making. It is worth noting that the clerk can perform all of these tasks without ever exercising formal leadership in the commonly understood manner.

The corollary is also true: a manager can show leadership without enjoying the formal attributes of authority. One can exercise leadership because of one's influence. Ultimately, the manner and style of leadership depends on the personality, style, will, and strategy of individuals and their understanding of the context in which they find themselves.

*A Few Styles of Leadership*

Jim Collins writes that leadership is often seen as the modern-day equivalent of medieval witches: leaders are held responsible for everything that goes right and wrong in organizations.[5] The concept of leadership has developed in five long stages that have given the term equally distinct meanings.

The *authoritarian* leader, according to Chester Barnard,[6] defines himself: *I am the leader and they must follow me.* This personalized style imposes a hierarchical power of constraint while emphasizing a formal authority on the interplay of forces or on the charisma by which those who 'follow' will abandon their autonomy to the leader who will personally take charge of situations.

*Participatory* leadership commits the leader to consulting followers in order to create a consensus that will support the choice of actions and attitudes. The saying 'to lead the people, one must follow them' best illustrates this form of leadership.[7]

*Adapted* leadership, as described first by J.M. Burns and then by Bernard M. Bass and others, is part of a transactional form that uses rewards and punishments[8] and captures the leader's ability to adapt to different levels of maturity among followers (in any organization, employees vary considerably in terms of maturity). Responding to situations as they present themselves, the leader will apply more direction, or delegate more, according to the circumstances.[9]

*Transformational* leadership[10] gives to the leader the ability to provoke change and to guide employees through change by involving himself personally in providing a vision for the future. It is to 'make them do things they would not have done on their own, because they did not see its usefulness.'[11] Stuart Hart and Robert Quinn identify four leadership roles among directors: creating a vision, motivating, analysing-strategizing, and task mastering.[12]

*Sustainable* leadership is the label of the '5th level' identified by Jim Collins.[13] This sort of leader presents a paradoxical blend of determination and humility in his behaviour, attributing success to the prowess of colleagues and assuming responsibility for difficulties and failures. This is authentic leadership, sincere and thoughtful. It makes decisions in light of the future needs of an organization, not for immediate show. It aims to create sustainable conditions for the success of an organization, even after the leader's departure, through a manifest concern for the organization's culture, succession, systems, personnel, and so on.

If leadership is a personal imprint on the exercise of power, the authority of the clerk is considerably different because it is derived from delegated powers. The clerk rarely operates in public, and seldom is the leadership of the office visible. 'A clerk-cum-leader understands his role and knows how to use his authority including when to remove himself from the scene and to hand off to others (colleagues or staff) on certain occasions,' said one former clerk. This analysis could not apply to any executive position in the public service since the clerk holds a strategic position in the decision-making process and performs a unique figurehead role.

The leader draws on many of these abilities within the course of the day and applies a mixture of them in responding to a given situation. These styles, therefore, do not exclude each other. The art of leadership is to know how to use any and all of these styles according to the leader's judgment of a particular issue. The leader's ability to perceive and to judge personalities plays a vital role in this regard. The leadership of the clerk is founded on values, on a total personal commitment, and especially on an ability to assess situations.

## Leaders or Managers?

Many have used these terms as opposites. There are directors who, because of their personalities, are also of executive calibre. Others are managers who have characters that make of them leaders.[14] It is difficult to sustain this dichotomy nowadays.[15] The leader who has no ability to manage becomes superficial, issuing dictates in a vacuum and jeopardizing the sustainability of his accomplishments. In other terms, vision is not a substitute for action. The manager who has no ability to lead will likely micromanage and this will ultimately undermine his ability to manage resources and lead to missed opportunities to act. We are 'overmanaged and underled,' writes Warren Bennis, giving voice to the exasperation of front-line employees and managers.[16] A number of converging reflections from former clerks and deputy ministers show that various clerks have been seen as change managers in policy, while others have chosen to provoke change in areas of operational management. And still others have opted to devote themselves to both tasks. The degree of autonomy demonstrated, and the choice of priorities that became the object of focused attention, would seem to distinguish the form of leadership practised by the clerks.

The relations between the clerks and the deputy ministers, because of their professional maturity and power, illustrate the clerk's specific leadership, making them resemble what James Elloy has called super-*leaders* who operate autonomous organizations.[17] Peter Drucker defines eight rules that must be put into place by the effective leader and confirms the role of 'leader' as central in defining the task of the manager: 'They asked: What needs to be done? What is right for the organisation? They developed action plans; they took responsibility for decisions and for communicating; they were focused on opportunities rather than problems; they ran productive meetings (decide in advance what kind of meeting it will be); they thought and said "We" rather than "I" ... You owe to the organisation not to tolerate nonperforming people in important jobs.'[18] Leadership at this level demands clarity, courage, and humility. 'Be capable of delegating in areas where you are not competent,' advises Drucker.[19] In an ideal world, managing and leading must be integrated. Some of the clerk's tasks require more leadership and others more management.

### The Particular Need of Leadership in the Public Sector

The exercise of leadership is important for all types of organizations and the public service is no exception. How are public-service needs different? First, the Canadian public-sector executive derives authority from his career. He was nominated without the fanfare or media interest that can accompany private-sector promotions. The holder must make a name and stake a claim, and create interest around his arrival. He must conciliate the sometime divergent approaches to the public interest: among politicians, between ministries, or between politicians and public servants. The deputy minister must ensure that the best policy analysis and decision-making processes are provided to the minister, argues former clerk Paul Tellier.[20] It is the clerk's leadership that will allow recommendations to be made in accordance with a certain vision of the public good that is both consistent and continuously adapted to the changing needs of public organizations.

Those who follow this leadership, both as subalterns and as colleagues, will enjoy more job security and more professional stability. This is not the case in the private sector, where unionization levels are much lower and where legal obligations are more flexible. All the directors of the public sector enjoy, in theory, a heavier burden in inspiring and motivating their workforce and in transmitting to them a need to meet new expectations. Secondly, many in the public sector have a vocational approach to their job. It is easier to believe in the cause of victims of violence or poverty, for instance, than to commit oneself to the production of widgets. To be sure, the commitment of public-sector directors to their work often prevents them from seeing the full range of governmental engagements on social and economic issues. The successful public-sector executive must be able to place the cause and mission of his department within the context of governmental constraints and opportunities.

The public organization, by its nature and shape, offers particular challenges to leadership: it frequently pursues goals that are difficult to quantify and often abstract, and it does so in an environment that is leaden with contradictory rules. The public-sector executive must offer a coherent vision of the usefulness of the department's mandate to society's goals.

Secondly, the public organization anchors its actions in a number of legal constraints that inevitably diminish the enthusiasm of employees. In public-sector organizations, employees often have the impression that their purpose is to satisfy process requirements, instead of reaching objectives. Their leader must explain, value, and justify these constraints, coach subordinates on how to manage them, and ensure that the workforce maintains its commitment to the attainment of results. Leadership compels the executive to find, identify, and maintain a balance among a complex set of objectives, in terms both of results and of process. Public-sector organizations are often large and their employees feel the need to see how their work contributes to the achievement of goals. It is incumbent on the leader to highlight the significance of each employee's contribution to the result. The leader must be able to promote this perception and, above all, recognize the importance of communication with the employees who ultimately report to his office.

Working in a highly partisan politicized environment also creates important challenges for leadership in the public sector. The joint pressures of interest groups and both friendly and less-friendly lobbyists can create challenges for the leadership. Ministers often must adjust their plans as they re-read their political environment and the evolution of the government. Naturally, they are the ultimate directors, and democracy cannot tolerate public servants who continually feel victimized or immobilized by undue pressures. Public leaders must offer and communicate values and ethics as well as a sense of purpose for society, regardless of decision making that seems all too often focused on the short term. Ruth Hubbard and Gilles Paquet[21] attribute a 'social architect' role to the clerk. The specific needs that justify policy and programs change constantly as social needs evolve and understandings become more scientifically precise. Employees often feel as though they must repeat work they thought they had done earlier, and the effect of such a realization can be paralysing. A public-sector leader, such as the clerk, must become a champion of continuous improvement and adaptation, or change, and of lifelong learning.

The popular image of the public sector is often negative. The tax-funded, favourable working conditions are consistently condemned and the media feast on errors or unfortunate cases, while politicians focus on government waste and inefficiency. The context is almost entirely negative: the public sector painted as ineffective and inefficient. The role of a public-sector leader, in such an environment, is to communicate a sense of vision and pride in the work. He communicates this to the staff but also acts as their spokesperson in society. The clerk who exercises real leadership will concoct a strong message of encouragement, pride, and confidence.

### The Roles of the Privy Council Office

In administrative terms, the Privy Council Office is a government department whose minister is the prime minister and where the clerk is the deputy minister.[22] The secretariat of the PCO is, in effect, the ministry of the prime minister and the secretariat of cabinet.[23] The PCO, however, was not founded on a legal principle or a tangible act of Parliament. Its existence and legitimacy rests on a sketchy constitutional provision as well as a 1940[24] decree and a few conventions.

W.E.D. Halliday argued that the PCO is concerned with the 'machinery' of government as a committee. In other words, it exists to ensure that formal mechanisms and procedures translate the executive will into actionable recommendations to the Crown (agenda, memoranda, minutes, transmission of cabinet decisions, liaison among cabinet committees) while also providing secretariat services for inter-ministerial relations and various other committees of the public service.[25] In 1982 Murray Hay concluded that it had acquired two new roles: providing policy continuity and counsel to the cabinet, its committees, and the prime minister.[26] Modern times have enlarged its role even more, the PCO website asserting that 'the primary responsibility of the PCO is to provide public service support to the Prime Minister, to Ministers within the Prime Minister's portfolio, and to the Cabinet in order to facilitate the smooth and effective operation of the Government of Canada.'[27] In sum, the PCO provides support for the prime minister so that he can direct effectively (and as coherently as possible) the activities of government. It is the hub of government actions as well as the point of convergence for the actions of the whole of the public service.

Since the PCO acts as the secretariat of cabinet and of its subcommittees as well as 'the system as a whole,'[28] it must maintain close and sustained contacts with all ministries and Crown agencies. The objective is to facilitate the efficiency of their work, to ensure continuous consultation, and to coordinate action. This aspect of its mandate is often the subject of controversy. Even though the PCO asserts that it does not duplicate the activities of ministries[29] (Gordon Robertson even established the principle 'Stay off the field; Plans work through operations'), the line departments still consider the PCO too interventionist, fickle, and costly in terms of time and administration.[30] Paul Tellier has described the direct but 'subtle' influence of the PCO on policy formulation.[31] The clerk, as leader of the organization, must incite the PCO staff to maintain a certain liaison style. 'I insisted that it was not our role to rival, or to compete with, departments, but it was our role to know all the right questions about everything coming forward, and to cover it in our briefing of the prime minister,' writes Gordon Robertson.[32] According to a former deputy minister, the PCO will occasionally act as regent for a ministry in crisis. The best-known case was Paul Tellier's actions in the Department of Immigration.

Beyond the issue of style, it is important to note the nature of the structures that manage relations with ministries: their size has been noted by Robertson[33] and by Donald Savoie[34] and deplored by Arthur Kroeger.[35] The refinement of central agencies is aimed at improving the coordination and the capacity of line ministries. This has been the case in Ontario, Alberta, and Saskatchewan, where the quality of the central agencies is beyond dispute.[36]

As the hub of government action as well as the point of convergence of the public service, the PCO provides cabinet with a decision-making nexus. To cabinet ministers, it offers 'whatever aid and assistance it can to permit individual and collective judgment to prevail ... and sound policy to emerge.'[37] This support, and the opinions articulated by the PCO, are meant to be non-partisan,[38] and the public-service executive must abide by its decisions, even if they are inconsistent with the recommendations emanating from line departments.[39] Charlotte Gray has explained that the distrust of the PCO by the Mulroney government in its first year led to an important reduction in the PCO's role, to the point where it was likened to a post office. It would take the Pacific salmon crisis of 1985 to reinvent the office by bringing about Paul Tellier's appointment as clerk.[40]

## The Evolution of the Clerk-Secretary Portfolio

At the risk of borrowing an expression normally applied to ministers, the clerk-secretary's portfolio consists of an array of responsibilities that are conferred on the position by a number of laws (rules, decrees, and regulations) and also by conventions, customs, and practices as well as by decisions made by the prime minister. It varies to the point that three provincial governments have chosen to split the role among two people: one as deputy minister to the premier, the other as clerk and secretary to cabinet. This decision has had an impact on the 'shared leadership' of the clerk and of the deputy minister to the premier. In general, however, one person assumes these functions. It is important to note that in the government of Canada these responsibilities are defined more by conventions than by formal rules. Most provinces have legislated the functions of the office, giving more definition to the role of the clerk.

The clerk supports the prime minister or premier in the near totality of his functions: 'The Clerk of the Privy Council is the most senior non-political official in the Government of Canada, and provides professional, non-partisan support to the Prime Minister on all policy and operational issues that may affect the government.'[41] The clerk also supports the cabinet's collective decision making and the execution of its decisions, a function he performs as well with respect to members of the Council of Ministers.[42] The role of the prime minister inside the cabinet inevitably affects that of the clerk: 'The position of the prime minister is one of exceptional and peculiar authority. He has been called the keystone of the cabinet, or the sum around which all the planets revolve. [He] is naturally master of the cabinet in all matters of organization and procedure. It has been said the office of prime minister is what the holder makes of it.'[43]

The documentation of the government of Canada specifies three titles for the clerk, in addition to holding him responsible for the administration of the PCO: clerk of the Privy Council and secretary to cabinet, deputy minister to the prime minister, and head of the public service. The history of the position shows that these three titles contain a mix of six distinct roles.

*Clerk of the Privy Council (1867)*

The clerk provides technical support to the Council of Ministers: he gives it shape by swearing in the members, giving it consistency,[44] convening it, and, of course, 'taking notes and delivering minutes and OCs [orders-in-council].'[45] Mitchell Sharp recalls that, until Arnold Heeney assumed the position in 1946, meetings were barely recorded and few

archives were preserved. Indeed, before the 1960s, 'ministerial committees were less important than interministerial committees of deputy
ministers.'[46]

The clerk now has the responsibility of collecting the archives of cabinet and its files for the use and benefit of subsequent administrations.
In this instance, he is entrusted with the task of preserving cabinet confidentiality and of assessing when and how cabinet secrets can be un-
veiled.[47]

*Deputy Minister to the Prime Minister (1985)*

The clerk advises the prime ministers in all areas of the latter's purview
– that is, in all aspects of his functions and privileges (such as nomina-
tions, representations, exercise of legal, conventional or traditional
authority, and so on). He provides support to the prime minister and
counsels him on the issues that concern the executive cadre of the public service, such as hirings, rankings, salaries, departures, promotions,
and evaluations. The prime minister, for example, in his role as a minister accountable to Parliament, expresses his expectations of ministers
through the critically important mandate letters.[48] Thus, the prime minister consults the clerk to identify the topics on which cabinet can articulate expectations and to determine ministerial responsibilities. It is the
PCO, rather than the Prime Minister's Office (PMO), which drafts and
finalizes the mandate letters.

The prime minister is also the chief of the government, an institution
not explicitly described in the constitution. The fact that government is
based on convention and tradition rather than statute implies a certain
flexibility in the way it can define and pursue its work; the clerk can
mould it by his ability to seize chances and by affecting its institutional
memory. The clerk also shapes the government agenda, and its articulation by the prime minister, by making use of technical expertise and
policy advice. 'This includes advice on appointing senior office holders
in the public service and organizing the government, on the Cabinet
decision-making system, overall policy directions, intergovernmental
relations, and the management of specific issues.'[49]

The clerk's power is derived from the prime minister.[50] According to
Savoie, this function took on the importance it today enjoys because of
Paul Tellier's influence in 1985.[51] Yet, at early as 1963, Gordon Robertson
spoke of his daily meeting at 9 A.M. with Prime Minister Pearson and

Tom Kent (his chief of staff) to discuss 'government and policy.'[52] Michael Pitfield saw Prime Minister Trudeau every morning during the 1970s. Many have debated the partisan nature of Michael Pitfield. He certainly had joined the public service long before Pierre Trudeau had been elected in Ottawa,[53] but the two had been close personal friends for a long time before 1968, when Trudeau assumed the mantle of prime minister.[54] Trudeau's patronage 'helicoptered' Pitfield through the ranks, creating no small measure of envy among the senior ranks of the public service.[55] According to some, Trudeau was the hero figure Pitfield had long sought, explaining, perhaps, his extraordinary personal devotion to the prime minister. Trudeau, in turn, showed unlimited confidence in his clerk. Pitfield was thus a hybrid of bureaucrat/politician.[56] To distance himself from the Liberal Party machinery, he asked to be named to the Senate as an 'independent' – a rare case in the modern history of that chamber.

Many former occupants of the post have stated that the clerk is not formally the deputy minister of the prime minister, except in the most minimal sense, as titular head of the PCO. 'He is not the deputy to the Premier only to manage the PCO. He is rather his closest adviser. Ninety-nine per cent of his work is not done as a deputy, but more as an adviser.' P. Foster cites the reflection of a former minister in the Trudeau-Pitfield years: 'Whenever you were dealing with the PCO or PMO, you had to ask yourself: is this question really coming from Trudeau or is it coming from Pitfield?' Foster shows the degree to which the delegation of powers was complete and to which it was difficult to distinguish who really was in charge!

The clerk makes use of the PCO in a manner that is, in almost all aspects, similar to that of deputy ministers. The difference comes from a limited interpretation of the prime minister's role as minister of this office. As one former clerk puts it: 'As a deputy minister to the prime minister, his case is not the same as any other DM, except for when it comes to the management of operations of his department, the PCO. In contrast to other deputy ministers, his authority cannot be held as a substitute to that of the prime minister. The only exception is the management of PCO.' In those roles, tied to the roles and privileges of the prime minister, the clerk is not personally held accountable for the successes and failures of the prime minister. In the areas in flux, the clerk will likely act with his own leadership style, rather than exercising a classic form of management.

*Secretary to Cabinet (1940 – Arnold Heeney)*

The second title, 'secretary to cabinet,' was formally added in 1940.[57] The importance of the roles that accompany this title evolved in four distinct phases, in 1946, 1963, 1964, and 1968, as the range of activities of the federal government grew as part of the expansion of 'the new interventionist state.'[58] A state that is more interventionist will legislate more and execute more. As the cabinet becomes more active, and its challenges more complex, its secretariat becomes all the more crucial. J.L. Granatstein describes the experience of the war cabinet in the Second World War as a basis for the launch of a greater role for the PCO within cabinet operations.[59] Robertson corroborates this perspective: 'Arnold Heeney used it [the PCO of the 1940s] as the base on which to establish the secretariat for War committee ... [The result] was so obviously valuable that Mr King was brought, reluctantly, to agree that it should carry on the same role for the cabinet when peace came.'[60]

For a long time, meetings of the Council of Ministers required little technical preparation. Robertson recalls that the prime minister could pull a sheet of paper from his jacket and announce what decisions the cabinet would be taking. This situation changed in 1963, when Lester Pearson asked the clerk to meet him regularly on Tuesdays to prepare the agenda of the next meeting.[61]

Granatstein notes the rise of the role of secretary as adviser to the prime minister between 1941 and 1960. More important, the cabinet recognized, and used on a continual basis, Arnold Heeney's expertise in organizational development.[62] The secretary was firmly rooted in its role as prime cabinet adviser. Subsequently, as Robertson has described, nine specialized cabinet committees were created in January 1964.[63] From that point on, committees vetted the options presented to cabinet, thereby increasing the strategic and coordinating role of the clerk.

In 1968 Prime Minister Trudeau installed an elaborate and complex style of decision making, which he hoped would be more 'rational' and structured but which elicited little enthusiasm from Robertson. It aimed to reinforce the roles of the PCO and the secretary to cabinet.[64] As the secretary, the clerk was to provide a functional support to cabinet decision making, as well as to its members, by offering technical and legal advice and briefings. The clerk, in sum, facilitated the cabinet's work. According to the PCO website: 'As Secretary to the Cabinet, he or she assists the Prime Minister in maintaining the cohesion of the

Ministry and giving direction to it. In this role, the Clerk of the Privy Council provides support and advice to the Ministry as a whole to ensure that the Cabinet decision-making system operates according to the Prime Minister's design.'[65] The PCO website also states that the clerk is responsible for 'ensuring the continuity of government between successive administrations; keeping custody of the records of previous administrations; and enabling the government of the day to understand and recognize the established conventions of Canada's constitutional monarchy.'

As 'head' of cabinet, the prime minister is advised by the clerk, in the latter's exercise of his chairmanship of the group. A former clerk expressed the complexity of the role:

> The role regarding cabinet is exceptional. You are serving a group that is chaired by the prime minister. You are constantly on guard to determine where the PM's prerogatives begin and end and where those of cabinet begin and end. There is also the role of preserving the prerogatives and powers of cabinet. Sometimes the PM has to be told: this issue you are looking at seems fine ... but it is the cabinet's business! You have to craft each of these interventions. You can't be seen by members of the cabinet as the servant of the prime minister. Yet you also have to keep your distance from cabinet. In this role, you are serving ministers as individual members of this institution. Sometimes you tell a minister that his or her proposal cannot come to cabinet, because it is his or her prerogative to act independently.

The clerk also plays a role of double-representation. He represents the public service to the cabinet and the prime minister, and, inversely, represents the prime minister and cabinet to the public service. He 'presents, explains and promotes' the characteristics, constraints, and projects of one to the other. In this regard, the consensus seems to have been that Michael Pitfield was mostly the representative of the prime minister to the public service, rather than the opposite.[66]

*Head of the Privy Council Office (1940)*

Like all deputy ministers, the clerk is also held responsible for the management of a central agency (such as it is in Ottawa) or of a minister (as in many provinces), be it the PCO, the Office of the Executive Council, or the Ministry of the Executive Council. In all cases, these support the cabinet or Council of Ministers, as well as their committees.

*Head of the Deputy Minister Community*

The clerk is 'traditionally regarded as the senior deputy minister of the public service.'[67] Savoie notes that 'much like Mitchell Sharp, a retired deputy minister reports that, during the 1960s, the clerk of the Privy Council and secretary of cabinet did not dominate in Ottawa.' But 'things changed with Michael Pitfield's appointment.'[68] Sharp, a former deputy minister himself, recalled that the positioning of the clerk as the chief executive of the public service had started with the Trudeau government and evolved further though the 1970s and 1980s.[69] As such, the clerk assumed the orientation and coordination of the deputy ministers as a management corps, as a professional group (who hold similar functions), and as a community (as a relational group). He looked after the introduction and orientation of new members, the coordination of actions, the development of long-term policy and reflection, and the implementation of the government's agenda; he also monitored performance, provided individual support, encouraged collaborative approaches, maintained a community spirit, and organized critical parts of the social calendar.

The professionalization of the lives of deputy ministers became especially evident in the 1960s as the clerk began to exert a special influence. As Savoie writes: 'When my respondent became deputy minister in the early 1970s, he claims that he "would not have recognized one-third of my colleagues had I come across them on the street ... It was very rare that you had dealings with the clerk, perhaps a couple of times a year. You had a job to do with your minister, and you went and did it." There was no such thing, for example, as a mandate letter from the clerk. But things began to change in the 1970s, particularly when the clerk started to chair monthly luncheon meetings with deputy ministers. Things changed again in 1985, when the clerk added weekly breakfast meetings, and again later when deputy ministers' retreats were organized.'[70]

Mitchell Sharp argues, though, that inter-ministerial meetings dominated the 'political scene' under Mackenzie King, St Laurent, and Diefenbaker.[71] He refers to a group of five or six particularly important senior deputy ministers. It also seems as though that there were two groups of deputies: the senior DMs, who worked collaboratively, and the junior DMs, who remained in their silos!

By 1969, the informal lunch meetings of mandarins no longer sufficed to buttress the initiative of the prime minister, given the growth in the role and mission of the federal government.[72] The systematic holding of monthly meetings, convened by the clerk, began around 1970.[73] The performance evaluation of peers, sponsored by the clerk, started in 1969,[74] and the retreats started around 1970.[75] The notion of corporate leadership and the weekly breakfast meeting started in 1985, under Paul Tellier.[76] In 1994 Jocelyne Bourgon accentuated this role by organizing retreats for reflection,[77] in part to fuel discussion on corporate learning, policy capacity, management planning, and corporate results.[78] In the provinces, Saskatchewan was the first to establish formal apparatus for these objectives during the 1970s. A number of its executives migrated to New Brunswick during that decade and implanted the practice there. Informal groups of deputies met occasionally in the provinces. In Quebec, the most well-known case, during the 1960s, was the 'Groupe de l'Aquarium' or the 'Club du Georges V.'[79]

The involvement of the clerk in the community of deputy ministers varied from time to time, depending on the personality and level of interest of each individual. As one deputy minister frankly observed: 'He has the right to get actively involved, but he has no formal or direct legal authority on deputy ministers.' To exercise his role, the clerk defined, installed, validated, and adjusted the management system of the deputy minister community. This system involved formal committees of deputies, working groups, meetings to share information and coordination (such as the weekly breakfasts), events to trigger long-term reflection, such as retreats and learning initiatives, professional-support mechanisms, and individual coaching.

On some occasions, the clerk must mediate tensions between a deputy minister and a minister, or identify solutions when deputies disagree on priorities and solutions. According to those interviewed, the clerk is on occasion a go-between, an appeals court, and an arbiter. It depends on the jurisdiction, the particular circumstances, and the individuals involved.

*Head of the Public Service (1992)*

The head of the public service is responsible for the development of the organization. The website of the PCO offers two definitions of the role of the head of the public service. The first is generic: 'As Head of the Public Service, he or she serves as the principal link between the Prime Minister and the Public Service of Canada, and is responsible for the quality of expert, professional and non-partisan advice and service provided by the public service to the Prime Minister, Cabinet and to all Canadians.'[80]

This definition makes the clerk the guarantor of the quality of the support the public service can offer the political apparatus. The PCO website offers a second definition that seems more precise regarding the responsibilities of the clerk of the Privy Council as head of the public service:

> PCO supports the Clerk of the Privy Council and Secretary to the Cabinet as Head of the Public Service in:
>
> - advancing the government's public service management agenda, with particular emphasis on public service reform;
> - ensuring strategic management and planning of senior public service personnel;
> - serving as spokesperson for the Public Service; and
> - submitting an annual report to the Prime Minister on the state of the Public Service.[81]

This second definition insists more on the clerk's supporting role to the public service. It is only at the federal level, and in three provinces, that the clerk is formally recognized as the head of the public service. Savoie documents this bi-directional role as a link between the political directors and the public service as a whole. The *Public Service 2000* initiative had also recommended it.[82] For each of these roles, the clerk must call upon particular features of leadership that invoke vision, personal commitment to colleagues, and an ability to engage others.

### The Basis of the Clerk's Leadership: Leading Up, Down, and Horizontally

The clerk's leadership is defined as 'leading up' with political masters, 'leading down' with subordinates, and 'leading laterally' with colleagues and counterparts in the provinces, the business community, and, sometimes, actors on the international scene. As one clerk said: 'This is a credibility business. You cannot lead down if you are not seen as leading up ... and conversely.' Of course, leading up is not made of the same components as leading up or horizontally. As discussed above, the clerk has little formal authority and his few direct powers are not conferred by the positive affirmations of law. A clerk has few employees and little in the way of financial resources to lead directly, but, paradoxically, he is the leader of the entire public service. This is why the clerk leads through others: up through the PM and down through the DMs. The clerk exercises significant power, through his functions and through his influence: on the prime minister, cabinet, individual ministers, his colleagues, and the public service as a whole. To exercise this role, the clerk must proceed by a leadership of influence rather than of direction, in the classic understanding of the term. There are four categories of leadership levers exercised by the clerk.

The *reputation* of the individual's competence within the bureaucracy (especially among the public-sector executive but also among the senior management) – with ministers, across the country, and even internationally – will confer the necessary influence to exercise power and leadership.[83] Unless there is a reputation of excellence, reliability, discretion, and loyalty, the clerk cannot influence the prime minister, the ministers, his peers, or his employees. Gray relates how Paul Tellier's reputation as a performer, and an adapter, attracted him to the attention of Prime Minister Mulroney.[84]

*Personal efficiency and skilful management* also play a vital role in leading horizontally. Adrien Payette argues that the principal capital of the manager is his personal efficiency. Each holder of the office brings to the job a personality and a set of preferences, sensitivities, emotions, strengths, and weaknesses. It is clear that success depends on a personal ability to limit the damages of the weaknesses while capitalizing on the fundamental strengths. The importance of the clerk's role is dependent on the impact of his personal efficiency. It follows that the impact must be positive! The clerk must have a personality that lends itself to the exercise of influence (not timid, yet not so egocentric as to impede the creation of a rapport with others). The clerk must also enjoy sufficient experience that will allow him to anticipate and react in complex situations (after having witnessed how complex issues work themselves out). Finally, a clerk must possess a *savoir-faire* and a solid judgment (be able to decide what must be done, and how, in response to an extreme diversity of complex situations): 'You must know how to make trains run!' In those cases, the quality of leadership, being able to identify 'the right road to take,' depends on how often followers have been willing to go down that road. Each senior manager faces situations where individuals will choose to follow. If errors are made, or if actions are awkward, the followers will become more troubled, less attentive, and downright critical. In that case, the clerk cannot go forward.

For leading down and horizontally, *the confidence of the first minister and the cabinet* towards the clerk is key, since it creates access to the primer minister. It is, first, a material access. It is measured by how much time the prime minister devotes to the clerk, the timing of the meetings, and their spontaneity. Intellectual access to the decision makers undeniably creates a considerable leadership impact. The leader must be able to influence and to convince. The confidence that occasions the access to power is manifested in a number of aspects. It rests on perceptions of loyalty, technical and managerial capacity, and sound judgment. A former clerk stated: 'Without access, you're dead. If you lose access to the prime minister, others will go around you to get that access.' Problems arise as soon as interlocutors of the clerk perceive that he is no longer heard by the prime minister or premier. Inevitably, the moral authority of the clerk is questioned, rumours multiply in the upper ranks of the public service, and the clerk finds himself circumvented. At this level of management, there cannot be parallel tracks of influence.

Hard-won confidence does not imply blind subjugation of the clerk to the prime minister. 'The confidence must come from both the prime minister and the cabinet; if the cabinet is not confident in you, you cannot help the prime minister, because you cannot be heard by it,' said a former mandarin. Judgment, knowledge, values, and experience allow the clerk to choose his interventions to maintain the confidence of all actors. A responsive clerk, with little judgment, would be as effective as a reputed manager whose loyalty or judgment was suddenly questioned.

To lead down, *credibility and legitimacy* must be earned and constantly nurtured. As many former clerks have said, such qualities are crucial among peers – typically hardened veterans – who can be fiercely critical and whose confidence must be earned 'as low as possible in the government organization.' Vastel reports these words of an influential minister regarding Jocelyne Bourgon: 'She belongs to the new generation; she understands the changing role of government, has a very good judgment and is nobody's fool.'[85]

The clerk is not likely to be making only popular decisions and cannot please every interest. His recommendations to the prime minister, and to the cabinet, may please some but will create as many frustrations. His decisions to let some files mature will inevitably frustrate those promoting certain actions. His mediation between deputies can generate distrust among losers. Finally, his decisions to appoint, dismiss, and transfer colleagues, to evaluate their performance, and to recommend salary adjustments will not please everyone in a community of accomplished colleagues – most of whom the clerk has likely known his entire career. Worse, the clerk cannot always reveal all the circumstances and reasons that underpinned his decisions. 'The challenge is to keep it [confidence and legitimacy at the same time] ... across tough calls in complex situations when you have to protect secrecy.'[86] Clerks live in a village of political and bureaucratic clans and in particular they may find themselves among clans of not-so cooperative DMs, said one clerk, who referred to 'Sandinista' manoeuvres directed at hampering their authority.

## Instruments of Leadership

In some cases it is difficult to distinguish among instruments that lead up, down, or horizontally. 'The first instrument of the manager is his self,' said one clerk, paraphrasing Payette.[87] The management of one's self allows a person to calibrate emotions and behaviour in light of the situations that present themselves and everyday multiple microrelations. Henry Mintzberg shows that the executive's perspective implants itself in the organization through three means: managing, conceiving, and organizing knowledge (communications and control); mediums (concerting, directing); and actions (negotiating and acting).[88] This Mintzberg model applies well to the functions and role of the clerk.

*Managing and Leading through Information: Communicating and Controlling Systems*

There are three formal channels of communications and control: the machinery of the cabinet, the community of deputy ministers, and preparation of the annual report of the head of the public service. The clerk can exercise leadership through the various attributes of the position of secretary to cabinet: having minimal direct authority, the clerk can use his influence to a greater degree on the chief decision maker and the government agenda setter, because he has direct access. The clerk is the functionary with the most authority over the weekly cabinet meeting agenda. He sits with the cabinet, and ministers may solicit his point of view.[89] The exercise of authority, and decisions regarding policy options, belong to the clerk, because of his position in the decision-making chain. A clerk says of this tool for leading up and horizontally:

'There you lead and manage change, convey messages, make use of symbols and you reward.'

For leading the troops and leading horizontally, the clerk must enjoy considerable power vis-à vis the deputy minister community: in this case, his leadership is a function of his capacity to develop and maintain consensus on many issues. The clerk has access to the levers of internal coordination (such as meetings of senior executives), various central agency committees, DM committees, and performance contracts and evaluations. It is important to recognize that the DMs convey messages to each department's employees, while the clerk, in leading down, enjoys a 'podium privilege' (his speeches, letters, and communiqués are widely distributed) and, as head of the public service, prepares an annual report that contains a number of messages to the bureaucracy as a whole: it commits him to actions before the public service and before the wider public.

*Managing and Leading through People: Concerting and Directing*

The clerk is in charge not only of coordinating the work of the public service and the cabinet but also doing likewise with the community of deputy ministers and specific groups of public servants. This is particularly so when the clerk makes decisions on the number of committees, their mandates, their composition, and the frequency of their meetings.

The clerk also directs when making recommendations on personnel deployment. Foster identifies Michael Pitfield as the 'godfather' in this regard.[90] The clerk can involve himself in providing special support, coaching, or advice to new deputy ministers. This is evident in five provinces.[91] He can implement a corporate-learning agenda for deputy ministers and establish a system of retreats and seminars on government agendas, challenges, and opportunities that can be more or less rigorous, depending on circumstances.

*Managing and Leading through Deeds: Negotiation and Actions*

Like any director, the clerk negotiates constantly: within the public service, with the prime minister, with the ministers, with ministerial staff, with the leaders of central agencies, with individual deputy ministers, and with senior managers inside the PCO. 'Better to build consensus than to order!' as a former clerk once put it. The process of building a consensus often takes the shape of a subtle negotiation.

The clerk must also act. He applies pressure through his speeches and his interventions within the community (for example, Paul Tellier's searing speech after the Al-Mashat affair). He must follow the evolution of files and programs and express opinions as necessary. He also spends a lot of time making recommendations. His actions are either written or, more usually the case, spoken: the public service will evaluate his leadership in light of the coherence of his message, as well as the justifications for the actions and policies he has authorized. He must act to encourage confidence in the cabinet, in the prime minister, and in the community of deputy ministers. Ultimately, his behaviour will serve as a model and be judged as such.

Three types of factors may dilute the clerk's leadership towards the public service more broadly: some bear on actions, others on image, and still others on the chain of communication within the government. The clerk's leadership may be impaired by the government's priorities being seen as 'bad' by the troops. Similar results happen when priorities change too often or when no priorities are evident. In such a case, the government's decisions are interpreted in lockstep with the clerk's decisions: either the initiatives came from PCO or the clerk was unable to stop them. The conclusion is that the clerk has little or no influence. A second instance may emerge when the clerk develops a poor media image that reflects poorly on the public service's image. Media stories on the clerk may cause some damage and controversial speeches may be harmful. The PCO staff has become protective of the clerk's image, and, as a result, the clerk has to be very conscious of the potentially negative interpretations of all informal presentations. Finally, if the clerk's image and intentions are unenthusiastically relayed within departments, his leadership will be hampered.

### Relations with Politicians and the Management of Essential Organizational Change

The clerk's relations with politicians are first marked by the management of transitions, when a new team of ministers or a new prime minister assumes power. Political transitions of power occur regularly. In a narrow sense, they refer to the replacement of a government formed from one party by another team of MPs belonging to another party. The clerks emphasize, though, that the term 'transition' should be interpreted in a broader sense that includes situations where a member of a political party succeeds an individual from the same party or when a cabinet shuffle takes place. In all cases, the clerk supervises the preparation of transition memos within the ministries, as well as within the Prime Minister's Office and the Privy Council Office. It is necessary to recognize the necessary changes to the agenda, structures, and personnel (although not necessarily in that order, because structures often follow personnel decisions and agenda!). The clerk plays a critical role in contributing to the formalization of the governmental agenda and in establishing the operational machinery of the new structure of cabinet committees and of various ministries, all the while being actively involved in the nomination of candidates for senior posts.

In a transition setting, the clerk aims to ensure the smooth institutional process of installing a cabinet, although Savoie emphasizes that the process is ultimately the responsibility of the prime ministers.[92] In cases where ministers and governments have little or no experience, the clerk has two concerns: Will the public service cooperate with the new government? Will it try to impose its priorities on the new government? In the first case, the operative principle is that the public servant must loyally serve the democratically elected government, without prejudice, within the limits of a government of laws. To implement a change of policy, the clerk likely recommends a classic dose of continuity and innovation. He must define and implant organizational change and management methods, such as when the 'new managerial methods' of Trudeau[93] were implemented or when, in British Columbia, 'leadership [was] attentive to an active administrative policy.'[94] Foster cites the case of the new energy program of the Liberal Party in the 1980s, when a party taking power with few new ideas was vulnerable to public-service notions and adopted them in order to create a policy program.[95] The clerk plays a critical role to ensure that the specific objectives of the government are recognized and implemented as much as possible.

In the daily course of events, the key to clerk leadership is balancing access to the prime minister with intellectual independence. As a former clerk put it, 'one day I asked the chief of staff what the prime minister thought of me. He said that he liked me, enough, but [thought] that I was a too argumentative. I thanked him, saying that this was the greatest professional compliment he could ever offer me!' Generally, the political personnel expect, from the clerk, professional advice that is frank and direct. This intellectual liberty allows the political class to benefit fully from the competence of the individual they have named as clerk. A former deputy justified this prerogative on the grounds that the clerk's advice was likely to be based on a solid understanding of the state of knowledge, tradition, and institutional memory of the public administration. The clerks, however, have varied in explaining the full political implications of the policies they professed. Paul Tellier would have done it more than Gordon Osbaldeston.[96] Is it a question of the circumstances, of lessons learned, of personal style, or of the prime minister's expectations?

The clerk needs the courage to tell people, with the authority to end his employment, things that they would rather not hear about their pet projects. For instance, Vastel praises the courage displayed by Jocelyne Bourgon in establishing a demanding program review.[97] The clerk must first serve an institution, rather than the person who serves as prime minister or as president of the Privy Council. 'In these matters, the institutions must prevail on people,' says a former clerk. For example, one must resist the enthusiasms of some and put off cabinet considerations of projects that are not ready or that may trigger disputes among ministers.

Clerks must commit to making decisions that will have a great impact, that may be risky, and that may destabilize the system. They must make decisions instead of pretending to ignore them, to 'let the time pass,' or to sweep difficulties under the carpet. Vastel writes that 'Jocelyne Bourgon proved she had the guts to wield the broom, even with the top ranks of the public service' (my translation).

### External Factors That Dilute Leadership

Leadership, of course, can be diminished or diluted when execution is faulty. Even the best leaders must work within particular contexts and within the constraints of 'external' factors – in this instance, those not related directly to the clerk or his actions. They can take the form of a potential rival influence when a prime minister seeks a third perspective because he is not entirely satisfied with the clerk's performance or simply wishes to take advantage of a new stream of advice. There are two sorts of cases: first, those in which a sharing of responsibilities, or a sharing of audience, with a colleague will reduce the influence of the clerk; second, those in which the prime minister or premier's position weakens the impact of the clerk.

The sharing of power may involve a division of functions, such as with the chief of staff or a private adviser. It also may arise when the position of clerk and secretary to cabinet is divided in two. This was the case in 2006 in three provinces. A similar model was adopted temporarily in the government of Canada in the early 1990s, when the clerk's functions were shared by two individuals. The arrangement did not endure. It was felt that it created situations where the clerk and the secretary to cabinet could work against each other and harm clear and effective decision making and leadership, as well as fostering doubts in some minds regarding access to the prime minister or the cabinet and thereby reducing the credibility of the clerk. Finally, the division of power opened the possibility that one of the individuals would be challenged when a minister or a deputy minister was not satisfied with a position taken by either the clerk or the secretary to cabinet.

Power is also shared when access to the prime minister and the chief of staff may have a negative impact on the relations between the clerk and the prime minister. Will the clerk and the chief of staff become twins or rivals, accomplices, or enemies? Will there be peace, a war of attrition, or a guerilla war of traps and subterfuge? In 1971 Gordon Robertson felt the need to shed light on the 'parting of the waters' and reaffirmed that the Prime Minister's Office was partisan, politically oriented, and yet operationally sensitive. The Privy Council Office, in contrast, was non-partisan, operationally oriented, and yet politically sensitive.[98] Ministers and deputy ministers decode who occupies the spheres of influence around a prime minister and create their strategies of influence and pressure accordingly. Other ministerial offices will see in that relationship a model for their own political-administrative relations. Under Trudeau, the PMO enormously enlarged its personnel, and diversified its role, according to Marc Lalonde – one of his chiefs of staff.[99] These changes created a conflict and Robertson made a plea for 'greater harmony.'[100] It is worth recalling that similar conflicts erupted in 1983 when Mulroney's Progressive Conservatives took power.

Speaking of the provinces, Luc Bernier has written: 'There is a huge competition from PMO at times.'[101] Robertson recalls the need to establish a sound method of working, similar to the harmony that prevailed when Prime Minister Pearson and his chief of staff, Tom Kent, would ask the clerk to remove himself from cabinet meetings once discussions took a decidedly partisan tone.[102] There is also competition when many of the prime minister's advisers have a special status and are personally close to him. All prime ministers have had one or more privileged advisers, such as Eddy Goldenberg was for Jean Chrétien.[103] They inevitably will rival the access and influence of the clerk and will dilute the impact of his leadership.

Another type of threat can weigh on clerks in the relations they maintain between the prime minister and certain ministers. If the prime minister has trouble imposing his authority on a minister, or on a number of them, it will be more difficult for the clerk to exercise his leadership vis-à-vis the relevant deputy minister. It is rare in Canada for a minister to defy the prime minister. There are, though, three exceptions to the rule: when public opinion polls show a particular minister is more personally popular than the prime minister;[104] when time in office inevitably erodes the popularity of a prime minister;[105] and when the prime minister, having announced his departure (the Chrétien case of 2004 comes to mind), will not leave, creating leadership rivalries that affect cabinet unity.[106]

### The Performance Zone: Clerk as a Relay (Political and Administrative), a Pivot (All Departments), and a Traffic Controller (Shot-caller, Pacemaker, Culture Promoter)

The perimeter of functions in which results are expected from an employee is referred to as 'performance zone.' A range of actors that is more or less measurable, depending on the level of the position, will judge performance – qualitatively and quantitatively. The organization expects the officer to plan and organize work in a manner that will occupy the whole 'zone' and to accomplish that work in a way that will benefit the organization. This could get tricky and contradictory in the politico-bureaucratic context, since expectations are not always clearly spelled out and some may appear contradictory and may change suddenly. The clerk's performance zone is expressed in terms of the contract that is agreed to with the prime minister. Whatever its formality, this contract reflects six types of leadership opportunities.

*Counsel to Political Officials: Leading with Clairvoyance and Courage*

The clerk must support the cabinet's discussions by supplying data, facts, studies, and objective analyses. Based on the information that is gathered and collated, advice is provided to the prime minister on opportunities and the feasibility of various policy projects. The clerk can advise on political management by validating what is at stake in any issue and in shedding light on what can be done to ensure that projects move forward once the prime minister and cabinet have come to a decision. This increases the cabinet's capacity. The clerk brings a horizontal and corporative perspective to bear on discussions and helps to optimize resources and opportunities, bringing coherence to the group and efficiency in collective action.

The leadership of the clerk demands a vision and no small measure of courage. In some instances, the clerk must plead for a longer time frame for the implementation of policy, warning the prime minister against haste. In some interventions, it behooves the clerk to understand the many roles and personal constraints of the prime minister. The clerk must know how to manage his time with the prime minister and accept the constraints of an individual who is also the head of a party, a member of Parliament, a minister, the head of government – and a person with a private and family life!

*Implementing the Vision in the DM Community: Leading with Engagement and Providing Support*

The second zone of the clerk's performance is his rapport with the community of senior mangers, deputy ministers in particular. His first responsibility is ensuring that the government's agenda is implemented. He must interpret that agenda by creating a plan of action for the senior level of public-sector leadership. His leadership invariably means that he will be personally implicated. He cannot simply act, as Jim Collins has expressed it, as a tennis referee, perched at the net, counting points and staying neutral on the outcome.[107] The clerk chooses the administrative structure that will enact policy, organizes the agenda of deputy ministers, and sees that the performance contracts of the relevant actors reflect the priorities of cabinet. As leader of the community, he sets, by verbal and written instructions, the tone and rhythm for communications. His decisions create examples, and he chooses the symbols to signal the importance of some issues, methods, and themes over others.

Secondly, he must define the method of dialogue for exchange with the community: as a leader, he must wish for consensus more than the imposition of his point of view. In so doing, he must intervene personally to affirm a style and to give an example to the community. For instance, Gray contrasts the styles of Robertson, Osbaldeston, Pitfield, and Tellier. The first two showed a preference for anonymity, focused on the integrity of process. Pitfield had a more interventionist style and would contest the wisdom, consistency, and rationality of ministerial submissions. Tellier's leadership was based on 'purpose and brain power building loyalty and trust between himself and both subordinates and seniors.'[108]

Thirdly, the clerk must choose, establish, and preserve a system by which the community will be managed. His key tools are committees, and he can shape their work – mandates, members, frequency of meetings, calendar – as well as manage relations among their members. It is critical to know when and how to intervene, when to avoid doing so, and when to detect or defuse conflicts. When necessary, the clerk must reinforce decisions of committees among the members of the deputy community.

Thus, leadership rests on the manner by which the clerk interacts with his colleagues, who are his equals and who, professionally, are competent and powerful in their departments, and sometimes outside of them. The clerk exercises leadership in part by an ability to intervene between colleagues and impose the will of his office.

### Directing 'Corporate Governance': Providing Vision and Diffusing Values

The third component of the performance zone is anticipating the challenges that a government must corporately manage, and ensuring that it deals with them promptly. The clerk must announce a perspective and ensure that the articulation of the policy is conducted in its light. The strategic role of counsel on priorities and planning is all the more important because most political leaders do not have all the necessary information or time, or the proper perspective, for effective action. Their perspective is legitimately narrower and shorter term and takes into account parliamentary concerns and the vagaries of public opinion. Pitfield wrote in 1976 that 'we have not viewed government sufficiently as a total system.'[109] In this context, the clerk's contribution is essential to complete the checkerboard of considerations that the political directors must acknowledge. J. Aberbach, R. Putnam, and B. Rockman have presented this complementarity through a model of 'energy-balance' of relations between the administrative and the political.[110]

The clerk must act corporately through the Privy Council Office, ensuring that the staff exercises its role but does not exceed it. The ideal is the coordination of energies, rather than coercion; dialogue, rather than imposition of directives; and support, rather than micro-management.

The clerk's third corporate role consists of protecting the cabinet by ensuring that inadequate decisions – legally dubious, insufficiently documented, or weakened by an incomplete consensus – are not submitted to it, or decided by it. The clerk must, as much as possible, prevent difficulties from becoming crises and choose carefully how – or if – to be involved in crisis management. Charlotte Gray recounts how Paul Tellier had barely installed himself as clerk before assembling all the deputy ministers to inform them that the PCO had to be alerted of all crisis possibilities that could embarrass the government.[111] Depending on the circumstances, the clerk may take control of the situation or keep a certain distance from it, providing help where necessary. As some clerks put it, 'crises have given clerks enormous shots of adrenaline. Others hated crises but loved to get involved in their management.'

The clerk also encourages teamwork in order to integrate the efforts of all the deputy ministers. He urges members of the community to get involved and assigns roles as circumstances necessitate; he uses tools to mobilize (again, the power of the pen, of persuasion); and he attends critical meetings and conveys to peers that teamwork is essential to good governance and that he supports the initiative in question. In some provinces, the clerk will mentor, coach, and support: tailoring his approach, being more pro-active with newcomers, signalling signs of difficulty with others, and tolerating individuals going through exceptional circumstances. He supervises the performance evaluation of his peers: some practise a rather holistic, rigorous approach, while others limit their efforts to a more formal one.

Ultimately, the clerk must ensure that his message, vision, expectations, and commitment impress as many minds as possible in the hierarchy. His concrete, supportive actions must be taken on as broad a scale as possible to counter the cynicism of many who argue that the senior ranks of the bureaucracy do not 'walk the talk.'

*Protecting Conventions: Demonstrating Candour, Rigour, and Confidence*

There are few legal documents that describe the job of the clerk, and even fewer concrete laws shape the prerogatives of the prime minister and the cabinet.[112] Yet the clerk's role is to protect the institutional rule of the executive. The Canadian constitution is composed of positive law, conventions, customs, and precedents. Jurisprudence brings interpretation to this situation and binds the lower courts when facts and laws reflect earlier situations and court decisions. Some have estimated that 90 per cent of the rules that govern the executive are unwritten. These conventions are derived from the Westminster-style Parliament and, to a remarkable degree, the Whitehall model of the executive, 'enabling the government of the day to understand and recognize the established conventions of Canada's constitutional monarchy.'[113] Nicholas D'Ombrain writes that 'prime ministers and cabinet secretaries should ... ensure that the institutions over which they preside respect the Constitution' (including 'the principles, conventions, and practices of parliamentary and cabinet government'). He further states that the 'machinery of Government is the guardian of precedent ... the genius that respects precedents without impeding progress.'[114] This includes ministerial responsibility, the role of the prime ministers and cabinet, ministerial solidarity, the application of the rule of law, the professional and non-political character of the public sector, and so on. These rules must also be applied to the values of the public service; they are the bedrock of its culture.

The clerk, as first adviser to the prime minister and the cabinet, must first defend that institution, rather than the individuals who serve in it. He must know the rules and see their import in providing consistency, stability, and the legitimacy of a government of laws. It is essential that he apply them in light of their fundamental goals, and to political directors as well as administrators. These rules and regulations are alive. The clerk must know when to allow them to evolve or, by interpreting them in light of contemporary challenges, to bring precision to them and to ensure that they are all well understood. For example, it is important that the working relations with the prime minister's chief of staff and the cabinet maintain a distinction between the interests of a party and those of a state administration. On some occasions, the clerk will have to defend a deputy minister before a minister who oversteps the political-administrative boundaries – thus allowing the senior public service to do its work within a zone of confidence and comfort. These delicate situations can often prove difficult, since the clerk advises deputy ministers using information they may not like to hear. As one former clerk put it, 'we must remind them of principles of democracy when, in good faith, they come out of their zones of authority.'

*Making Difficult Decisions, Providing Commitment, and Rallying the Troops*

The clerk expresses the courage of leadership when he directs the attention of decision makers to a long-term public good or raises fundamental questions by recalling public-service principles. He will offer arguments on such issues and will write formal memoranda to mark their importance, as Jocelyne Bourgon did in reminding Prime Minister Chrétien that the policy of maintaining the sponsorship program was under his authority, even though he left another minister to handle the file.[115] The clerk must assume the risk of creating a conflict, and of losing the confidence of some political directors, who would like to take short cuts or satisfy immediate political needs. As one former clerk puts it: 'Sometimes you have to say it: we can't and won't do it!'

On other occasions, the clerk must act as confessor and as a guide. 'We feel he's ready to support us and to help us get the support we need – it's a good sign,' a few deputy ministers said, in 2001, regarding Clerk Mel Cappe.[116] It happens often that the clerk has to resolve disputes between deputy ministers, well aware of their respective competences and personalities. Leadership, in such cases, is to find solutions to tough situations and, at the same time, manage to rally the troops.

The tough choices involve naming individuals to top jobs – transfers, evaluation, bonuses, and so on – in some cases disappointing those who have been long-time professional partners. Jim Collins explains that the most common misunderstanding in human-resource management is the notion that recruitment is the most important decision, when, in fact, it is deciding who should be maintained in a given position.[117]

Ministers do not always have an idealized perception of the public service. Many are critical of its slowness and indifference to political concerns. Every now and then, however, it falls to the clerk to remind them of the importance of the public service. In such cases, he must argue for the well-being of the public service and of its employees. In that capacity, the clerk becomes their spokesperson.

*Guiding the Public Service in Transformation: Broadcasting a Sense of Mission and Valuing Employees*

At the federal level (and increasingly across the provinces), the head of the public service must present an annual report to the prime minister, as well as to the public service itself. As one former clerk states, '80 per cent of public servants will never know the name of the clerk, and will never see his face! That is why the clerk must work through the senior executives to bring about change.' As head of the public service, he must broadcast a vision and learn to adapt it to the variety of audiences he will speak to in any given week.

To the prime minister, the clerk must demonstrate where progress has been made, where challenges lie, and where support will be necessary. To the public service, the second audience for the clerk's annual report, the clerk must be a credible spokesperson, demonstrating accomplishments and also showing confidence and engagement. K. De Vries writes that the leaders of an organization must pursue five strategies: create a sense of mission, take hold of destiny, transmit to employees how important they are, value the development of competencies, and value the sharing of common corporate values.[118] The clerk clearly fulfils this mission and must also act to ensure that his decisions and gestures are consistent with his words.

The public service expects the clerk to react clearly, quickly, and convincingly during any crises that can damage morale. He must be present constantly: even though his days are more than full, and likely unpredictable, he must travel to visit employees, attend important events, and celebrate the success of the organization with its people. His personal behaviour must be exemplary at all times, and in all ways.

Nobody in the public service is more visible, observed, obvious, or interpreted than the clerk. 'The impact of my speeches always surprised me,' said one former clerk. 'If I gave a speech on globalization, groups of young public servants would congregate to discuss the topic. If I talked of values, there would be a whirlwind of messages and reactions on the topic on the next day.' The clerk's speeches are broadly exploited. 'We point to the clerk's speech to get what we want!' said one deputy minister. Owing to his position, informal influence, and tools, the clerk has an unmatched impact on the public service. Consequently, the way he wields leadership is vitally important.

**Conclusion**

The evolution of the clerk's role has shown a number of trends. First, acting literally as a clerk to the cabinet, he has become its prime counsel and the director of the corporate-government apparatus. The reasons why the clerk plays such an important role today are a reflection of the fact that the state has grown larger, inter-ministerial cooperation has grown more critical, government files have grown more complex, and government must move more quickly to respond to situations than ever before, especially in times of minority government.

The clerk requires commitment to keep the system on an even keel. He plays a pivotal role in preserving various responsibilities and in developing a chain of accountability between the prime minister and the ministers of the cabinet, between cabinet and individual ministers, and between ministers and deputy ministers. He willingly goes against the grain to insist that transparency be optimal while at the same time being highly sensitive to the needs of cabinet secrecy and solidarity, with all the legal implications this may entail. He assumes the responsibility of performance reporting, with all that these activities imply. He grapples with the future and prepares the state's response. He must be pro-active, rather than content with a prudent and reactive mode. He must commit to implementing the government's agenda, and he must obtain results that show that the public service is responsive. He must make personal adjustments, as well as corporate adjustments, to fit political and ideological currents. The clerk must also meet personal performance objectives set with the prime minister. Horizontal management has become a key priority among clerks. As one puts it, 'I spent a lot of time at COSO [Committee of Senior Officials] pleading that deputy ministers who acted horizontally, collaboratively, and who committed themselves to the community, be subject to good performance bonuses.'

The clerk is the champion of public-sector values and is personally responsible for their promotion. Through his values, commitment, discourse, decisions, presence, and leadership, he must inspire new generations of officers and managers.

The tasks of the clerk translate into many forms of leadership (see appendix 2). For example, on a legal or constitutional question, a clerk's counsel to the prime minister could become key to ensuring that wrong decisions are avoided, but, in that case, he would become a party to the decision making. The chart in appendix 2 aims to illustrate the advisory capacity required to exercise leadership in certain situations, with certain interlocutors, and to establish a transformative style. A clerk must master the various styles of leadership, recognize different kinds of situations, and demonstrate a solid judgment on the correct options to follow.

The evolution of leadership depends on the evolution of the challenges in the position. In the clerk's case, there is no doubt that leading the community of deputy ministers and the responsibilities of corporate leadership have most recently shaped the position. This is manifested in the challenges of modern government: permanent change, globalization, and demands for transparency and more efficient service. Leadership thus requires a clear vision of the challenges, an engagement with the government agenda and a commitment to implementing it, the stimulation of enthusiasm, the confidence of peers and employees, and the protection of institutional conventions.

## Appendix 1
## Titles and Functions of Clerks

| MODELS 1 Title | | | | | | | | 2 Titles | 2 Titles |
|---|---|---|---|---|---|---|---|---|---|
| Clerk + | Clerk + | | Clerk + | | Clerk + | Clerk CE | | Greffier | Clerk |
| DM of PM+ | DM of PM+ | DM of PM+ | | Sec Office | | Sec to Cab | | DM of PM | DM to Premier |
| Sec to Cab + | Sec to Cab | Sec to Cab | DM, Office of the Exec. Comm. | of the Exec. Committee / MCE | Sec to Cab + | | | Sec to Cab/Exec Committee | |
| Head of the PS+ | Head of the PS+ | | | | Head of the PS | | | (*) Separate | |
| Resp for PCO | | | | | | | | | |
| Canada | Alta. | BC | Nun. Yuk. | Queb./NB | Ont. | PEI | Man. | Nfld. NS | Sask. |

## Appendix 2
## The Principal Traits of Leadership and the Clerk's Functions

| | Authoritative | Participative | Adaptive | Transformational | 5th type sustainable |
|---|---|---|---|---|---|
| Adviser to PM | | | x | x | |
| Adviser to cabinet | | | x | x | |
| Adviser to ministers | | | x | x | |
| DM | | x | x | x | x |
| Community Head of PCO | x | x | x | x | x |
| Head of public service | | | x | x | x |

NOTES

* The author wishes to express his thanks to the Université du Québec à Montreal, the École nationale d'administration publique, the Canada School of Public Service, and the Institute of Public Administration of Canada for their support, as well as to the many public-service executives who kindly agreed to be interviewed. The author thanks, too, Simon Dupuis for his assistance. This article was originally published as 'Les facteurs contributifs au leadership du greffier dans la fonction publique du Canada' in *Canadian Public Administration*, 50, no. 4 (2007), and was translated by Patrice Dutil. For the purposes of this book, minor editorial modifications have been made to the text of the French article.

1   Michel Vastel, 'Miss Canada fait le grand ménage,' *L'Actualité*, 19, no. 17 (1994): 28.

2   For New Brunswick, see Stewart Hyson, 'Governing from the Centre in New Brunswick,' in Luc Bernier, Keith Brownsey, and Michael Howlett, eds., *Executive Styles in Canada: Cabinet Structures and Leadership Practices in Canadian Government* (Toronto: University of Toronto Press, 2005), 90.

3   PCO website, accessed March 2006.

4   Public Service Commission of Canada, *Assessing for Competence* (Series) (Ottawa: Queen's Printer, 1998–2003).

5   Jim Collins, *Good to Great: Why Some Companies Make the Leap and Others Don't* (New York: Harper Business, 2001).

6   Chester I. Barnard, *The Functions of the Executive* (Cambridge, Mass.: Harvard University Press, 1968).

7   R.R. Blake and J.S. Mouton, *The Managerial Grid: Key Orientations for Achieving Production through People* (Houston: Gulf Publishing, 1964).

8   See J.M. Burns, *Leadership* (New York, Harper and Row, 1978); Bernard M. Bass, 'From Transactional to Transformational Leadership: Learning to Share Vision,' *Organization and Dynamics*, 18, no. 3 (1990): 19–31.

9   P. Hersey and K.H. Blanchard, 'You Want to Know Your Leadership Style,' *Training and Development Journal*, 28, no. 2 (1974): 22–37.

10  OCDE, *Développer le leadership dans le secteur public pour le 21e siècle* (Paris: Comité de la gestion publique and PUMA, 2001).

11  J. Bourgault, *The Contemporary Role and Challenges of Deputy Ministers in the Government of Canada* (Ottawa: Canadian Centre for Management Development, 2003).

12  Stuart Hart and Robert Quinn, 'Roles Executives Play: CEO's Behavioral Complexity and Performance,' *Human Relations*, 46, no. 5 (1993): 114–22.

13  Collins, *Good to Great*.
14  A. Zaleznik, 'Managers and Leaders: Are they Different?' *Harvard Business Review*, 55, no. 5 (1977): 67–78.
15  R. Saner, 'La Mondialisation et son impact sur la qualification des cadres de l'administration publique,' *Revue internationale des sciences administratives*, 67, no. 4 (2001): 739–53.
16  W.G. Bennis and B. Nanus, *Leaders: Strategies for Taking Charge* (New York: Harper and Row, 1985), 21.
17  James Elloy, 'The Influence of Superleader Behavior on Organization Commitment, Job Satisfaction and Organization Self-Esteem in a Self-Managed Work Team,' *Leadership Organisational Development Journal*, 26, no. 2 (2005): 120–7.
18  Peter Drucker, 'What Makes an Effective Executive?' *Harvard Business Review*, 59 (2004): 61.
19  Ibid., 62.
20  Paul Tellier, 'L'évolution du Bureau du Conseil privé: commentaire,' *Administration publique du Canada*, 15, no. 2 (2005): 377–9.
21  See chapter 3.
22  W.E.D. Halliday, 'The Executive of the Government of Canada,' *Canadian Public Administration*, 2, no. 4 (1959): 233.
23  Executive powers in Canada belong to the Crown as a result of royal prerogatives or by constitutional law (ss. 8 and 11 of the BNA Act, 1867). The prerogatives are delegated to the governor general, acting on the advice of the Privy Council. The latter is a large body, consisting of former and current members (all for life), prime ministers of the Commonwealth, and former speakers of the House of Commons and Senate. These council members do not meet; instead, the committee of the Privy Council consisting of actual ministers (members of Parliament recommended by the prime minister to be sworn in by the governor general) reports to the governor general in council. It exercises the executive power of the governor general by issuing orders-in-council, commissions, or proclamations. The Privy Council is a legal designation, while cabinet is the functional expression of executive power that makes decisions and coordinates the action of ministers. It is through cabinet that ministers exercise responsible government. Halliday, 'The Executive of the Government of Canada,' 229–33.
24  See Gordon Osbaldeston, '1992 341: BNAA (SC 1867, s.130).' Prepared for the Cabinet secretariat: PC 1940–1121, 25 March 1940.
25  Halliday, 'The Executive of the Government of Canada,' 235–41.
26  Murray A. Hay, 'Understanding the PCO: The Ultimate Facilitator,' *Optimum*, 13, no. 1 (1982): 6.

27  Accessed March 2005.
28  Gordon Robertson, 'The Changing Role of the Privy Council Office,' *Canadian Public Administration*, 14, no. 4 (1971): 504.
29  See the PCO website.
30  Bourgault, *The Contemporary Role*, 124.
31  Paul Tellier, 'L'Évolution du Bureau du conseil privé: Commentaire,' *Administration Publique du Canada*, 15, no. 2 (!972): 378.
32  Gordon Robertson, *Memoirs of a Very Civil Servant* (Toronto: University of Toronto Press, 2000), 257.
33  Robertson, 'The Changing Role,' 492–3.
34  Donald Savoie, 'The Federal Government: Revisiting Court Government in Canada,' in Bernier, Brownsey, and Howlett, eds., *Executive Styles*.
35  A. Kroeger, from a speech delivered at IPAC's 'Leadership Lessons of Secretaries to Cabinet' conference, Toronto, May 2005.
36  Ted Glenn, 'Politics, Personality and History in Ontario's Administrative Style,' 169; Keith Brownsey, 'The Post-Institutionalized Cabinet: The Administrative Style of Alberta,' 221; and Ken Rasmussen and Gregory P. Marchildon, 'Saskatchewan's Executive Decision-making Style: The Centrality of Planning,' 207. All in Bernier, Brownsey, and Howlett, eds., *Executive Styles*.
37  Robertson, 'The Changing Role,' 508.
38  Jeffery Simpson, *Discipline of Power: The Conservative Incertitude and the Liberal Restoration* (New York and Toronto: Dodd, Mead, 1980).
39  Robertson, 'The Changing Role,' 500.
40  Charlotte Gray, 'The Fixer,' *Saturday Night*, December 1985, 13–17.
41  PCO website, accessed March 2005.
42  It is commonly understood that cabinet assembles all the members of the Council of Ministers as well as others designated by the prime minister. Thus, all ministers of departments created by legislation – such as Agriculture, for example – are members of the Council of Ministers; others who hold portfolios not created by legislation – such as a Secretary of State for the Elderly – do not sit at the Council of Ministers but do sit at the cabinet. Jean Chrétien applied this distinction between 1993 and 2004. See Nicole Jauvin, 'Gouvernement, ministres, macro-organigramme et réseaux,' in J. Bourgault et al., *Administration publique et management public: expériences canadiennes* (Publications du Québec, 1997), 43–57; and Christopher Dunn, *The Institutionalized Cabinet: Governing the Western Provinces* (Montreal and Kingston: McGill-Queen's University Press, 1995).
43  Halliday, 'The Executive of the Government of Canada,' 232.
44  Hay, 'Understanding the PCO,' 6.

45  Robertson, *Memoirs*, 216.
46  Mitchell Sharp, 'Decision-making in the Federal Cabinet,' *Canadian Public Administration*, 19, no. 1 (1976): 3.
47  For example, the Gomery Commission followed legal precedents and conventions to seek the information it required to carry out its investigations.
48  Savoie, 'The Federal Government,' 34–5.
49  PCO website, 'Roles of the Clerk of the Privy Council,' accessed March 2005.
50  Savoie, 'The Federal Government,' 25.
51  Ibid., 37.
52  Robertson, *Memoirs*, 217.
53  C. McCall-Newman, 'Michael Pitfield and the Politics of Mismanagement,' *Saturday Night*, vol. 97, October 1982, 27. Pitfield was not the first clerk whose political affiliation was well known. Jack Pickersgill, whose Liberal partisanship was never in doubt, was the most prominent. See J.L. Granatstein, *The Ottawa Men: The Civil Service Mandarins, 1935–1957* (Toronto: Oxford University Press, 1982).
54  P. Foster, *The Sorcerer's Apprentices: Canada's Super-Bureaucrats and the Energy Mess* (Toronto: Collins, 1982).
55  McCall-Newman, 'Michael Pitfield,' 26.
56  Ibid., 28, 35.
57  Foster, *The Sorcerer's Apprentices*, 54.
58  Granatstein, *The Ottawa Men*, 3.
59  Ibid., 207.
60  Robertson, *Memoirs*, 216.
61  Ibid., 207.
62  Granatstein, *The Ottawa Men*, 207.
63  Robertson, *Memoirs*, 217.
64  Ibid., 255.
65  PCO website, accessed March 2006.
66  Savoie, 'The Federal Government,' 37.
67  Hay, 'Understanding the PCO,' 15.
68  Savoie, 'The Federal Government,' 54.
69  Sharp, 'Decision-making,' 1.
70  Savoie, 'The Federal Government,' 5.
71  Sharp, 'Decision-making,' 1.
72  Gray, 'The Fixer,' 14.
73  Savoie, 'The Federal Government,' 40.
74  J. Bourgault and S. Dion, *Comment évaluer un haut fonctionnaire? La réponse des sous-ministres fédéraux* (Ottawa: Centre Canadien de Gestion, 1993).
75  Jacques Bourgault, *The Contemporary Role and Challenges of Deputy Ministers*

*in the Government of Canada* (Ottawa: CCMD, 2003; www.csps-efpc.gc.ca/research/publications/html/cont_role/cr_3_e.html); and Savoie, 'The Federal Government.'

76  Savoie, 'The Federal Government,' 40; and Gray, 'The Fixer,' 17.

77  Vastel, 'Miss Canada,' 28.

78  J. Bourgault, *Corporate Management Practices in Governments of Canada: A Fact-finding Report and Networking Initiative* (Government of Quebec, Ministère du Conseil Exécutif, March 2005). This report was initially delivered on October 2004 with the title *Les structures de gestion des emplois supérieurs et la gestion corporative au niveau des sous-ministres au Canada.*

79  This was a restaurant in Quebec City reputed to be the haunt of influential senior executives in the Quebec public service.

80  PCO website, accessed March 2006.

81  http://www.pco-bcp.gc.ca/default.asp?Language=F&Page=aboutpco

82  Savoie, 'The Federal Government,' 37.

83  J. Bourgault, 'Paramètres synergiques du pouvoir des hauts fonctionnaires,' *Revue canadienne de science politique,* 26, no. 2 (1983): 227–56.

84  Gray, 'The Fixer,' 17.

85  Vastel, 'Miss Canada,' 28.

86  Gordon Osbaldeston, *Organizing to Govern* (Toronto: McGraw-Hill, 1992), 135.

87  Adrien Payette, *L'efficacité des gestionnaires et des organisations* (Quebec: Presses de l'Université du Québec, Sillery, 1988).

88  H. Mintzberg and J. Bourgault, *Managing Publicly* (Toronto: University of Toronto Press and IPAC, 2000), 20.

89  Foster, *The Sorcerer's Apprentices*; Robertson, 'The Changing Role.'

90  Foster, *The Sorcerer's Apprentices*, 52–3.

91  Jacques Bourgault, *Les structures de gestion des employs supérieurs et la gestion corporative au niveau des sous-ministres au Canada* (Quebec: Gouvernement du Québec, ministère du Conseil executive, 28 October 2004), 55.

92  Savoie, 'The Federal Government,' 33.

93  Robertson, *Memoirs*, 256.

94  Norman J. Ruff, 'The West Annex: Executive Structure and Administrative Style in British Columbia,' in Bernier, Brownsey, and Howlett, eds., *Executive Styles*, 239.

95  Foster, *The Sorcerer's Apprentices*, 55.

96  Gray, 'The Fixer,' 17.

97  Vastel, 'Miss Canada,' 28.

98  Robertson, 'The Changing Role,' 506.

99  Marc Lalonde, 'The Changing Role of the Prime Minister's Office,' *Canadian Public Administration*, 14, no. 4 (1971): 529.

100 Robertson, 'The Changing Role,' 506.
101 Luc Bernier et al., 'Conclusion: Executive Institutional Developments in Canada's Provinces,' in Bernier, Brownsey, and Howlett, eds., *Executive Styles*, 247.
102 Robertson, *Memoirs*, 207.
103 Vastel, 'Miss Canada,' 29.
104 Bernier et al., *Executive Styles*, 151, 246.
105 Christopher Dunn, 'The Persistence of the Institutionalized Cabinet: The Central Executive in Newfoundland and Labrador,' in Bernier, Brownsey, and Howlett, eds., *Executive Styles*, 73.
106 Robertson, *Memoirs*, 257.
107 Collins, *Good to Great.*
108 Gray, 'The Fixer,' 15–17.
109 Michael Pitfield, 'The Shape of Government in the 1980s: Techniques for Policy and Instruments for Policy Formulation at the Federal Level,' *Canadian Public Administration*, 19, no.1 (1976): 19.
110 J. Aberbach, R. Putnam, and B. Rockman, *Bureaucrats and Politicians in Western Democracies* (Cambridge, Mass.: Harvard University Press, 1981).
111 Gray, 'The Fixer,' 14.
112 Halliday, 'The Executive of the Government of Canada.'
113 PCO website, accessed May 2005.
114 Nick D'Ombrain, 'Ministerial Responsibility and the Machinery of Government,' *Canadian Public Administration*, 50, no. 2 (2007): 195–218 (203–13).
115 See, for example, the testimony and evidence produced by the Gomery Commission.
116 Bourgault, *The Contemporary Role*, 134.
117 Collins, *Good to Great*, 44.
118 Manfred K. de Vries, *Les Mystères du Leadership: vendre l'espoir* (Paris: Village mondial, 2000).

# PART TWO

## Leadership in Transformation

# 3 Clerk as *Révélateur*: A Panoramic View

RUTH HUBBARD AND GILLES PAQUET

... he was born poor, died rich,
   begat a new form of art
and hurt no one along the way
                    – Duke Ellington at Louis Armstrong's funeral

The way a socio-economy governs itself is defined by a composite of private, public, and social mechanisms, practices, norms, organizations, institutions, and regimes. This amalgam constitutes an ecology of governance: 'many different systems and different kinds of systems interacting with one another, like the multiple organisms in an ecosystem.'[1] As W.T. Anderson suggests, such arrangements are not necessarily 'neat, peaceful, stable or efficient ... but in a continual process of learning and changing and responding to feedback.'

From the time it became a country, in 1867, Canada has had a variety of ecologies of governance. The relative importance, and the architecture, of the public sector (the machinery of government, organization, processes, and personnel) have evolved as a result both of external and contextual circumstances and of the transformation of the guiding principles and norms in good currency at any particular time. The public sector (federal, provincial, local) acquired an increasingly significant weight over this period. Some have argued that it was because the public sector could do most things better than other sectors.[2] In the recent past, this sort of assumption about the superiority of the public sector has been questioned, but the public sector remains a significant factor in the governing of the country.

The last three decades have brought new, and even more daunting, challenges for the public sector: the need to accommodate deep and growing diversity, globalization, and citizens' rising desires to be 'kept in the loop' have increased the pressure to adjust both more substantially and more rapidly.[3] This has led to public-sector reforms throughout the world.

The clerk of the Privy Council (hereafter, the clerk), who is also the secretary to cabinet and head of the (federal) public service in Canada, is a central figure in the federal government-cum-state governance apparatus. The incumbent sits at the heart of the 'federal government' and holds many of the key levers that can redefine the 'shape' of the public sector.

The current duties of the clerk are wide-ranging and are described as follows by the Privy Council Office (PCO): 'the most senior non-political official in the Government of Canada ... provides professional, non-partisan support to the Prime Minister on all policy and operational issues that may affect the government ... [and] also has particular responsibilities with respect to: ensuring the continuity of government between successive administrations; keeping custody of the records of previous administrations; and enabling the government of the day to understand and recognize the established conventions of Canada's constitutional monarchy ... [Acts as] Deputy Minister to the Prime Minister ... [offering] advice on appointing senior office holders in the public service and organizing the government ... Secretary to the Cabinet ... [and] Head of the Public Service.'[4]

In a Westminster-type system, the prime minister, as leader of the political party that forms the government (the executive), is quite powerful. The executive formally 'governs' with the consent of Parliament, and many key positions (including those of deputy ministers and many heads of Crown corporations) are filled de facto by the prime minister. The power carried by the position is especially great if the distribution of seats in Parliament is based on a 'first past the post' system of election (as is the case in Canada). Such a system tends to produce a majority for one political party in the legislature. In such situations, the clerk also can carry enormous power and influence within the formal machinations of government.

Following the evolution of the role of clerk through history can provide interesting insights into the ways in which Canada has coped with the challenges of change. The clerk is obviously neither the sole site of power nor necessarily the most important in a federal system that leaves much of the public sector under provincial and local *dominium*, but the incumbent has a privileged vantage point.

He/she can observe the interactions among the different forces at play (private, public, and social; federal, provincial, local), as well as the strains that they impose on the existing governing architecture, and the incumbent has a vast array of direct and indirect levers with which to influence the strategies that have been designed by all these actors to cope with these strains.

These levers are dependent – for their weight, usefulness, and scope – upon the goals and character of the prime minister whom the clerk serves, as well as upon his/her own. Like a seismograph, the clerk registers much of what happens in the environment and perceives and acts on both challenges and opportunities with varying degrees of effectiveness.

Our strategy is to look at the clerk as *révélateur* (i.e., as a syncretic character that reveals, through its pattern of activities and more or less explicitly stated priorities, the way in which the existing forces in the broader socio-political terrain are aligned, somehow kept in balance, and harnessed to allow progress). Some of this pattern is ascribable to external pressures but much of it is an echo of an internal reconciliation of the different principles and power sources at play. This approach aims at making more explicit some of the latent or hidden or emergent tensions that would not necessarily be reflected in official statements but are prime movers in the dynamics involved.

Since one may presume that the clerk is likely to be more fully aware than most other actors of the tensions at work, and since his/her job is to ensure that they remain under control, his/her statements and action plans (even when they are somewhat cryptic and revealed in oblique ways) may be regarded as indicative of the main zones of friction in the ecology of governance and of the strategies to deal with them.

We use this approach to provide a panoramic view of the evolution of the clerk's role at the federal level, in Canada, since Confederation. The first section sketches some key aspects of the evolving context; section two identifies the different clerks and prime ministers who worked in tandem, highlighting some markers for the different periods. In the third section, we put forward hypotheses about the contextual forces at work, and the demands that they impose on societal governance, and suggest ways in which these forces have shaped the evolution of the core role of the clerk. The fourth section provides a 'windshield survey' of the different periods in support of the plausibility of our hypotheses.

Finally, we speculate on the future of the clerk's function and the governance it underpins.

## An Evolving Context

Before exploring the evolution of the role of the clerk, it is crucial to identify a number of interdependent sets of forces that have shaped the social architecture of governance in Canada over the last century or more.

First, external forces have rocked the country: two world wars, the Depression of the 1930s, the internationalization of production, decolonization, and so on. These have produced a number of important transformations in the governance system. Moreover, the frames of reference have evolved and gradually transformed Canada's very notion of its capacity to govern itself. The emergence of Keynesian economics turned economic thinking on its head with the notion that government could and should manage 'aggregate demand.' This has underpinned the rise of the welfare state in the developed world. Later, as governance failures came to be ascribed to the failures of the public sector, 'New Public Management' swept the Western world and modified the very notion of the public sector.

Secondly, the various shocks that hit the Canadian socio-economy revealed that the federal governing arrangements hammered out in the nineteenth century were not satisfactory for coping with twentieth-century crises. A long series of commissions – from the one on the relationship between capital and labour in the nineteenth century to the Rowell-Sirois Commission established in 1937, along with a variety of task forces and working groups – have suggested ways to respond to the need to take better account of significant imbalances and major dysfunctions.

Thirdly, the role of the state itself has changed as a consequence of these developments: from being an important player operating in a relatively narrow range of the governance terrain to one that occupied more of the center stage in the 1950s and 1960s. It has actively (and some would say intrusively) set up programs to give expression to the welfare state and has presumed itself to be the premier spokesperson and guardian of the public interest.

More recently, concerns about government overload and declining legitimacy, along with social limits to growth imposed by the welfare state, have given rise to experimentation with new ways of governing

Table 1
The drift from G to g

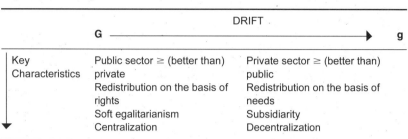

| | DRIFT | |
|---|---|---|
| | G ⟶ | g |
| Key Characteristics | Public sector ≥ (better than) private | Private sector ≥ (better than) public |
| | Redistribution on the basis of rights | Redistribution on the basis of needs |
| | Soft egalitarianism | Subsidiarity |
| | Centralization | Decentralization |

strategically.[5] After almost a century when the idea of the centrality of the state seemed to grow boundlessly, there has recently been a reversal of the trend: one can observe an underlying drift from big (G) Government to small (g) governance. Table 1 illustrates some important characteristics of this drift.[6]

The old assumption that the public sector could always outperform the private sector has been challenged. In lieu of a top-down, state-engineered, soft egalitarism, based on rights and predicated on centralization (i.e., in order to be able to redistribute resources, one must first bring them to the centre), a new bottom-up governance framework has emerged in response to weakening east-west economic ties and rising, deep diversity among segments of the country. This new framework of governance has been woven around the notion of needs and the principle of subsidiarity.[7]

These strands of experience suggest a provisional partitioning of the Canadian experience into four distinct periods characterized by particular patterns of challenges and responses. To use a very crude architectural metaphor, one might say that the first period (1867–1940) can be seen as one of basic construction of the federated house; the second (1940–75) as one of dramatic expansion of the house with key rooms being added; the third (1975–94) as one during which the house becomes more and more ill-suited to the family's needs; and the more recent, fourth, period (1994–2006) as one in which the federal house is gradually restructured into condominiums, but *dans le désordre*. Some key events for these four periods are highlighted in Table 2 to provide a basic background for our discussion.

This commingling of forces has given rise to two 'meta-phenomena.' The first is the evolution of the relative importance of the federal gov-

Table 2
Three interdependent threads: Some examples

| Period | External forces | Strains on the federation | Role of the state |
|---|---|---|---|
| I (1867–1940) G<br>Building the<br>house | ♦ Gaining the authority to<br>govern itself: WW 1,<br>Charnak (1922), Imperial<br>Conference (1923)<br>♦ Westminster Act (1931)<br>♦ social programs sweep<br>Europe<br>♦ Keynesian economics<br>(1936) | ♦ Early wounds:<br>Manitoba schools<br>(1880), Riel Rebellion<br>(1885), conscription<br>(1917), residential<br>schools<br>♦ Rowell-Sirois<br>Commission on fiscal<br>imbalance begins work<br>(1937) | ♦ Activist government: last<br>half of the 19th century –<br>1920s (infrastructure<br>railways, harbours,<br>navigation) and tariffs)<br>♦ Maritime subsidies and<br>special freight rates<br>(1926) |
| II (1940–75)<br><br>Expanding the<br>house and<br>finishing key<br>rooms | ♦ WW II<br>♦ Canadian Supreme<br>Court final arbiter (1949) | ♦ Rowell-Sirois rejected<br>(1940) except for UI<br>♦ Tax powers borrowed<br>in WW II took decades<br>to return<br>♦ Conscription (1944)<br>♦ Status Indians get the<br>right to vote (1960)<br>♦ White paper on Status<br>Indians rejected (1969)<br>♦ Peter Lougheed,<br>Alberta (1971) | ♦ Rise of welfare state: UI<br>(1940), family<br>allowances (1945), OAS/<br>GIS (1951), modern<br>equalization (1957),<br>medicare (1966), CPP<br>(1966), the DREE (1969)<br><br>♦ Rise of individual rights:<br>Bill of Rights in federal<br>jurisdiction (1960), OLA<br>(1970). |
| III (1975–94)<br>House ill-suited<br>to the family's<br>needs | ♦ Thatcher (1979–90)<br>♦ Reagan (1981–9)<br>♦ New Zealand reform<br>(IMF driver)<br>♦ UK executive agencies<br>♦ Australia – 5-yr terms for<br>deputies | ♦ Regional maturity:<br>– René Lévesque,<br>Que. (1976)<br>– Frank McKenna,<br>N.B. (1988)<br>– Ralph Klein, Alta.<br>(1992)<br>♦ Aboriginal aspirations<br>acknowledged (1991)<br>♦ Quebec opposes<br>patriation (1982)<br>♦ Quebec referenda:<br>getting closer to 'yes'<br>♦ Meech Lake (1987),<br>Charlottetown (1992) | ♦ Belt tightening begins,<br>late 1970s<br>♦ NEP (1980)<br>♦ Charter of Rights and<br>Freedoms (1982) |
| IV (1994–2007)<br>Condos? | ♦ Blair – devolution<br>♦ North American<br>economic integration<br>accelerates | ♦ Provinces/territories<br>start saying no (Gun<br>Registry (1995) and<br>Kyoto (1998))<br>♦ Nunavut (1999)<br>♦ Council of Federation<br>(2003)<br>♦ B.C. Citizens'<br>Assembly On Electoral<br>Reform (2003) | ♦ Program Review (1994)<br>♦ Deficit eliminated (1995–<br>6), not to return<br>♦ Big, centralized<br>government with<br>differences:<br>– innovative funding<br>– restructuring,<br>retooling, reframing<br>– infrastructure<br>♦ Fiscal imbalance again<br>(three levels)<br>♦ Federal money flows to<br>problems: health, cities,<br>'have not' provinces |

g

ernment within the public-sector apparatus in Canada. As major infrastructure projects proved essential, and world wars and economic
crises unfolded after Confederation, the federal government had to
shoulder an ever-greater portion of state action. Indeed, by the end of
the 1930s, a need was felt for fiscal transfers from the provinces to the
federal government to enable it to do its job. The valence of the federal
government within the public-household sector in Canada grew
steadily until the 1960s.

Since then, as social issues (such as health, education, and quality of
life) have come to dominate the state agenda, provinces and local communities have faced increasing strains and have demanded and
received a growing portion of the fiscal pie. Moreover, as provinces/
territories have acquired new capabilities, the relative importance of
the federal portion of the public sector has declined. Recent discussions
about the problems of fiscal imbalance call for yet more fiscal transfers
from the federal to the provincial and local governments, so that they
can perform their legitimate job adequately.

The second meta-phenomenon is the slow and silent revolution that
has seen the executive branch acquire more and more real power and
control over the public sector. One might legitimately speak of a drift
from a parliamentary democracy to a governmental democracy. This
drift is not unique to Canada, but, in this country, the executive branch
has absorbed the power of the legislature to a greater extent than elsewhere: Parliament has become more and more a spectator to the government's operations. Importantly, as well, within the executive in
Canada, power is increasingly seen as concentrated around the Prime
Minister's Office (PMO).

These two meta-phenomena have had a significant impact on the
role of the clerk. On the one hand, the slippage in the valence of the federal government has reduced the scope of the clerk's power and transformed his/her role into one calling for a greater capacity to cooperate
(a shift from power *over* to power *with*). On the other hand, the growing
authority of the executive, and the centralization of power around the
PMO, has significantly increased the clerk's power and relative influence.

On balance, the potential for the clerk's influencing the federal public
sector's architecture and operations (and therefore the whole governance system) has probably grown. This does not mean, however, that
the political masters of the day have allowed the clerks to employ the
full sweep of their potential powers, nor does it mean that their usable

powers have been exploited as well as possible, or to the fullest extent that they might have been.

## The Honour Roll

In the period from 1867 to 2007, twenty clerks (nineteen men and one woman) have occupied the position of clerk of the Canadian Privy Council, and they have served governments led by twenty-two different prime ministers. To help keep the names, relationships, and challenges of the time in mind, Table 3 (A-D) co-relates the clerk-prime minister tandems for this long historical stretch, partitioned into four periods, with a sample of the challenges faced by the governance apparatus of Canada in each time frame.

The clerk has been called upon to play quite different roles in each of these four eras. We shall attempt, in the next two sections, to identify the dynamics underpinning this broad evolution, and to probe each of these periods provisionally to gain an appreciation of the *vraie nature* of each period, as well as the ways in which the clerk can serve as a useful *révélateur* of the constellation of forces at work, of the *habitus* of the period, and of the propensity to deal with issues in a particular way.

### Through an Iconoscope: A Guiding Hypothesis

To explore the evolution that has taken place, we would like to use an instrument similar to a nineteenth-century iconoscope – a crude optical instrument that accentuated differences the better to appreciate them. The design of our iconoscope is inspired by the work of F.E. Emery and E.L. Trist (1965), J.E. McCann and J. Selsky (1984), and L. Metcalfe (1998). It borrows some elements of their neo-institutional approach and uses them to co-relate some of the central activities connected with the different governing and management functions of the clerk with the texture of the environment.

Our basic hypothesis is that, as a society moves from a placid to a clustered- or disturbed-reactive and then to a turbulent and even an hyper-turbulent environment, the nature of its governance changes and the role of the clerk (with the predictable leads and lags) registers and reflects, with varying degrees of accuracy, the way in which the environment has been transformed, the extent to which the governing apparatus has evolved, and the extent to which it has kept up with the

Table 3A
Canadian clerks through history: Period I (1867–1940)

| Year | Clerk | Prime minister | Key events |
|---|---|---|---|
| 1867–72 | W.H. Lee | J.A. Macdonald (C) (1867–73) | British North America (BNA) Act. Power split: UK parliament, fed. & prov. governments |
| 1872–80 | W.A. Himsworth* | | Activist state last half 19th century, first two decades of 20th. Federal focus on infrastructure (railways, harbours, navigation) and tariffs. |
| | | A. Mackenzie (L) (1873–8) | |
| | | J.A. Macdonald (C) (1878–91) | |
| 1880–2 | J.-O. Côté | | |
| 1882–1907 | J.J. McGee | | |
| | | J.J.C. Abbott (C) (1891–2) | |
| | | J. Thompson (C) (1892–4) | |
| | | M. Bowell (C) (1894–6) | |
| | | C. Tupper (C) (May–July 1896) | |
| | | W. Laurier (L) (1896–1911) | |
| 1907–23 | R. Boudreau | | External affairs established (1909) |
| | | R.L. Borden (C,U) (1911–20) | WW1 (1914–18). Canada full partner at Paris peace conference. |
| | | | Conservative-Liberal coalition (begins 1917) |
| | | | Civil service reform (1918–19); modern Civil Service Commission (PSC) begins |
| | | A. Meighen (U) (1920–1) | Coalition formally ends |
| | | W.L.M. King (L) (1921–6) | Charnak crisis (1922) |
| | | | First Crown corporation: CNR (1922) |
| | | | Imperial War Conference (1923). Another step to independence |
| 1923–40 | E.J. Lemaire | | King/Byng affair (1926) |
| | | A. Meighen (C) (June–Sept. 1926) | Brief minority government |
| | | W.L.M.King (L) (1926–30) | Great Depression (1929–39) |
| | | R.B. Bennett (C) (19305) | Westminster Act (1931) cuts apron strings |
| | | | Bank of Canada & public broadcasting (1935) |
| | | W.L.M. King (L) (1935–48) | Rowell Sirois established 1937 |
| | | | WW II (1939–45) |

* Note: The PCO website incorrectly spells his name "Hinsworth."

Table 3B
Canadian clerks through history: Period II (1940–75)

| Year | Clerk | Prime minister | Key events |
|---|---|---|---|
| 1940–9 | A.D.P. Heeney | King continues | Provinces relinquish tax room for WWII<br>Rowell-Sirois reports 1940 (Que., Ont. & Alberta boycott it)<br>Rise of the welfare state: UI (1940)<br>Family allowances begin (1944) |
| | | L. St Laurent (L) (1948–57) | |
| 1949–52 | N.A. Robertson | | Supreme Court becomes final arbiter (1949)<br>OAS/GIS begins (1951) |
| 1952–53 | J.W. Pickersgill | | |
| 1954–63 | R.B. Bryce | | Modern equalization program begins (1957) |
| | | J.G. Diefenbaker (PC) (1957–63) | Height of Cold War, Cuban Missile Crisis<br>Glassco (1962): 'let managers manage' |
| 1963–75 | R.G. Robertson | L.B. Pearson (L) (1963–8) | CPP begins mid-1960s (QPP analogue)<br>Medicare begins 1960s<br>Constitutional-reform efforts begin 1960s |
| | | P.E. Trudeau (L) (1968–75) | DREE established  (1969)<br>OLA (1970)<br>Alberta starts asserting itself (Lougheed, 1971) |

challenges to be met. In a relatively placid environment, self-conservation and preservation prevail and tactical moves suffice; when the environment is placid-clustered, strategic adjustments are required; when the environment is disturbed-reactive, governing entails some adjustments in the functioning and operations of the organization.

When the environment becomes turbulent, however, and the ground is in motion, more fundamental modifications are in order: social learning is necessary. It is not any longer sufficient to tinker with tactics, strategies, and operations. One must adjust the very structure and mission of the organization in order to ensure that it responds adequately to the changes in circumstances. Social learning entails not only a mod-

Table 3C
Canadian clerks through history: Period III  (1975–94)

| Year | Clerk | Prime minister | Key events |
|---|---|---|---|
| 1975–9 | P.M. Pitfield | Trudeau continues | PQ first elected in Quebec (1976) |
| 1979–80 | M. Massé | J. Clark (PC) (1979–80) | Minority government |
| 1980–2 | P.M. Pitfield | Trudeau (L) (1980–4) | NEP (1980) |
| 1982–5 | G.F. Osbaldeston | | Quebec referendum defeated  (1980) Constitution patriated effective 1982: last ribbons of empire, no Quebec support, Charter, symbolic recognition of aboriginals Canada Health Act  (1984) |
| 1985–92 | P.M. Tellier | J. Turner (L) (June–Sept. 1984) B. Mulroney (PC) (1984–93) | FTA implemented (1989) Frank McKenna NB premier (1988–98) PS 2000 TFs – 1989 Nielsen TF Meech Lake reform failed 1990 RCAP (1991) |
| 1992–4 | G.S. Shortliffe | | Quebec referendum defeated (1992) (smaller percentage) Ralph Klein (1992–2007) Charlottetown Accord defeated (1992) Aboriginal as third order of government End of constitutional reform attempts |
| | | K. Campbell (PC) (June–Nov. 1993) J. Chrétien (L) (1993–2003) | Radical structural change, 32 departments to 23 |

Table 3D
Canadian clerks through history: Period IV(1994–2007)

| Year | Clerk | Prime minister | Key events |
| --- | --- | --- | --- |
| 1994–9 | J. Bourgon | Chrétien continues | 2nd Quebec referendum defeated (1995) 50.4% to 49.6% response to RCAP (1996) Post-Kyoto process approved (1997) Canada signs Kyoto (1998) Program Review to eliminate deficit, renewal of policy capacity, La relève |
| 1999–2002 | M. Cappe | | Alberta opposes fed/prov communiqué on climate change Nunavut established (1999) Romanow & Kirby on health care (2001) |
| 2002–6 | A. Himelfarb | | B.C. Citizens' assembly electoral reform begins (2003) Council of the Federation (2003) |
| | | P. Martin (L) 2003–6 | Sponsorship scandal, strengthening public management, democratic deficit, cities agenda |
| 2006 | K. Lynch | S. Harper (C) 2006– | Minority government takes power Feb. 2006 |

ification of the means and ways used in the pursuit of the general objectives of the organization, but also a reframing of the notion of the business the organization is in, an adjustment of its very mission, objectives, and ends.[8]

In the language of C. Argyris and D.A. Schön,[9] social learning is truly double-looped learning: in its efforts to adapt to new circumstances and to cope, the organization must first learn new ways to reach its objectives, but it must also be ready to reframe those very objectives and invent new ones when the circumstances come to show that the old ones are no longer useful. For it is only through social learning leading to an overhauling of the structure and mission of the concern that it may hope to survive.

In the face of a turbulent environment, double-looped social learning therefore leads to fundamental innovation as a surviving strategy – through a morphological transformation in the structure of the organization but also through the very redefinition of what business the organization is in. In addition, such modifications normally lead to building on collaborative strategies with groups that might have been competitors in normal times but now become partners because they see that collaboration is required for survival.

If and when hyper-turbulence threatens to become endemic, collaborative strategies may fail to harmonize member goals around shared principles and appreciative skills: collaboration may be so expensive, threatening, ineffective, or counterintuitive that only social triage will do – i.e., a partitioning of the environment and of the system into domains varying radically in terms of turbulence and adaptive capacity in an attempt to better allocate and protect the limited adaptive capacity.[10]

In a relatively placid environment, with state power clearly allocated to multi-level governments that can operate in relatively airtight compartments, the clerk can be a simple note taker and recorder of decisions taken by his/her federal political masters. As the environment becomes more complex, though, it requires different governance capabilities and interventions. To meet this need, the clerk (and his/her entourage) becomes the co-leader (with the prime minister of the day) of the architectural team, and is also a key member of the strategic team. While the compartments of different levels of government can still operate relatively effectively, some overhaul is essential.

In turbulent environments, the ground is in motion and the reference can no longer be set goals and means because they turn out to have to be revised substantially as the environment changes. The reference becomes some shared focal points that serve as the basis for orientation maps. These focal points are principles not shared values. The reference to shared values is an echo effect of folk sociology. It is quite difficult to find such shared values in a pluralistic society. One may reasonably state, as Joseph Heath has done in the 2003 John L. Manion Lecture,[11] that this is a myth based on the false presumption that 'social integration is achieved through value-consensus,' that shared values are what make people cohesive as a group, and that the state exists to promote these values.

While most sociologists have by now abandoned the theory of shared values, 'shared values theorists' continue to thrive. Indeed, one of the main problems with the way in which the Canadian Charter of Rights and Freedoms has been interpreted is that it has been regarded as a system of values rather than of certain principles (efficiency, autonomy, subsidiarity, and so on) deemed to help maintain a neutrality of the state and other institutions vis-à-vis different notions of the good.

In a world in which hyper-turbulence lurks just around the corner, even agreement on principles and effort at collaborating fail. The only survival strategy then is to collect and protect the available resources and skills in the hands of those best able to utilize them, and to sacrifice those portions of the concern less likely to survive. It is tantamount to the sacrifice of a limb to save the rest of the body. Such partitioning is always agonistic, and the allocation of resources gives rise to some dis-aggregation of the organization: in the language of McCann and Sel-sky,[12] certain segments (social enclaves) with better adaptive capacity are strengthened by being provided with additional resources, while other segments (social vortices) with less adaptive capacity are literally sacrificed and allowed to disintegrate.

This sort of partitioning may not be desirable for ethical reasons, but, as members become aware that by selective decoupling they can create a defensible space as well as a shared identity for defending scarce resources and skills from both real and perceived threats, social enclaves will materialize, if only to avoid catastrophic collapses.

Leadership in turbulent environments amounts to identifying prin-ciples likely to provide the requisite coordination, integration, and stewardship: an agreement on a few guideposts likely to permit the conversation to proceed, to facilitate double-looped learning, and to ease the required structural changes. In high-risk environments, com-bining uncertain threats with unimaginable ones,[13] hyper-turbulence may become commonplace and major transformations are in order. The shift from G to g becomes not just useful but necessary. However, it is not always easy to effect: major forces of dynamic conservatism (persons and groups who would be badly served by the changes) may effectively slow down the process of reform for quite a while.

As the degree of turbulence in the environment increases (Type 4, in the language of Emery and Trist),[14] operational, tactical, and strategic management reforms are no longer sufficient. Required is the develop-ment of capacities for collaborative action in managing large-scale reor-ganizations and structural changes at the macro level.[15] In such environments, the ground is in motion. The private, public, and social sectors and the multiple levels of government acting independently not only cannot ensure effectiveness but may make things worse and amplify tendencies towards disintegration. What is needed (in the lan-guage of Emery and Trist) is collective action by 'dissimilar organiza-tions whose fates are, basically, positively correlated.'

If such collaboration were to fail, the emergence of great strain would lead to partitioning – to the emergence of social enclaves and vortices – and eventually to the collapse of the system. In a catastrophe-theory-type graph, Metcalfe has synthesized the predicament that a shift to a truly turbulent environment raises for organizations, and he depicts the major aspects of the issue in three dimensions: the degree of complexity of the environment, the degree of sophistication of management/governance capacities, and the level of governance effectiveness (Figure 1).

He shows that, as complexity increases, management capacities must improve to avoid disintegration. If these capacities already exist, they must be brought into use (a-b); if they do not exist, they must be developed (e-b). If they do not exist and no development effort is made (e-f) – or if the capacity building is inadequate (e-c-d) – then disintegration ensues. A Type 4 environment requires innovations that strengthen *collaborative* relationships.[16]

This framework shows how the tasks of group mobilization and building capabilities are integrally related. The architectural team and the strategic team charged to make use of the new structures are profoundly different: different in make-up (broader), in leverage (more indirect), and in scope (wider). It is not so much a team as *an ecology of teams* that gradually, circuitously, and experimentally, by trial and error, feel their way forward (learning well or poorly along the way). The emphasis is on the need for creative politics, for innovative institutions, and for new modes of coordination.[17]

The clerk, who stands at the interface between the environment and the political process, will 'register' the tremors in the environment and should/will be called upon to 'respond' by playing a key role (directly or indirectly) in 'shaping' the governance capabilities (and safeguarding the integrity of key state processes). It is possible that in disturbed environments the response may be made sharply and effectively at the operational level, and that the appropriate stewardship may ensue. Turbulent environments, however, are a different matter. What is called for is a new form of leadership that may require much more than simple retooling and restructuring. Collaboration may necessitate a whole reframing of the situation, an enlightened capacity to eliminate the significant obstacles to collaboration, and much imagination in mobilizing reluctant partners through getting them both to visualize the benefits of collaboration and the costs of disintegration and to embrace the proposed network governance.

As different environments materialized, the clerk's burden of office

Figure 1
Metcalfe's catastrophe-theory framework

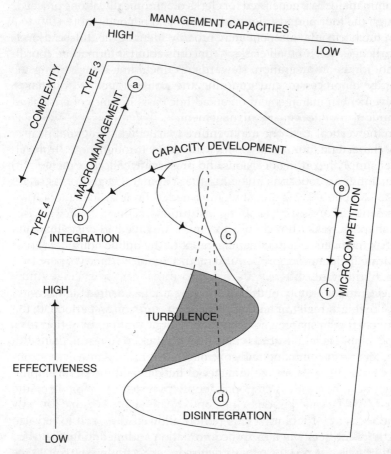

Source: L. Metcalfe, 'Flexible Integration in and after the Amsterdam Treaty,' in M. den
Boer, A. Guggenbühl, and S. Vanhoonacker, eds., Coping with Flexibility and Legitimacy
after Amsterdam (Maastricht: European Institute of Public Administration, 1998), 28.

has obviously had to evolve. But it would be naive to expect that the
adaptation has always been perfect. A mix of differences of opinions
about the state of the environment, together with problems of personalities and crises, has generated a greater or lesser goodness of fit
between clerks and circumstances materializing with shorter or longer
lags. Indeed, one may even be bold enough to hypothesize that a pattern

of evolution may be detectable in a two-dimensional tableau stylizing the mix of roles played by the clerk horizontally, and the sort of persona or dominant focus it generated for clerks diachronically, as one proceeds through the four periods identified above and beyond (Table 4).

On the horizontal axis, one may broadly identify the different kinds of challenges faced by all clerks – concerns about information, coordination, forms of integration, stewardship (including safeguarding the integrity of processes and guarding the political/policy boundary), involvement in management on an ad hoc basis in times of crisis, and continuous monitoring and management.

On the vertical axis, one may venture to label what might appear to be a characterization of the clerk's function through time: from an officer simply recording decisions and preserving collective memory to more ambitious functions involving the shaping of cognition as secretary to cabinet, serving an active intermediary role at the federal-provincial interface, shaping enabling institutions, acting as policy adviser and shaping policy directions, becoming involved in crisis management as the overseer of the management of the public household, participating in operations proper, and moulding the attitudes of people in the public service.

The centre of gravity of the role of the clerk has drifted significantly from the role of registrar and recorder of information, in period I, to the role of partner in shaping institutions and organizations in period II. In period III, the federal fortress came under attack. As a result, there was a blunter use of command and control. This translated into even stronger links between the prime minister of the day and the clerk, emphasizing the dimension of 'personal deputy minister,' as opposed to the others.

The shift in focus during this period allowed the clerk to indulge directly or indirectly in a mix of coordination and meddling: the coordination role revealed the new difficulty in orchestrating the collaboration among the different levels of government and among the private, public, and social sectors, while the meddling in operations became more and more prevalent as the search for mechanisms likely to help in meeting these challenges seemed to lead more and more often to stalemates.

This drift in the centre of gravity in period III has been ascribable both to the failure to develop fully a sound diagnosis of the malaises generated by the new environment, and to the growing lack of capacity for a renewed macro-management/governance of issues. As a conse-

Table 4
The clerk as *révélateur* of the evolution of governance

| FUNCTION OF CLERK | Discontinuities | ROLES OF CLERKS | | | | | |
|---|---|---|---|---|---|---|---|
| | | Information | Coordination | Integration | Stewardship | Meddling | Management |
| | | | Secretary to cabinet (shaping cognition) | Inter-provincial coordinator (shaping institutions) | Social architect & engineer (shaping organizations) | Managing crises | Systems/processes/public-service reform (shaping culture) |
| I Clerk as registrar | Secretary to Cabinet | CLERK AS REGISTRAR | | | | | |
| II Clerk as partner | Deputy to PM | | CLERK AS COORDINATOR | CLERK AS INTEGRATOR | | | |
| III Clerk as mercenary | Spin matters | | | | CLERK AS STEWARD | CLERK AS CRISIS MANAGER | CLERK AS MANAGER |
| IV Clerk as fixer | | | | | | | |
| V Clerk as network | | | | NETWORKED (provinces, territories, big cities) | | | |

Note: Degree of emphasis in role increases with intensity of colour

little | some | heavy

quence, towards the end of that period, the federal government was led to piecemeal experimentation with management instruments at the micro level – such as alternate service delivery (ASD) vehicles.

The most recent period (IV) has been as chaotic as period III, but in a less obvious way. By period IV, the shift from big (G) government to small (g) governance had become a fact of life. The state in advanced democracies everywhere had begun slowly and painfully to move away from centre stage towards the smaller (but absolutely crucial) role of nurturing, supporting, enabling, catalysing, and acting as societal failsafe.

Political leaders in Canada have been in denial both about the inevitable decline in the role of the state and about the lessening of federal influence within the federation. Even had the clerk understood what was happening, he/she would have been discouraged from speaking up (even privately), prevented from stimulating and encouraging the overhaul of governance of the country as much as was required, and forced into a good deal of social work as the public service and the provincial/territorial and local governments were savaged in the name of deficit and debt reduction.

The developments of period IV led, in turn, to the clerk involving himself/herself in human-resources management to a greater degree than heretofore, helping to put out brush fires, and emphasizing process over substance. Indeed, to some extent, in period III, and most importantly in period IV, the clerk developed a bifocal approach to his/her burden of office: on the one hand, putting an emphasis on shaping cognition as secretary to cabinet and deputy minister for the prime minister, and, on the other hand, meddling in detailed files as crisis manager and person responsible for the public service. This has meant a relative retrenchment from the core function of integration and stewardship.

If this reasoning holds, the clerk of the future may have to refocus his/her burden of office on the central functions of integration and stewardship, and to recognize that, in any event, such a burden of office can no longer be carried out in one place. The clerk may have to move to a postmodern version of the network governance of period II.

## A Windshield Survey

A serious review of the last 140 years of Canada's experience, through the lens of the clerk, would require a book-length exposé. A more detailed analysis will have to await a more extensive examination of the historical files.

What we can present in these few pages is a 'through the windshield' view of this experience that seems to support our hypotheses. We are quite conscious that this broad-brush survey may appear cavalier to some and as not providing a full-scale and rigorous test of the broad hypothesis sketched in Table 4. Its purpose is to provide a plausibility test. While the body of ethnographic evidence marshalled may not satisfy or please many, it is quite substantial and we feel confident that subsequent work will support our provisional assessment of the extent to which any clerk's work may have been less than adequate and why.[18]

## The World of the Clerk

According to Gordon Robertson, who held the office from 1963 to 1975, a good clerk must have 'apart from a sound record and knowledge of the public service, good judgment, a temperament compatible with the prime minister's, and complete reliability.'[19] To be successful, Robertson explains, it is necessary to have 'the sure confidence of ... the prime minister [and] of ministers and heads of departments.'[20]

This point of view is unduly limiting. It speaks only about a portion of the clerk's world. It does not throw much light on the role of the clerk as *révélateur*.

Our view of the clerk's world is more complex. In our reading of the evolution of the function, we adopt a fuller perspective that recognizes the centrality of the clerk's role as a mix of maven, connector, and salesman,[21] and as a person in need of a sextant that takes into account the three sets of constraints imposed by the environment, the governance capabilities available, and the character of the prime minister.

To the extent that his/her knowledge base is incomplete, and the learning process stunted, to the extent that the community of practice of which he/she is a part is limited, and to the extent that the ability for contagion and charisma is inadequate, the clerk is less than ideal: he/she will have a lesser grasp of the richness of the environment and will be less able to tap fully into a larger community of practice, to communicate effectively with all those who are meant to carry out the various stewardship functions, and to inspire them.

In a world of learning, connection, and persuasion, the clerk has to balance three sets of forces in defining viable strategies (Figure 2).

First, the environment (external forces, i.e., strains on the federation and the role of the state) imposes its diktats. The clerk will have to be

Figure 2
The clerk's world stylized

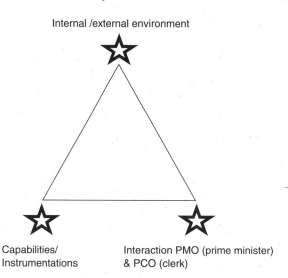

Internal /external environment

Capabilities/
Instrumentations

Interaction PMO (prime minister)
& PCO (clerk)

well informed about its changing parameters. Not all clerks have been equally adept at this capacity for profound appreciation of context. Furthermore, as the complexity of the environment has grown, more and more sophistication has been required for there to be any reasonable degree of understanding.

Secondly, the capabilities and kinds of instrumentation that are available to cope with the environmental challenges have to be appreciated. At first, much of the apparatus (and the community of practice underpinning it) was informal, fluid, and highly personalized. As the country matured, though, and the environment became more complex and more turbulent, there was a gradual crystallization of these capacities. They were instituted in organizations that gradually acquired a life of their own. Eventually, rigidity set in, and loyalty to the broader underlying purpose gave way to loyalty to the organization/institution itself. As a result, over time, change came to be experienced by the apparatus as an attack on its vested interests, and the clerk had to gain an appreciation of the extent to which he/she might or might not be able to make use of it.

Thirdly, the continuing tension between the prime minister of the day and the clerk, between the politicians and the bureaucrats, is omnipresent. Depending on personalities and on the fit between their personal values and plans, the tension may be greater or lesser, but it is never absent. Over the last 140 years, the prime minister has not always been at one with the clerk: in some cases, this led to the clerk leaving the post entirely. Also, as the public sector expanded, additional sources of expertise arose within, and prospered outside, government, so that politicians could and did benefit from advice from many sources other than the clerk.

Thus, the clerk requires a great deal of environmental intelligence, a mental agility that enables him/her to make the highest and best use of existing capabilities, and a large reserve of wisdom to dovetail his/her work with the priorities, predilections, and style of the prime minister of the day. When broad changes in any of these contexts are registered, the clerk has to retriangulate his/her own position and redefine what is likely to succeed.

## The First Two Periods, 1867–1975

During the first period (1867–1940), internal and external pressures forced the Canadian state to adjust rapidly. Canada was continuously gaining authority and independence from Britain throughout this period, while also building internal capacity (e.g., income tax during the First World War, Civil Service Commission of 1918–19). The federal government's intention to take an active role in the fight against poverty, social injustice, and inequalities was on the agenda even by 1919. It was, though, mainly the need to react to the ravages of the Great Depression that triggered a new kind of activism.

In the pre-1940 era, the basic social architecture that had existed since before Confederation was periodically 'tweaked' on an ad hoc basis. The clerk does not seem to have played any role of great significance – other than the traditional one of registrar that he had played since before Confederation. Politicians had their hands firmly on the rudder, and the degree of complexity was not such that it required a particularly elaborate governance apparatus. Crises were handled by special committees of inquiry, and there were pieces of legislation in which the clerk must have had a hand, but only to the extent of rigorous and careful processing.

There appears to have been little overwhelming accumulation of knowledge having an impact, little intermediation, and little in the form of leadership. Indeed, some holders of the office seem to have taken pride in their lack of interest in policy. In short, the clerks were not called upon to be the mix of maven, connector, and salesman, – or even help-mate – to the prime minister of the day, until the role of secretary to cabinet was added to their functions at the beginning of period II.

Faced with external and internal challenges, Mackenzie King reached for a few people to help, calling on those persons (like A.D. Heeney – the first clerk to acquire the role of secretary to cabinet – and O. D. Skelton) who had impressed him, This led, over time, to the arrival on the scene of 'social architects' such as Skelton (under-secretary of state for external affairs, beginning in 1925) and then Clifford Clark (deputy minister of finance, beginning in 1932) and Graham Towers (first governor of the Bank of Canada, beginning in 1935). In this way, the seeds were planted for the development of the network of intelligent generalists who helped make the effectiveness of period II (1940–75) possible.

The activism triggered by the Great Depression, and the challenges created by the Second World War, dramatically changed the terrain of operations. Momentous challenges like these could not be handled by gifted amateurs. Something needed to be done to address King's notorious lack of organization in the face of the need to take decisions and execute them quickly. The dual mandate of clerk and secretary to cabinet that King gave to Heeney in 1940 meant that the clerk (and a network of mandarins around him) was able to redesign significantly the governmental house between 1940 and 1975.

There were important weaknesses in capabilities and instrumentation. Heeney found cabinet operations inadequate when he arrived in 1940: 'There was no agenda, no secretariat, no official present at meetings to record what went on, no minute of decisions taken, and no system to communicate the decisions to the departments responsible to implement them ... It was obviously a system that could operate only where the pace of events was relatively slow and where matters requiring decision were not overly intricate or complex. Even so, it was a singularly inefficient and unfair way for a collective executive to reach decisions for which all would share responsibility.'[22]

J.L. Granatstein describes Heeney's contribution: 'Almost single-handedly Heeney had carried the Canadian government into the modern era ... In the process of doing this ... [he] had converted the Privy Council Office from a minor functionary's post into an executive secretaryship that handled the whole range of government business. He made the Clerk of the Privy Council and the Secretary to the Cabinet the invaluable servant of Prime Ministers, ministers, and the government, as well as an official with significant power in his own right. And Heeney established the non-partisan nature of the joint post, making its incumbent a civil servant like the others.'[23] Granatstein further notes: 'In the East block itself, the mandarins created the mechanisms – notably in the Privy Council Office and the Prime Minister's Office – through which the Prime Minister and Cabinet could shape, direct, and control the course of events in Canada to the extent they chose or were able. In the process they also created a central government structure and system in which great power flowed to them as well – a necessary, and probably not entirely unwelcome or unplanned, concomitant.'[24]

Heeney had an enormous impact on both organization and policy, but other senior players (part of the network around him) were crucial as well: among them, Lester Pearson, Jack Pickersgill, Norman Robertson, Clifford Clark, Gordon Towers, W.A. Mackintosh, and, a bit later, Bob Bryce. The dimension of guardian of the political/policy boundary in dealings with the government and the prime minister of the day, as well as of classical 'guardian' values, were natural consequences. In effect, the public service as an institution, with the clerk as its head, became a part of the checks and balances of the formal governance system.[25]

It was an era of collective leadership, based on friendship and trust by a group constituting an old boys' network, which was well connected nationally and internationally. Its members wielded enormous power, and in this respect the network of partners was a mirror image of the clustered world of politics. The very fact that one clerk could become a minister of the Crown is a good indication of the closeness of the partnership, although, at the same time, clerks and other group members stood their ground as 'keepers of the integrity of the system.' More importantly, this collection of people (along with some ministers) seems to have been imbued with a strong sense of the need to construct a propulsive state. In that sense, they reflected the Keynesian spirit of the times and the confidence that institutions could be built to manage the political economy.

It was only with Diefenbaker's arrival in 1957 that signs of diffraction began to appear. The then-clerk, Bob Bryce, earned Diefenbaker's confidence but was reportedly the conduit for virtually all of the other mandarins, who were never able to overcome the prime minister's mistrust.[26]

Gordon Robertson, Bryce's successor, was the last clerk of this era.

He was like the mandarins in terms of education (law at Oxford on a Rhodes scholarship), entry to the public service (External Affairs in 1941), and admission into the 'corridors of power' as secretary to King in 1945, in the form of a public-service secondment to the PMO (headed by Pickersgill), and later as adviser in the Privy Council Office to St Laurent. [27]

But the times were different, and the period was drawing to a close. The grand era of the mandarins, and of the *clerk as partner*, was coming to an end. Robertson's contributions included adding more formality and structure to the functions of the PCO and the PMO.

The 1972 election – which Trudeau nearly lost – seems to have played an important role in determining the shape of government at the very end of this period and the beginning of the next. The authors were told that, when Gordon Robertson left the position in 1975, it was for two reasons. The first was that Trudeau had lost interest in domestic politics. This is consistent with what Bliss reports: '[The] crass, highly political, lavish, desperate side of Trudeau Liberalism emerged after [the nearly lost election of[ 1972.'[28] Secondly, Robertson disagreed profoundly with Trudeau about Quebec. His departure heralded a shift in the role of the clerk towards that of helpmate that has only deepened with time.

## The Next Two Periods, 1975–2006

The underlying drift from G to g was beginning to be fully felt during period III (1975–94). As early as the late 1960s and early 1970s, broad worldwide forces (inflationary pressures, the oil crisis) disrupted the environment and revealed the inadequacy of the traditional understanding both of the context and of government's capabilities and means to cope with these new challenges.

The mid-1970s was a time of major upheaval. International integration, urbanization on the national scene, and Keynesian policies had served Canada well until the 1950s. By the 1960s, though, a Canada-made recession (à la James Coyne, governor of the Bank of Canada) and world inflationary pressure, along with the demographic destabilization generated by the baby boomers, the oil crisis, and an exuberant and dangerous monetary policy in the early 1970s, were ushering in a period of hyper-turbulence on many fronts. Instability on the international stage, a misguided pursuit of aggregate-demand policies in the face of aggregate-supply crises, and a consequent decline of credibility in government, and in the public service, led to much chaos at the centre.

Period III was dominated by two strong and determined prime ministers, Trudeau and Mulroney. Trudeau was in power until 1984 – with the brief interregnum of a minority Clark government in 1979 – and was followed very briefly by John Turner. He has been described as a 'fighting intellectual [and] a man with an extraordinarily clear vision of the structure of the Canada he wanted to mould.'[29] This was a man who told the Canadian Bar Association, in 1967, that 'the power of both the federal and the provincial governments would be restrained in favour of the Canadian citizen,'[30] and who would have Ottawa 'patriate Canada's Constitution, with an amending formula and a Charter of Rights and Freedoms, whether the provinces liked it or not.'[31] He chose Michael Pitfield as his clerk; this appointment has long been viewed as significantly shifting the balance towards greater valence for the role of deputy minister to the prime minister. Indeed, 'Pitfield came to speak more (and more), whether to ministers or to departments, in the name of the prime minister.'[32]

Trudeau's appointment of Pitfield was contentious among politicians[33] and, the authors were told, many senior bureaucrats left as a result. The fact was that there was no longer a network of expertise in Ottawa working as a knowledge-accumulation machine. As a result, every segment of the governmental house was building its own partial and feeble information base. This was the time when, in the face of impending economic disaster, an array of different economic forecasts, based on incomplete information, was leading to actions that were disconnected both from one another and from broad economic realities.

Not only was the diffracted knowledge not generating cumulative and effective learning, but, in addition, despite its claim to be in charge, the centre seemed to be becoming more and more disconnected from its environment. While disasters on the national and international front were papered over by a good deal of rhetoric, the role of the clerk was no longer one that included acting as connector, as it had before. As for persuasion, it no longer seemed to be seen as necessary: the leader knew best.

At the same time, the expansion of the federal public sector, especially towards the end of period II, had raised important management challenges. The 1976 auditor general's report advised that 'parliament had lost control of the public purse.' There was a clear need to manage this sprawling 'empire' better. In its 1979 report, the Lambert Commission highlighted weak accountability and extolled meta-management – eventually giving rise to the Program and Expenditure Management System (PEMS). Numbers of experienced professional managers were brought into the public service to help the government to get a better grip on controlling and managing public expenditures.

Trudeau was a fan of these new managerial methods,[34] and Pitfield strove to impose a rational system of setting objectives and making adjustments. He was responsible for introducing the heavy PEMS (envelope) system in 1977 during the brief minority government of Joe Clark, and then embellished it when Trudeau returned and reappointed him.

Pitfield's successor was Gordon Osbaldeston. The epitome of the 'professional manager,' he tried more practical managerial improvements, including dismantling the worst excesses of the PEMS system, during John Turner's brief interregnum as prime minister. Unfortunately, Osbaldeston's low-key, and somewhat laid-back, temperament did not match that of Brian Mulroney, and he did not survive beyond the transition to the majority Progressive Conservative government that arrived in 1984.

Mulroney's choice as his first clerk was Paul Tellier: a bright, quick, and experienced manager, whose effectiveness was ascribable to his singular understanding of people – rather than a reliance on the lens of ideas or systems. Like his predecessors, Tellier saw it as important for the clerk to continue to safeguard key processes, but he also saw the importance of acting as backstop for the deputy-minister cadre, so that he could delegate a good deal to them (which is exactly what he did).

Tellier was not a person likely to wait for cumulative social knowledge to come forth, nor to scan the environment for ways to enhance and enable it. The co-leader role stayed submerged (not to reappear to this day). He valued networking and, thus, adapted well to the style of the person for (or with) whom he worked. Yet his network was not as wide-ranging as it had been in period II. It also tended to focus on internal issues.

By this time, as New Public Management swept over most advanced democracies, the political leadership in Canada (as well as citizens generally) were pushing for change in the 'culture' of the public service. Tellier, and then Glen Shortliffe, tried to effect change by reducing the size of the public service or through organizational reform. Tellier's approach was to institute a series of deputy-led task forces (*Public Ser-*

*vice 2000*), but he neglected to take into account the fiscal difficulties that would swamp other efforts – including a six-year wage freeze – and he failed to understand the profound effect that the Al-Mashat affair of 1991, and other events, would have in undermining the unwritten contract between the senior public service and both its political masters and the country. He also failed to realize to what extent the public service had become resistant to change.

Shortliffe, who succeeded Tellier, kept the focus on internal state reorganization and instigated the secret de Cotret Task Force. This initiative, with support from the 'machinery of government' portion of the PCO (possibly at the behest of Mulroney), was intent on accomplishing organizational change that would improve decision making through a 'quick and dirty' reform of the public sector.

The frame of mind in place during most of this period was a focus on internal reorganization of the state and attempts to impose a rational regime of control on it as a way to cope with a new world where the state was no longer in charge. The relative failure of this period may be ascribed, to a great extent, to the role of clerk having lost much of its capacity for social learning, its broad connections through sectors and social groups, and its interest in – or sense of responsibility for – persuasion (e.g., the exhortation of elites, including its political masters). The clerk's function became more and more personalized and high profile. As a result, besides not playing the role of maven, connector, and salesman well, the clerk also became less of a steward.

Period III was an era in which the clerk had ceased to be at the core of a brain trust advising the politicians: the clerk was often charged with implementing ideologically inspired and ill-informed policies, imbued by a state-centric view of the world and immune to social learning. The clerk was no longer the architect and designer of Canadian governance: he was the engineer, charged with implanting the wishes of the political masters.

By the end of this period, and the beginning of the next, the breadth of what was expected of the clerk was no longer 'a part of the oral tradition of the senior public service.' One might even say that the guidance to ministers and bureaucrats on fundamentals like accountability began to reflect an increasingly distorted version of some basic principles.

Jean Chrétien swept into office with a majority in 1993, having defeated Paul Martin for the leadership, and was re-elected twice. His first choice for clerk was Jocelyne Bourgon. At the end of his ten-year tenure, he turned over the leadership of the Liberal Party to Paul Martin, in late 2003.

Period IV (1994–2006) – and the Chrétien-Bourgon tandem – began with the mortgage of momentous public deficits at the federal level that could no longer be ignored. Expediency trumped rationality: Canada's Program Review in the mid-1990s was the occasion to devolve responsibilities both to non-state actors and to junior levels of government in the name of deficit fighting and fiscal expediency. It was done *dans le désordre*, but it generated a large number of loose collaborative regimes where separate facilities and rigid organizational forms had previously prevailed.[35]

Bourgon was a superb personal deputy minister to the prime minister. Not one who had learned to be effective either by networking or by delegating, she nevertheless acted decisively to institute the necessary repairs and was remarkably successful on a number of internal fronts. For example, she recognized the dramatic weakening of policy capacity and worked on rebuilding it. She saw the need to recruit new talent at all levels to replace managers about to retire, and identified the deficit on the values and ethics front.

Nevertheless, her tenure was in strict continuity with the philosophy of carrying out only internal repairs and refurbishment as a response to the need for a much broader transformation of governance more broadly. This internal focus, and the refusal or inability to recognize the mammoth changes in the environment, led to the clerk's being confirmed as a fixer.

The growing turbulence of this period may have included accusations of waste, mismanagement, and corruption, but it also gave rise to significant instances of retooling (e.g., the Canadian Food Inspection Agency in 1997), restructuring (e.g., airport-administration devolution framework in 1994), and reframing (e.g., Nunavut in 1999).[36] Still, these initiatives did not seem to echo (except in an accidental way) the emergence of a new philosophy of governance.

Experts have observed that public-sector reform should proceed in three stages: first, a systematic review of government programs so as to retain only those that are necessary and appropriate; second, an organizational review to determine how best to organize to get that work done; and, finally, a service-delivery review to determine the most efficient and effective ways to deliver services.

Unfortunately, the federal government carried out these stages in exactly the reverse order of what would appear to be called for. First, in

1989, came Tellier's *Public Service 2000*, with its several deputy-led task forces to tackle key systems and 'service to the public'; then came Shortliffe's organizational reform, likely stemming from the de Cotret Task Force work of 1992-9; and finally came 'Program Review' in Period IV, with the appointment of Bourgon.

Bourgon was replaced, in 1999, by Mel Cappe, who limited his sights to one area of change for the public service – human-resources management – and gave the other deputies room to devise other improvements as they thought best. He succeeded, where many had hitherto failed, in changing the human-resources management system – although some argue that the change did not go far enough.[37]

Alex Himelfarb replaced Cappe in 2002 and served for the remainder of this period, as well as during the transition that resulted from the winter 2006 election, which brought the Conservatives to power with a minority government. He seems to have performed a kind of 'universal joint' role for handling crises à la Bryce, despite his ability to do more.

The Himelfarb years were a rather tragically gripping illustration not only of the centrality of the clerk's role but also of the fragility of the function in the absence of strong political leadership. He was appointed at the end of the Chrétien era explicitly to breathe a new policy soul into a tired government. But political infighting, national fractiousness, and a blind commitment to a centralized mindset crippled the prime minister. Survival became the dominant underlying theme of the latter days of the Liberal Chrétien-Martin governments, and the clerk, despite a strong interest in policy development and great skill at mediation, was reduced to the role of fixer and bricoleur.

Whatever the pace and structure of the clerks' interventions in these two periods, they have all proved to be internally focused on overhauling the state, and may be said to have generally failed to meet the challenges of the clerk's maven, connector, and salesman function. As a result, the job of clerk has lost its crucial place and failed to mount the sort of network of expertise that would help to shape the new Canadian governance. During all these years, the PMO trumped the PCO, and the clerk's role has been fundamentally eroded.

Yet there was a significant discontinuity between periods III and IV. In period III, there was a denial on the part of both politicians and bureaucrats that a new world was emerging, and much of the bafflement and frustration came from futile internal efforts to cope in a quixotic way with the very forces whose existence was denied. In period IV, the clerks have been conscious of their elusive powers in this new environment, and of the need to govern differently, but, given the fact that federal politicians were still in denial about the need to do so, they have had to be satisfied with coping – with the hope that they might do some good by bricolage here and there.

*The Dawn of Period V, 2006–*

This section is, of necessity, speculative. While the discussion of the performance of past clerks has shown that there has been considerable erosion of their functions in the recent decades, only time will tell if the role of the clerk is going to be refurbished or allowed to become counterproductive.

With the election of the Harper government in early 2006, and the nomination of Kevin Lynch, hopes were high. This was the case both because of the different mindset of the new government (more prone to defend decentralization) and because of Lynch's reputation as a person with a strong intellect, a capacity to listen, and a demonstrated focus on ingenious and effective execution in the face of increasing environmental turbulence.

Federal politicians are no longer in denial about the need to govern differently. Emphasizing the importance of the real collaboration that has become essential in today's world, the Harper government's first Throne Speech embraced an open federalism, including dealing with the fiscal imbalance.

The conjunction of a policy-driven prime minister with a clerk who is also policy-driven would appear to provide an ideal moment to bring back the sort of joint venture that Canada lived through in the post-1940 years of period II – of clerk as partner – and that could again provide Canada with the momentum to redesign its governmental house to meet the emerging challenges of the day.

What made period II a success was an alignment of ideas and principles combined with a capacity for grand design and the necessary execution skills. If the current opportunity is to be used well, the Harper government must embody the best of that period. But it must do it in a different way and in a more difficult environment. It must find new and creative ways to harness the energies of many more players (across levels of government and sectors), using an alignment of ideas and principles that resonates with a much more diverse Canadian population. It must execute well despite much greater complexity and diffusion of responsibility than ever before. Moreover, it must employ a new kind of leadership – one that is mostly based on meaning making[38] rather than trying to control from the top.

Like period II, period V is fraught with internal and external challenges. The presumption seems to be that the infrastructure and the mindset of the day are similar to those that prevailed in period II. But such is not the case. Over the decades, the adaptive capacity of the senior bureaucracy has diminished, constrained by an increasingly sclerotic infrastructure and a mindset focused to a growing degree on pursuit of its own interests. At times, this may create major blockages to the wishes of both the prime minister and the clerk.

The echo effects of decades of a centralized mindset being the order of the day must be overcome as well as the well-entrenched culture of risk aversion on the part of the senior bureaucracy and its growing degree of political correctness. All these factors dramatically reduce the capacity to transform the public-governance apparatus at a time when what is needed is a better alignment with reality.

### Conclusion

It is difficult to do justice in a few pages to a phenomenon as complex as the evolution of the clerk of Privy Council, an institution that has mirrored the evolution of Canadian society while helping to change it. Our purpose has been to provide a broad overview of the phenomenon and to suggest a hypothesis about both the evolution of Canada and the role of the clerk.

The elusiveness of the clerk's role and the fact that it is the locus neither of *imperium* (absolute power) nor of *potestas* (real power) but simply of *auctoritas* (authority, but not power) makes it difficult to pin down. *Auctoritas* is based on an impersonal capacity to augment, safeguard, and add value to what exists, which is embodied in the person charged with that role.

This elusiveness explains why each clerk has had to reinvent the role in different contexts and circumstances, and why whatever has been invested in the role at a given time has not carried on to his or her successor. *Auctoritas* comes from the person: whatever emanates from such a person is less than an order but more than simple advice.[39]

The evolution of the role of the clerk, and the variety of forms taken by its *auctoritas*, has revealed much about the times. The role reached a pinnacle in period II, when a network of mandarins exercised it fully: the Great Depression, the Second Word War, and the great leap forward of the post-war era made it possible for such authority to be very effective.

With the decline of the power of the state (and of the federal government within it), and the emergence of polycentric governance, such *auctoritas* has proved more difficult to exercise. The role of integrator and steward has been first diffracted and then largely submerged. The elusive authority of the clerk has ceased to have a determinant impact and has come to be overshadowed by the role of helpmate to the party in power.

It may well be that the only way to give the clerk more robust roots in the new context is through the recognition that the law of requisite variety has wide applicability. As Ashby's law puts it, the variety in the control system must be equal to or larger than the variety of the perturbations in order to achieve control.[40] So, in a tumultuous world, marred by diffraction, it may well be that any form of *auctoritas* designed to augment, safeguard, and add value will require governance (effective coordination when power, resources, and information are widely distributed) by network.

In that sense, the experience of network governance in period II may deserve some in-depth examination and suggest some directions for the future. It should also be clear, though, that the new network governance will bring together a new array of actors that transcends the confines of the federal-level state-centric apparatus.

Whether the arrival on the scene of a new prime minister and a new clerk will trigger a move towards clerk as network *auctoritas* and lead to a transformation of the institutional and organizational architecture of Canada – a real perestroika – remains to be seen.[41] But if it were not to materialize, and if such network governance were not to assure the requisite degree of collaboration, hyper-turbulence might be around the corner and social enclaves and vortices may ensue.

Some (more cynical than we are) already see signs of such social triage and even catastrophic disintegration on the horizon. But our hopes are greater than their fears at this time. Decentralization, polycentric governance, social learning, and moral contracts[42] may still provide the basis for effective governance. However, one cannot easily see how this will materialize without a good deal of adaptive-capacity development and without the clerk as network *auctoritas*.

NOTES

1  W.T. Anderson, *All Connected Now* (Cambridge: Westview Press, 2001), 252; R. Hubbard and G. Paquet, 'Ecologies of Governance and Institutional *Metissage*,' *Optimumonline*, 32, no. 4 (2002): 25–34.

2  H. Hardin, *A Nation Unaware* (Vancouver: J.J. Douglas, 1974).

3  R. Hubbard and G. Paquet, 'Betting on Mechanisms: The New Frontier for Federalism,' www.optimumonline.ca, 35, no. 1 (2005): 2–25.

4  www.pco-bcp.gc.ca. Accessed 11 July 2007.

5  G. Paquet, 'The Strategic State,' *Ciencia Ergo Sum*, 3, no. 3, 257–61 (Part 1); 4, no. 1, 28–34 (Part 2); 4, no. 2, 148–54 (Part 3) (1996–7).

6  R. Hubbard and G. Paquet, *Gomery's Blinders and Canadian Federalism* (Ottawa: University of Ottawa Press, 2007).

7  G. Paquet, *Governance through Social Learning* (Ottawa: University of Ottawa Press, 1999).

8  Ibid.

9  *Organizational Learning: A Theory of Action Perspective* (Reading, Mass.: Addison-Wesley, 1978).

10  F.E. Emery and E.L. Trist, 'The Causal Texture of Organizational Environments,' *Human Relations*, 18 (1965): 21–32; J.E. McCann and J. Selsky, 'Hyperturbulence and the Emergence of Type 5 Environments,' *Academy of Management Review*, 9, no. 3 (1984): 460–70; G. Paquet, *Gouvernance: une invitation à la subversion* (Montreal: Liber, 2005), chapter 5.

11  J. Heath, *The Myth of Shared Values in Canada* (Ottawa: Canadian Centre for Management Development, 2003).

12  'Hyperturbulence and the Emergence of Type 5 Environments.'

13  Y. Dror, 'Beyond Uncertainty: Facing the Inconceivable,' *Technological Forecasting and Social Change*, 62 (1999): 151–3.

14  Emery and Trist, 'The Causal Texture.'

15  L. Metcalfe, 'Flexible Integration in and after the Amsterdam Treaty,' in M. den Boer, A. Guggenbühl, and S. Vanhoonacker, eds., *Coping with Flexibility and Legitimacy after Amsterdam* (Maastricht: European Institute of Public Administration, 1998), 11–30.

16  Ibid., 29–30.

17  G. Paquet, *The New Geo-Governance: A Baroque Approach* (Ottawa: University of Ottawa Press, 2005), part II.

18  Much of the work we have done to gain a good ethnographic sense of the world of the clerk is based, not only on the limited written works on this subject that we quote, but also and most importantly on interviews carried

out with a variety of persons who have had the opportunity to work closely with different clerks. Information obtained in this latter manner was supplemented by a number of 'safe-space' discussions (forums where confidentiality is ensured) with authoritative persons in order to ascertain whether our reading of the different situations was accurate. In toto, the views of some twenty 'witnesses' have been sought.

19  G. Robertson, *Memoirs of a Very Civil Servant* (Toronto: University of Toronto Press, 2001), 215.
20  Ibid., 305.
21  M. Gladwell, *The Tipping Point* (Boston: Little Brown, 2000).
22  Robertson, *Memoirs*, 76.
23  J.L. Granatstein, *The Ottawa Men: The Civil Service Mandarins, 1935–1957* (Toronto: University of Toronto Press, 1998), 207.
24  Ibid., xxii.
25  For example, on one occasion, in period III, the authors were told, the secretary of the Treasury Board intervened when political advisers wanted the president of the Treasury Board to issue a public report on expenditures in a way that downplayed or obscured 'bad news' and set things out in the most flattering light for the government. The secretary advised the president that this overstepped the political-public interest boundary and would not be an acceptable action for the latter to take. Thus, it could not be supported by the secretary. The president agreed and the credibility of the office was preserved.
26  Granatstein, *The Ottawa Men*, 270–1.
27  Robertson, *Memoirs*.
28  M. Bliss, *The Right Honourable Men* (Toronto: Harper Collins, 2004), 260.
29  Ibid., 246.
30  Ibid., 253.
31  Ibid., 266.
32  Robertson, *Memoirs*, 310.
33  Ibid., 309.
34  Ibid., 256.
35  Paquet, *Gouvernance*, chapter 15.
36  G. Paquet, 'Innovations in Governance in Canada,' *Optimum*, 29, nos. 2–3 (1999): 71–81.
37  R. Hubbard, 'Public Service Modernization: Fixing the Cart May Not Suffice,' *Optimum*, 33, no. 2 (2003): 8–15.
38  W.H. Drath and C.J. Palus, *Making Common Sense* (Greensboro, N.C.: Center for Creative Leadership, 1994).

39  G. Agamben, *Etat d'exception* (Paris: Seuil, 2003), 130.

40  W.R. Ashby, *An Introduction to Cybernetics* (London: Chapman and Hall, 1956).

41  G. Paquet, 'Gomery as Glasnost,' *Literáry Review of Canada*, 13, no. 7 (2005): 12–15.

42  G. Paquet, 'Betting on Moral Contracts,' *Optimum*, 22, no. 3 (1991): 45–53.

# 4 Capacity, Complexity, and Leadership: Secretaries to Cabinet and Ontario's Project of Modernization at the Centre

BRYAN EVANS

Ideas, institutions, and the structures that link them together are profoundly significant for the political management of the state. In the post-Second World War era, Keynesian-trained economists and policy analysts institutionalized a new state orthodoxy. The ideas of Keynes had legitimated state intervention and in doing so 'shifted civil servants away from the more passive conception of their role towards a more active interest in planning.'[1] Since the 1970s and the formative work of the Committee on Government Productivity (COGP), through the deep recession of the 1990s and the consequent Ontario Public Service (OPS) Transformation Project, various initiatives to drive change from the centre have endeavoured to construct a different way of doing government. Australian Michael Pusey has observed that, 'along with elected politicians and some types of intellectuals, top public servants are the "switchmen" of history; when they change their minds the destiny of nations takes a different course.'[2] To think that the most senior-ranking public servant in Ontario, or any jurisdiction for that matter, is either a 'valet' or a 'lackey' is needlessly provocative.[3] To lead and manage change necessitates an enabled centre of government.

What is clear is that the relationship to the political leadership is critical. There is a symbiotic relationship between the cabinet as a centre of political power and the Cabinet Office (CO) led by the secretary of the cabinet. It is the fundamental role of the secretary of the cabinet to negotiate this differentiated relationship. However, this relationship is historically bound and conjunctural. That is to say, the senior political and public administrative executives come to reflect and be shaped by the personalities, dominant or emergent ideas, and balance of political-economic forces present during a specific period. This is the project of modernization as a response to environmental or exogenous pressures for change. The state apparatus evolves and transforms as a means of managing and adapting to change. Christopher Dunn's continuum of cabinet evolution – from traditional cabinet, which precedes the administrative state, to the departmentalized cabinet, which emerges in a period where 'government departments and ministers were the engines of public sector expansion,' to the institutionalized cabinet that is characterized by complex cabinet committee and support structures[4] – captures the growing complexity of cabinet in response to environmental complexity.

Donald Savoie has identified a further evolutionary step, which is the emergence at the federal level of a 'prime minister-centred' cabinet that represents a dramatic centralization of power and the erosion of collegial decision making.[5] Savoie's observation is equally applicable to Ontario. Since the early 1990s, there has been a trend towards centralizing power at the apex of the Ontario state. This is true not just for the premier and the Premier's Office (PO) but for their public-service counterparts, the secretary of the cabinet and her/his machinery (the Cabinet Office).

The story of Ontario's secretaries of the cabinet, all twelve of them since 1948, is the story of post-war Ontario's struggle to fashion and refashion the shape and logic of the Ontario state. Ontario's secretaries of the cabinet are neither valets nor mandarins but rather, as in Pusey's account of Australian public-service executives, the 'switchmen' of Ontario's policy trajectory. This project of 'modernization' involved, and continues to involve, adapting the state to a series of integrally related changes in the economy and political structures. It can be summed up as a process of working towards a 'normalization,' to re-establish continuity out of a period of discontinuity and change. Modernization, thus understood, is concerned with a continuous process of rationalization – of new rules, new ideas, and new values – which are more appropriate to a new set of circumstances. In short, modernization is adaptation to a changed environment. This is, indeed, the challenge of modern governance. In this context, the lessons of leadership generated by those serving as secretary to the cabinet in Ontario are intertwined with the modernization project and the need for a 'centre' to provide leadership and manage public-sector reform in response to economic, political, and public administrative complexity. In addition, it is impossible to consider the office of secretary of the cabinet, and those individuals who occupy that position, without linking this function to the evolution of the Cabinet Office and the Premier's Office. The basic role of the secretary of the cabinet and the Cabinet Office, from its inception, has been to serve as the link between cabinet (the site of political decision and leadership) and the administrative state. And, in turn, it is not possible to make sense of this vital central agency without consideration of the political and economic context. It is not happenstance that the establishment of Ontario's Cabinet Office via order-in-council on 23 September 1948 coincides with the project of post-war reconstruction and the emergence of Ontario's welfare state. Since the 1970s, as the Keynesian era waxed and waned, the economic and political context has necessitated a different approach and through it all the secretary of the cabinet served to broker the provincial state's role in the political management of change.

### The Formative Years, 1948–71: The Departmentalized Cabinet and Growing Complexity

It is difficult to reconcile the Cabinet Office of the mid-1990s with the one that existed between 1948 and 1971. One is particularly struck by the partisan/policy fusion at the apex of the provincial state. Demonstrating this point, the first three Ontario secretaries of cabinet (Lorne McDonald, W. Malcolm McIntyre, and Keith Reynolds), spanning the period between 1948 and 1971, also served as deputy minister to the prime minister.[6] For this period, the deputy minister to the prime minister and the secretary of the cabinet were one and the same person. This may be explained by a number of factors, including the role of the province as a delivery arm of federal policy decisions (the provinces as 'policy takers'). In this context there was little need for strong policy capacity at the provincial centre. Instead, policy making at the provincial level was housed in the line departments. The second factor is the rather remarkable longevity of the Conservatives in government (1943 to 1985) and the comfort that would have been built up over a long period of association between key public-service and partisan leaders.

A third consideration is that the congruence between the deputy minister and secretary to the cabinet roles may also have been a function of the administrative 'support' role allocated to the Cabinet Office with respect to the functioning of cabinet and the Premier's Office. Ultimately, this fusion is in part understood as a logical consequence of the evolution of the role of secretary of the cabinet, which originated in the role of the provincial secretary following the Second World War. As F.F.

Schindeler states: 'Prior to the war, most of the functions now per-formed by a civil servant were the responsibility of the provincial secre-tary, who was a member of the cabinet.'[7] The provincial secretary functioned as the de facto secretary of the cabinet, which involved man-aging the business transacted within and between cabinet and the var-ious departments and ministers and decisions recorded as orders-in-council.[8]

Ontario's first secretary of the cabinet, Lorne McDonald (1948–53), was the architect of Ontario's Cabinet Office. Immediately after the Sec-ond World War, the then-provincial secretary, Roland Michener, saw that the demands of post-war reconstruction required more formal pro-cedures in the conduct of cabinet business.[9] The existing arrangements were all a little too chaotic for Michener, who tasked McDonald to advise on how cabinet business was dealt with in the United Kingdom and in Ottawa.[10] McDonald, borrowing from Whitehall, introduced the recording of cabinet decisions and, most significantly, instituted a sys-tem whereby the secretary would sit at the cabinet table as one of the premier's 'silent men.'[11]

It was during this period that Ontario's economy was transformed and the welfare state incrementally constructed. Important policy areas such as health, education, and transportation fell within provincial jurisdiction. Thus, there was an increase in demand for services as the provincial state became involved in more and more expensive areas. Between 1951 and 1971, the Ontario public service had expanded from slightly more than 20,000 employees to nearly 65,000, and provincial expenditures, reflecting the growing role of the provincial state, soared from $340 million to $6.1 billion.[12] Between 1963 and 1969, provincial expenditures were growing at an annual rate of 16.8 per cent.[13] The socio-economic expansion of Ontario necessitated an expansion in the state and, consequently, in the complexity of the issues and policy prob-lems. To address this growing complexity, the size of the cabinet was expanded from approximately twelve, in the 1940s, to twenty-one min-isters by 1971.[14]

Cabinet Office, under the leadership of William McIntyre (1953–69), Ontario's second secretary of the cabinet, could no longer be immune from the need to manage this growing complexity. In his dual roles as secretary to the cabinet and deputy minister, McIntyre added an eco-nomic-research capacity as well as a media-relations unit to his office. While the preparation and management of cabinet agendas remained a prime function of the secretary of the cabinet, McIntyre had also begun to concern himself, and his premier, with the gathering of 'strategic intelligence' and the tools of political management.[15] However, from a capacity perspective, an office of 12–15 staff (CO and PO combined) was not equipped to provide policy support to cabinet.[16] Analytical- and policy-support capacity was decentralized and housed, to some degree, in the line departments. Consequently, it was expected that ministers would be briefed on issues by their own ministries. It was becoming clear that 'Government could no longer meet the large demand for government programs and services; nor could provincial revenues keep pace with the increasing financial burden caused by the provision of these activities.'[17] In 1967 Premier John Robarts 'expressed concern regarding the operational efficiency and effectiveness of the government' and 'recognized that the workload demands on ministers' time were becoming significant and that this was impeding the policy decision-making process.'[18] Former secretary of the cabinet Peter Barnes has observed that 'in the 1960s and 1970s, Ontario departments were viewed as some of the best delivery agencies in the world – policy was not their strength.'[19] The result was to be the most comprehensive review of capacity in the Ontario public service and a prelude to a series of efforts at adapting the Ontario provincial state to a changing economic and political environment.

### The Committee on Government Productivity: The Dawning of the Limits to Public-Sector Growth

On 20 February 1969 Charles McNaughton, treasurer of Ontario and minister of economics, rose in the legislature to announce the formation of the Productivity Improvement Project, stating: 'During the 1960s this Legislature has approved an increasingly broad range of public services, greatly expanding its contribution in such areas as health, education and welfare.'[20] The third secretary of the cabinet, Keith Reynolds (1969–71), who served both as secretary to the cabinet and as deputy minister to the premier, like his predecessors, would participate in Ontario's first massive rethink of the role of the provincial state.

Prompting this comprehensive review was Premier Robarts's view that 'no matter how talented the government's staff, its antiquated organizational forms were unequal to the tasks of modern public administration.'[21] The incremental and ad hoc post-war construction of the welfare state resulted in a significant expansion of the public sector and consequently 'public administration grew commensurately more difficult as the size of the provincial budget increased.'[22] The result of this largely line department-led expansion was a series of structurally related dysfunctions. First, the line departments were not capable, either structurally or culturally, of working across sectoral boundaries. Thus, problems of coordination emerged. Secondly, the complexity of managing in this context contributed to an impoverishment on the policy-formulation side. Thirdly, the productivity problem within the public sector became more obvious as it consumed an ever-increasing volume of resources with little indication of greater production of public goods and services.

Moreover, the context for these developments was a growing recognition that a narrowing of options and possibilities was occurring as the ideas of 'scarcity and rationality' ascended and displaced the sense of an 'unrestricted freedom to pursue diverse and conflicting social and economic goals.'[23] The model of the post-war social contract was reaching its limitations. The Committee on Governmental Productivity was created to address these issues through a three-pronged effort to: 1) transform the provincial cabinet into a cabinet-committee system; 2) transform the 'silos' of the line departments into a more horizontally oriented policy-field structure; and 3) transform the policy process into a much more rational and structured system.[24] A 'new management philosophy' guided this reform initiative, which posited a more anticipatory and future-oriented state possessing the capacity to adapt and innovate.[25] The tasks of modern public administration indeed were changing and the COGP was a forward-looking attempt to manage expectations and resources strategically by creating more 'rational' decision-making structures and greater capacity at the centre to enable 'horizontal coordination and control.'[26]

Still, at its most fundamental level, the COGP was about limiting the growth of the public sector; the objective of this project was 'to cut the costs of government administration by whatever means can be recommended.'[27] The motivation in establishing the COGP was, as Charles McNaughton states, a concern with the growing level of state intervention and the concomitant costs associated with it. One unpublished discussion paper circulated internally set the context as one where 'projections of government costs and revenue into the immediate future indicate that costs are rising much faster than revenues. This implies that government managers should become more cost-conscious for cost factors will loom larger in decisions on proposed new activities.'[28]

The thrust of the COGP framework was to reassert the doctrine of the politics/administration dichotomy through a new governmental structure based upon the principles of political control of policy (particularly at the cabinet level) and the establishment of a distinction between policy development and program delivery as a means of constraining public-sector growth.[29] The principles of political centralization and delivery decentralization foreshadow the work of David Osborne and Ted Gaebler some twenty years later,[30] both conceptually and in expression. Two proposals in particular are significant: strengthened subcontract mechanisms and reprivatization.

### Austerity as Orthodoxy: The Special Program Review Committee

Ontario first began the process of rethinking its version of the post-war social contract with the 1974 budget in which the treasurer stated that 'the most important problem facing us today is inflation.'[31] With those words, Ontario was embarking on the first steps towards an incremental rupture with the post-war Keynesian order. However, the watershed between the eras of public-sector expansion and public-sector retrenchment was the budget of 1975, which marked what has been deemed the beginning of 'Ontario's rather protracted struggle with the mid-1970s end of the great long-boom that followed the Second World War.'[32] With this budget the government of Ontario set out on a concerted program of retrenchment to combat inflation. The treasurer made clear his conviction that 'one of the root causes of the current inflation problem in Canada is excessive government spending and unnecessary growth in the size and complexity of the public sector.'[33] The overall commitment was to limit the growth in public expenditure to 16.8 per cent and a 2.5 per cent shrinking of the Ontario public service.[34]

A more muscular approach to public-expenditure constraint was deemed necessary and, in June 1975, Premier Bill Davis appointed a Special Program Review Committee (SPRC) 'to enquire into ways and means of restraining the costs of Government, through examining issues such as the usefulness of programs, alternative lower cost means of accomplishing objectives, and the problem of increased public demand for services in an inflationary period.'[35] If one can point to a defining 'moment' in the post-war politics and history of public policy and management in Ontario, where in Pusey's words the 'state changed its mind,' this document, and the government's response, is it. At its core the 'SPRC looked at social and economic issues through the lens of neoconservatism.'[36] This was the first major study within the

province to do so. It unambiguously identified inflation as the key pol- .
icy problem and linked this explicitly to public expenditure. In other
words, from this assessment, it really was a public 'expenditure problem' that was feeding inflation.

The overarching policy goal set by the committee was that 'the
expenditures of the Ontario Government as a percentage of the gross
provincial product should decline.'[37] And, in this respect, the challenge
for government 'is not merely to exercise extraordinary vigilance in
containing current spending, but to face up to the difficult job of cutting
it back.'[38] The principles proposed by the committee, to guide the government towards this goal, envisioned a much more broadly 'mar-
ketized' future for the public sector. The committee ruled against any
expansion of public services and instead urged that consideration be
given to 'the possibility of transferring back to the private sector some
of the activities that it currently undertakes' and that the 'Government
should act more in its regulatory capacity and less as a provider of services to accomplish its objectives.'[39]

Upon succeeding Robarts as leader of the Progressive Conservative
Party and as premier of Ontario in 1971, Davis had appointed Reynolds
to be his deputy minister and asked Carl Brannan (1971–3) to take the
role of secretary to the cabinet. Although there were now two distinct
roles for the deputy minister and the secretary to the cabinet, there was
no structural differentiation between the Premier's Office and the Cabinet Office. 'Public servants continued to be involved in activities which
we would now regard as political functions.'[40]

### Institutionalizing the Ontario Cabinet: Structured
### Collegiality in the Davis Era

It was left to Brannan, and particularly his successor, James Fleck
(1974–6), to implement the recommendations flowing from COGP.
Prior to his appointment as secretary, Fleck had served two years as
'chief of staff' (his formal title was 'chief executive officer') to Premier
Davis. While Davis maintained the de facto separation of senior public
servant and political operative by appointing Dr Edward Stewart to the
position of deputy minister to the premier (thus symbolically sustaining the politics/administration dichotomy), it was clear that the movement from an essentially political role to a senior public-service
position was indeed rather fluid.

Under Fleck, Cabinet Office proper maintained staffing at a modest twenty to twenty-five positions, with a budget in the $1.0–1.3 million range. Structurally, it began to reflect the COGP-inspired reorganization of the cabinet-committee system. A Policy and Priorities Board, with its own secretary, was appointed together with coordinators for the policy-field committees (Social Development, Resources Development, Justice) and for the 'coordinating' committee. In turn, the 'Provincial Secretariats' had been established and staffed with approximately ten positions in each. Fleck has observed that the task of implementation was made easier by his being 'known' to the premier through his work on the COGP. 'Davis,' he says, 'liked the recommendations and ideas coming out of the COGP as he came into the premiership. That's how I became his chief of staff because he knew I could carry out the implementation.'[41]

Steering the COGP reforms was one of Fleck's greatest personal accomplishments, but doing so was not an entirely individual project. Its success 'required good political leadership – Robarts, Davis, McNaughton, and Carl Brannan who was secretary of the cabinet before me. They all saw the importance of doing this and strongly backed it.'[42] Thus, for Fleck, it is clear that the secretary and the premier, and by extension the senior-management cadre and the ministers, must share a common vision and be equally prepared to row in the same direction. To build this common vision and broad consensus, the style of decision making is critical. Fleck notes that 'in the Davis era the decision-making model was collegial. That is, there was opportunity for deputy ministers to broaden discussion at cabinet.'[43] According to Fleck, the role of the secretary is not that of 'policy maker' but rather 'to critique policy proposals coming from the ministries.'[44] The role of the secretary of the cabinet is to provide advice to the premier on the implications of policy recommendations coming forward.

In January 1976 Premier Davis appointed Edward Stewart, his deputy minister in the PO since 1974, to the position of cabinet secretary (he would continue as deputy minister to the premier, holding both posts from January 1976 to July 1985). Once again, the Cabinet Office and the Premier's Office became closely linked and would remain so until Stewart's departure in 1985. Davis's decision to merge the office of a key political adviser with that of the secretary of the cabinet was a clear demonstration of his comfort with, and confidence in, Stewart.

The Davis-led governments, between 1971 and 1984, were 'unapologetically activist and interventionist, extending the reach of government into social and economic realms previously thought outside the

province's domain.'[45] Total provincial expenditures during Davis's tenure grew from $5.9 billion in 1971–2 to $26.4 billion in 1984–5.[46] The
number of public servants employed directly by the Ontario government also grew, from 65,000 in 1971–2[47] to 80,000 in 1985.[48] The result of
this expansion was that the provincial deficit increased from $624 mil-
lion in 1971–2 to $3.1 billion in 1983–4.[49]

These were also years of growing economic instability, characterized
by 'stagflation,' as the Keynesian tools of demand management broke
down in the face of double-digit inflation and unemployment. For
example, between 1973 and 1975, inflation ran above 10 per cent, reaching a high of 12 per cent in 1981–2.[50] Given the activism of the Davis
governments from 1971 to 1984, and the increasing uncertainty with
respect to the economic future, there can be little doubt that fusion at
the apex of the 'centre' was based less on the premier's comfort in his
deputy than on the need for increased direction and management from
the centre.

Over the nine years that Stewart served as secretary of the cabinet
and deputy minister to the premier, he presided over a period of modest expansion in the organizational complexity in the PO/CO. Staffing
in the Cabinet Office ebbed and flowed between twenty and thirty-five
positions and the budget incrementally expanded from $1.0 million in
1976 to $1.6 million in 1984. In 1976 the position of associate secretary of
the cabinet was created to provide coordination to the secretariats serving the Policy and Priorities Board and the policy-field secretariats. In
1978, in response to the growth in inflation and the introduction of
wage-and-price controls, a small anti-inflation unit was set up in the
Cabinet Office.

Through the 1970s, and into the early 1980s, the number of cabinet
committees proliferated as the number of policy challenges facing the
government grew and apparently overwhelmed the existing standing
committees. By 1984, there were, or had been, ad hoc cabinet committees established to address a broad spectrum of policy issues, such as
the state of Confederation (1977); mining communities (1978); emer-
gency planning (1979); native affairs (1979); Board of Employment
Development Fund (1979); race relations (1980); Board of Industrial
Leadership and Development (1981); manpower (1982); administered
prices (1983); and municipal assessment (1983). In addition, specialized
ad hoc policy/issues management units were established addressing
an equally diverse range of issues, including an advisory committee on
the economic future (1978); a customer-service and deregulation unit

(1978), which was a precursor to the Red Tape Secretariat, led by its own associate secretary of the cabinet; and a women's directorate (1983).

Recognizing the power of the media and messaging in such turbulent times, Stewart appointed a communications coordinator and established a communications unit. Simultaneously, two trusted political advisers of Premier Davis – Hugh Segal and John Tory – came to play increasingly prominent roles in a world that made few distinctions between politics and public service. Tory, who had served as principal assistant to the premier, moved into a variety of roles which would largely be considered public-service positions, including associate secretary of the cabinet for federal-provincial relations (1984); secretary for the Cabinet Committee on Federal-Provincial Relations (1984); and secretary for the Advisory Committee on the Economic Future (1984). Similarly, Segal became secretary of the Policy and Priorities Board of cabinet in 1979, replacing the previous public-service associate secretary of the cabinet – policy. In February 1985 Frank Miller replaced Davis as head of the Progressive Conservative Party and thus as premier of Ontario, and Stewart continued on in his dual role.

Stewart is rather sanguine about the degree of integration between the PO and CO during his period as Ontario's senior public servant. He matter-of-factly observes that he was 'working up to the end of forty-two years of Conservative rule. So the relationship that existed over that time between and among members of cabinet, senior public servants, the premier, and indeed, some of his outside advisers, was very different from that which has transpired with subsequent regimes.'[51] For Stewart, the Ontario Conservatives' long tenure in office strongly shaped the relationship between the senior public service and the political leadership. However, the general election of 2 May 1985 brought the forty-two-year-old Progressive Conservative dynasty to an end. While Frank Miller was able to form a fragile minority government for a few weeks, the historic 'Accord' between the second-place Liberals and the New Democrats allowed David Peterson to become premier.

Peterson asked Stewart to stay on as secretary of the cabinet, but Stewart declined, citing his having 'been with Davis and all those people associated with him all those years' as reason enough.[52] He doubted his motivation to adapt to another personality in the Premier's Office. Peterson then turned to a long-time public servant, and secretary of the Management Board, Robert Carman (1985–9), to take on the role of secretary of the cabinet on 31 July 1985. Carman's tenure as secretary marked a watershed in the history of the Ontario public service, and indeed Ontario. Not only had a forty-two-year-old political dynasty been replaced, but, more important for Ontario, which was a latecomer to neo-liberal-inspired public-sector restructuring, fundamental change was no longer avoidable. The prescient quality of Carman's perspective at the time reveals an understanding that the world, and Ontario, as part of that world, was indeed moving through a period of profound change – a paradigm shift. In an address to the Premier's Advisory Committee on Executive Resources in 1988, he summed up the tremendous challenge confronting Ontario as one where the province's economic performance had spared it 'the budget-slashing and continued restraint seen in other jurisdictions,' and he further warned that the welfare state 'can no longer be afforded, unless a new entrepreneurial economy can greatly increase a jurisdiction's productivity.'[53]

Carman understood that in this changing environment a new mode of public management was necessary. He characterized this as 'the challenge of breakthrough,' which outlined the type of public service Ontario would need. His four-part strategy entailed: 1) a review of basic businesses; 2) a shift in management theory and practices; 3) a transformation in leadership; and 4) a clear vision of a pace-setting public service. Carman's vision for reform required that direct delivery of services by government be replaced by a more pluralist model of service delivery; that there be a shift to leadership rather than administration (which is to say, replacing a command-and-control approach to management with management by vision and values); and that the relationship between the senior public service and the political leadership be transformed from a master servant relationship to a partnership.

In practice, this would mean a broadening and deepening opportunity for a larger number of senior public servants below the rank of deputy to participate in 'political conversation' with ministers. Finally, Carman's conception of a 'pace-setting public service' entailed a nine-point framework: 1) a shift from a task-driven management style towards one that was goal- and vision-driven; 2) moving from a functional, and ministry-based, approach to management and policy formulation to a cross-sectoral, horizontal one; 3) shifting from a focus on technical and professional skills to corporate-leadership skills; 4) acceptance of ambiguity and competing goals; 5) placing a high priority on human-resources management; 6) moving from command-and-control management to 'empowerment leadership'; 7) moving from segmented management to corporate management; 8) moving towards a more strategic rather than 'additive' approach to resource allocation ('working below the line'); and 9) de-emphasizing program development and delivery in favour of alternative means of achieving the intent of the government's policy agenda.[54]

While the COGP clearly understood the need for restructuring delivery and management, the actual reforms had focused on decision-making capacity and process at the centre. The new secretary's interest and focus was clearly beyond this: he was attempting to recover elements of the COGP that had been left behind. Moreover, it was in the area of human-resources management that he made an enduring contribution. Carman placed leadership in the public service on the agenda, but, in doing so, he was still working in the wake of the COGP, which had referenced human resources and the need for a new managerialism.

Structural change was not the centrepiece of the Peterson premiership. The COGP/Davis era structures were largely retained: 'the three large sectoral cabinet committees, the Policy and Priorities Board, and the Management Board.'[55] Yet it was not all a matter of *plus ça change*. The appointment of Carman was indicative of the new premier's interest in depoliticizing the most senior positions in the public service by re-establishing a clear delineation between the Cabinet Office and the political functions of the Premier's Office. Consequently, he eliminated the position of deputy minister to the premier. The new premier, said Carman, 'had a perception that the secretary of cabinet had become a little too closely involved with the Conservative Party.'[56]

Some of the functions performed by Ed Stewart, the former Davis-era secretary of cabinet, were restructured, resulting in a new relationship between the Premier's Office and the head of the public service, one that became known as the 'three legged stool.' What this meant, in functional terms, was that Peterson's principal secretary, Hershell Ezrin, would provide policy and communications leadership; Gordon Ashworth, as executive director of the Premier's Office, would provide management of the political and administrative relationship; and Carman exclusively would provide leadership to the Ontario public service.[57] This division of labour was designed to end the intertwining of political and public-service functions, which had been common under decades of unbroken Progressive Conservative government, and resurrect a politics-administrative dichotomy.

As a result, Carman was to become, whether by chance or design, a pioneer in substantially renovating and building the capacity of the

Cabinet Office. The restructuring of the roles of the secretary of cabinet, in the early days of Peterson's government, was critical to this evolution, according to Carman, who states that 'as a deputy minister of the premier – the capacity to act as a switch person declines.'[58] In practice, the secretary of cabinet could now be left to think and strategize about public-service transformation, rather than becoming consumed by political firefighting. Beyond this, Peterson made only minor adjustments to the cabinet decision-making system he had inherited from the Conservative administration.[59]

Carman inherited a modest Cabinet Office, with about thirty staff. By 1989, a more robust organization of more than seventy, supported by a budget of $9 million, was in place. Like Davis's, the Peterson government was an activist government. Provincial expenditure grew from $28.8 billion in 1985–6 to $41.1 billion in 1989–90 – a not insignificant 43 per cent increase! [60] The size of the Ontario public service also grew, from 67,845 in 1984–5 to 73,823 in 1989–90.[61]

Capacity at the centre was necessary, if only to manage the volume of policy proposals generated by the Accord with the New Democratic Party (NDP), between 1985 and 1987, and by the post-Accord ministry agendas.[62] In March 1989 Carman warned: 'Our traditional approaches to policy development, human resources and fiscal management, service delivery and management processes are beginning to groan from the weight of the complexity of government.'[63] While he said this only a few months before leaving the Cabinet Office, it does characterize his sense of urgency in advancing the transformation of the Ontario public service.

The COGP reports had spoken of the need for a new management style that would be more horizontal, strategic, and anticipatory, rather than reactive, but it was Carman who took a keen interest in developing a corporate managerialism in the public service. Managerialism, in this sense, refers to 'a radical reshaping of the culture and administrative structures of the public sector ... with the increasing adoption of private corporate practices concerning the delivery of "more with less," the rhetorical administrative reforms of restructuring and rationalization.'[64] Carman's vision anticipated the work of future cabinet secretaries, building a senior-management cadre that functioned outside sectoral and organizational silos: corporate management, in other words.

His thoughts on leadership were shaped by the observation that the 'feeder ranks' for the deputy-minister level were thin. The assistant-deputy ministers (ADMs), the obvious cadre in line to ascend to the rank of deputy, were particularly underdeveloped, according to Carman. He made it a priority to identify the five or six hundred people in the public service with deputy-minister potential and began to develop this group as a corporate resource. The problem, as diagnosed by Carman, was that 'a lot of ADMs had become subject experts in their own area. However, being a deputy requires a more generalist approach rather than a technical one.'[65] The solution was to provide 'high potential' candidates 'with developmental opportunities in other ministries, or even within their own ministries, but not in the area that they had held – this would broaden their experience and build generalist skills in management. Eventually we would have some bench strength.'[66] In this regard, he expanded the role of the Executive Development Committee, established by Ed Stewart, as a forum in which to develop and recruit deputy ministers, while also enlarging its purview to include appointments to the rank of assistant deputy minister.

To operationalize this focus on human resources, Carman initiated a number of innovations. First and foremost, he appointed an associate secretary of the cabinet responsible for executive resources. In addition, he established (anticipating what is today the Centre for Leadership) a Human Resources Secretariat, led by a deputy minister located within Management Board and mandated to provide leadership 'on human resources policy, planning, employment conditions, and practices.'[67] Moreover, a group of private-sector executives was constituted as the Premier's Advisory Committee on Executive Resources, to advise the premier on the development of public-service leaders in terms both of performance and of compensation.[68] Converging with, and working to shape, Carman's thinking on building managerial capacity within the public service was the influential work of a 1985 Price Waterhouse and Canada Consulting Group (CCG) study entitled *A Study of Management and Accountability in the Government of Ontario*. Another influence was an Imperial Oil executive-development manager, W.P. Moher, who was seconded to the Ontario public service 'to review the role and mandate of the Civil Service Commission, in the context of new and innovative management philosophy and techniques.'[69]

The Price Waterhouse-CCG study recommended that good performance be rewarded and that performance appraisals be the instrument to measure, motivate, and manage behaviour. Moher's 1986 report – *Managing Human Resources* – identified the strategic role of senior managers/executives as leaders in the difficult process of bringing about the kind of fundamental change that Carman knew was required. Moher wrote: 'Evolution must be driven by senior managers. Their beliefs and actions are at the core of organization culture, and their leverage is greatest ... The change to executive practices is an end in itself, but more importantly, it is also a necessary precondition to broaden change and to advance excellence in public service.'[70] With respect to Moher's report and his own perspective, Carman says, 'At least this was the philosophy and it was consistent with the recommendations of the Lambert commission at the federal level and Moher. In addition, we had the Price Waterhouse study [that] recommended a change in the working culture. So we had all these documents pointing toward the need to develop a new culture within the Ontario Public Service.'[71] With these studies, Carman understood the link between building a senior-management leadership and achieving a deeper cultural change. Achieving the latter required building the former. It was Carman's goal to move from 'command and control to a vision and values led organization,' and that was 'when we adopted the term "leadership" as opposed to "management."'[72]

Towards this objective, Carman pioneered not only new structures and institutions but also new practices focusing on performance rather than process at both the managerial and policy levels. Under his leadership, performance-based pay – tied to performance agreements – as recommended in the Price Waterhouse-CCG study, were instituted, and, at a policy level, budget allocations were linked to outcomes. This, too, was something that interested the premier, so Carman 'went forward with the proposal to link compensation to performance agreements.'[73] In 1987 the performance-agreement practice was pushed down to the entire senior-management group – which consisted of the top five hundred or so managers.

Long before he became secretary of cabinet, Carman also pioneered the introduction of Management by Results (MbR), which required that ministries submit business plans that specified how money was going to be used. This movement, in fact, had begun as far back as the early 1970s when Ola Berg, director of the Management Board resources branch, required that the Ontario Northland Transportation Agency submit a business plan, outlining objectives for the year, to support its annual budget submission. In 1972 Carman, then an executive director with Management Board, worked with Berg to introduce this concept as a general requirement for all ministries. The proposal was taken up with the treasurer, John White. White could not be convinced of the political merit of a results-based approach to management. Undeterred, Carman took the idea to Management Board and, in 1973, a four-year pilot project was initiated. By 1978, 95 per cent of Ontario expenditures were being measured against planned results.[74] However, Carmen found that moving to the next step of outcome measures met substantial resistance from deputy ministers.[75]

In all of this, Carman had taken the role of secretary of the cabinet much closer to the model of a corporate chief executive officer. He was less concerned with policy than with managerial reform. The presence of strong policy capacity around the Premier's Office allowed him to focus on institutional renovation, a project supported by the premier. Moreover, he acknowledged a policy-capacity gap within the Cabinet Office and so marshalled and relied on the capacity inherit in the Ministry of Finance to contest policy proposals coming from the line ministries.[76]

In 1989 Carman stepped down as secretary of the cabinet and was succeeded by Peter Barnes (1989–92), another long-time senior public executive. In many respects, Barnes would attempt to build on the platform for transformation left to him by his predecessor.

## Hard Times and the 'Prime Ministerialization' of the Centre

Barnes came into a Cabinet Office with about seventy staff and a budget in the range of $7 million. There were three associate secretaries responsible for executive resources, the Policy and Priorities Board, and operations, indicating a deepening organizational sophistication and a willingness to broaden executive responsibility and leadership in these core areas. However, the Ontario electorate – in part responding to a deepening economic malaise and frustration with political establishments of any stripe, in the wake of the failed Charlottetown Accord on constitutional reform – unpredictably (and, as Graham White says, incongruously) tossed out the Peterson Liberals in the election of September 1990, handing the government to Bob Rae's New Democrats.

The New Democrats came into government just as Ontario was sliding into the deepest recession since the Great Depression of the 1930s. Between 1990 and 1994 the unemployment rate hardly slipped below 10 per cent.[77] Provincial GDP shrank from $322.5 billion in 1989 to $304.5 billion in 1991,[78] and the provincial deficit grew from $3 billion in 1990–1 to $11.9 billion in 1992–3.[79] Given the economic climate and the politically problematic situation into which the social-democratic party had been thrust, the apex of the provincial state was expanded. Notably, this was the beginning of an important trend at the centre of the Ontario state. In 1990–1 the Cabinet Office grew to about ninety staff and the budget approached $11 million.

Reminiscent of the concerns driving the COGP twenty years prior, and those that had much more recently shaped Carman's thinking about restructuring, Barnes and the senior executives around him questioned the capacity of the Ontario state to respond to the demands and challenges of an age of discontinuity. Evert Lindquist and Graham White sum up Barnes's critique as one that viewed 'the "vertical silo" structure of government as outmoded and ineffective, moreover, it rejected a management philosophy premised on control and command imperatives, in favour of emphasis on effective service delivery.'[80] Carman's legacy – an enduring corporate interest in creating a leadership cadre committed to change – was expressed in Barnes's Tomorrow Project, which 'was primarily an attempt at changing organizational culture to accept and to manage change.'[81] The objective was to reorient senior management away from the administration of the status quo and towards leading a fundamental transformation in the function and organization of the Ontario public service. The Tomorrow Project was this and much more. One account characterized it as 'an enormous reorganization of the government that promised to slash the fat in the interface between ministries, potentially eliminating thousands of public service jobs and cutting hundreds of millions in annual cash requirements from the province's treasury.'[82] There were three discrete projects that together composed the initiative: service delivery, led by Glenna Carr, best practices, led by Art Daniels, and a central agencies review, led by Glenn Thompson.

Echoing and combining the managerial principle of 'let the managers manage,' greater management discretion and autonomy – advanced by the COGP and by Carman's project of developing a corporate-management perspective and practice within the public service – the Tomorrow Project comprised a vision of 'leadership from the center to promote change, but not the imposition from the center of specific solutions; instead, line ministries were to be encouraged to create their own solutions.'[83] Thus, in addition to the issue of leadership, the Tomorrow Project had several important objectives, including: improving the image of the public service, initiating a service-quality focus, slimming the public service, and updating the COGP recommendations. This was heavily influenced by the experience of the Netherlands and New

Zealand.[84] As the 1990 election approached, Premier Peterson agreed that, post-election, Barnes would go forward with a set of reorganization recommendations. But the September election, as noted, resulted in Peterson's Liberals being replaced by Rae's New Democrats. Before long, the question of trust and the need for a strong working relationship among the premier, his cabinet, and the senior public service would be tested in a manner not experienced in Ontario for some time.

First, the Tomorrow Project did not proceed as had been anticipated. As Barnes says: 'We had the Tomorrow Project ready to go but the NDP said they had no time for reorganization – they were concerned solely with policy.'[85] Given that any major reorganization may have resulted in some degree of job loss in the unionized public service, it is understandable that the New Democrats would not have been interested in pursuing such an agenda – at least at the outset. However, Barnes viewed the decision to abandon the Tomorrow Project as a lost opportunity. 'We lost five years when change should have taken place,' he notes. 'We would have had much more time and could have dealt with staff reductions through attrition and lay-offs would have been unnecessary.' [86] Secondly, unlike Peterson, who, while initially suspicious of the public service, quickly learned that this was in fact a very professional and competent organization, Rae (or, more pointedly, much of the NDP staff) 'was determined that the public service was against them.'[87] The New Democrats came to Queen's Park with a number of trade-union and social-movement activists for whom 'the bureaucrats were an integral part of the conservative establishment which impeded genuine reform.'[88]

The result was a growing structural parallelism at the centre of the Ontario state. While Peterson Premier's Office functioned with twenty-five to thirty-five staff, that of Premier Rae, in 1992–3, reached more than one hundred. This included the primarily public-service-staffed corporatist-type Premier's Council,[89] which was established under Peterson but became much more robust as a policy-development and brokering structure under Rae. However, there was a strong shift towards policy initiatives coming from the Premier's Office and the ministerial offices of other central agencies. In 1990 Premier Rae's principal secretary, David Agnew, and others 'were not satisfied that Cabinet Office was not much more than a secretariat' and, according to Agnew, 'one of the first decisions we made was to augment the resources and positions in Cabinet Office. We wanted to add a very strong policy capacity to it. I think this was partly because we were a new party to government. There was some thought that after a hundred years of rule by other parties, there needed to be a new capability at the center to interpret the wishes and desires of the new government.[90]

For many public servants, especially those accustomed to a centre more concerned with coordination than policy development, the NDP's centralization of control over the policy process was interpreted as a politicization of the public service.[91] The question of politicization during the Rae term is controversial; some may well contend that there was no more politicization (defined as the appointment of political allies to key positions) than in previous governments. Certainly, a number of key deputy ministers and assistant-deputy ministers (Michael Decter, Jim Thomas, Charles Pascal, Jay Kaufman, Jeff Rose, Grant Wedge, Rosemary Proctor, and Michael Mendelson) were actually or perceived to be personally aligned to the overall political orientation of the government. How qualitatively different these appointments were from those made under other governments, however, is debatable.[92]

A somewhat more nuanced view is that, for the NDP, the neutrality and professionalism of the public service notwithstanding, 'only bureaucrats sympathetic to democratic socialism could adequately serve an NDP government.'[93] Yet even some of those senior appointees who were seen to be political (such as Mendelson, Kaufman, and Proctor) were in fact appointed under Peterson. Others had careers in the public service that preceded Rae. Regardless, for Barnes, 'the role of Secretary of the Cabinet is to ensure coordination and smooth working relationships between key ministries – a good Secretary of the Cabinet has to work these relationships and balance them. It was difficult to play this role under the NDP. Some deputy ministers who were very close to the Premier were end-running me and going directly to him. Given this, I told Rae he had to replace me.'[94]

As if to confirm the view that the public service was becoming increasingly politicized under the NDP, Premier Rae turned to his principal secretary and the director of the NDP's successful 1990 election campaign, David Agnew, to fill the post of secretary of the cabinet on 21 September 1992. The decision to appoint someone so closely linked politically to the premier was, in Agnew's view, a practical one since 'the premier decided he needed a stronger linkage with Cabinet Office. He wanted to ensure that the government's message was getting through to the public service. Of course, at that point, we had already made some changes to the deputy-minister ranks. We had done some recruitment from the outside and so on. The fact remained we had work to do.'[95] Agnew's successor as secretary of the cabinet would be much more concerned with the symbolism of this appointment and what it meant for the reputation of the public service.

For Agnew and the NDP government, it was a matter of governing in hard times. The macro-environmental context – both economic and political – in which this government was fated to be situated was determinative of a tendency towards centralization and, consequently, an expansion of the means by which to control the state apparatus. And it was a tendency that was by no means unique to Ontario. Christopher Hood and Maurice Wright have related this trend to the rupture in the post-war boom and the construction of the welfare state: 'Modern ideas about government behaviour are largely based on the experience and presumption of government growth. But, increasingly, "big government" seems to be facing a crisis. The resources that it needs for maintenance and expansion of its activities are becoming harder to obtain as economic growth declines.'[96]

Carman had begun to caution that Ontario was confronting the same challenge. As the horizons of the Keynesian model narrowed, Ontario's New Democrats remained, at some level, committed to it. Donald Savoie's account of the Keynesian revolution that took place in the 1940s, wherein there was a strengthening of 'the hand of those who wanted an interventionist role for government in society ... [which] could also serve to strengthen the center of government,' might apply equally to the Rae government.[97] Agnew observes that, 'when the political and the economic environment become strained, it becomes more important for government to control its activities and its agenda.'[98]

This was the conundrum of Ontario's first social-democratic government; these were not Keynesian times. From Agnew's vantage point, the senior leadership of the public service was not 'up to the task of dealing with public management when resources were in decline. The Ontario Public Service was always able to find some money or people to solve the problem but in 1992 revenues dropped – this had never happened before. This was not just another recession, it was a fiscal wall. And people were not happy with dismantling what they had spent time building.'[99] The lesson, however, is that all revolutions, all paradigmatic transformations, if you will, require capacity at the centre to lead and direct change. In essence, it was a lesson that the COGP and Carman's focus on 'leadership' implicitly understood.

## The 'Common Sense Revolution': The Paradox of Shrinking the Provincial State and Building the Centre

Months before the 1995 election that brought the 'Common Sense Revolution' to power, the Conservatives assembled a transition team, which included former senior public servants, to lay the groundwork for taking control of the Ontario government apparatus. In January 1995 the transition team reported to party leader, and soon-to-be-premier, Mike Harris on how to deal with the public service and in particular its most senior members. Their recommendations were based on two criteria: competence and comfort with the policy direction of the Common Sense Revolution.[100] Whether or not 'comfort' was exactly the quality possessed by the next secretary of the cabinet is debatable, but the new government was clear that policy had been formulated and expressed in the platform and it would be the work of the senior public service to ensure it was implemented. Harris's transition team debated the question of politicization at the top of the public service. According to one transition-team member: 'I was one of the people who was involved at the time of the election of the Harris government in persuading them they should not politicize the public service and they should try to make better use of the public service. On the other hand, we also advised them that if you want to go forward with your pretty hard-nosed agenda, you're going to have to centralize even more or you'll lose control.' This was the problem for the Common Sense Revolutionaries: to pursue their 'grand enterprise'[101] of shrinking the role and influence of the provincial state while, at the same time, ensuring that the state was aligned to their agenda. The decision was made to find someone from within the public service; the new government went about interviewing a number of key deputy ministers. The process ended on 13 June 1995 with Rita Burak's appointment as Ontario's tenth secretary of the cabinet. Premier Harris's former principal secretary, David Lindsay, explains the decision as one based on the new administration's confidence in Burak's ability to align the public service with the new agenda: 'We went in with a clear foundation, a clear platform about what we wanted to do. We spent some time thinking about the deputy ministers and the inside public servants, we hired Rita Burak as the Secretary of the Cabinet. She is a long-serving public administrator and we gave her a free hand to do what she needed to do to put the civil service into the right position to implement this huge agenda. Rita quickly recommended a number of senior deputy ministers to take on a number of portfolios to help start implementing the agenda.'[102]

Indeed, as James Rusk stated in the *Globe and Mail* on 28 June 1995, five deputy ministers who were seen to be too close to the NDP were removed on 27 June. A change project of the magnitude proposed by the programmatic Conservatives required that the top leadership of the Ontario public service – the deputy ministers – be both capable and aligned towards implementing this agenda.

Burak's first priority was to restore the professional and non-partisan integrity of the Ontario public service by moving out 'partisan deputies or those who behaved as partisans. I wanted to dismantle the centre and decided I would rely on line deputies to implement the "Common Sense Revolution."'[103] More interestingly, the Cabinet Office staff complement was quickly shrunk by about 20 per cent as structures such as the Premier's Council were wound down.

As a means of ensuring the identification and development of senior leaders, Burak appointed an associate secretary to lead a new structure within the Cabinet Office dedicated to senior-management development: the Centre for Leadership (CFL). The CFL represented the institutionalization of the movement to create a corporate- management culture and practice within the public service by providing training, education, and development opportunities for senior managers. Susan Waterfield, associate secretary of cabinet, was appointed to lead the CFL and worked with Burak to develop and implement a 'Senior Human Resource Strategy.' The strategy increased salaries for deputy ministers and senior managers across the public service, but, in addition, reintroduced a performance-pay system. Performance contracts for deputy ministers were also reinstated by Burak. The total package was reviewed and approved by Premier Harris. Moreover (reflecting a recognition of the important role of mass communications, media, and information technology for both internal and external messaging), a new division of Communications and Corporate Services was established and led by an assistant deputy minister. An equally significant piece in Burak's modernization agenda was the creation and appointment of a new assistant deputy minister, responsible for policy coordination, in the Cabinet Office. Burak recognized the need to facilitate horizontal coordination across ministries as the line ministries moved into the role of policy implementers of the far-reaching provision of the Common Sense Revolution. Appropriate leadership and communications were to be key, given the transformative agenda of the new government, and Burak understood what needed to be done to bring the Conservative agenda and the public-service perspective together.

Signalling the need to quickly align the public service with the policy agenda of the government, a forum was held in late 1995, hosted by the Public Policy Forum of Canada and involving fifty private-sector leaders and twenty public-service deputy ministers. At this forum, Burak reviewed the evolution of the public service since the Committee on Government Productivity. She spoke about the challenges of meeting the new government's policy and fiscal agenda and, at the same time, held out a positive vision for the public service. A key feature of the challenge, noted Burak, would be the need to move on a 'faster and more significant downsizing than any other public service in Canada.'[104]

The discussion focused on the need for greater exchange between the private sector and the public service; a restructuring of the public service and its relations with transfer partners (municipalities, universities, schools, and hospitals); a plan to recruit and train future public-service leaders with skills in strategic thinking, business-mindedness, familiarity with change management, and entrepreneurialism; and the overhauling of the public-service recruitment and compensation system to better reflect the private sector.[105] Whereas Agnew, and the New Democrats, sought, perhaps one could say, to colonize the state with trusted advisers, the Common Sense Revolutionaries adopted a strategy of alignment that would impose a clear division of labour between the political leadership as policy makers and the public service as policy implementers. Burak recalls, 'The Harris government was very clear about wanting to actually implement the CSR [Common Sense Revolution]. The Premier wanted to be different from others by doing exactly what he said he'd do. The premier told this to deputy ministers at their first meeting with him. He was interested in their ideas on how to implement CSR initiatives, *but the government was going to implement its promises.*' Burak notes that implementing the Common Sense Revolution was a given, but, 'just before the government took office, I presented the premier with a multi-year plan to transform the public service. I wanted the OPS to once again be the respected public service that other jurisdictions sought out for advice in public administration.'[106]

In a presentation to a cabinet retreat in September 1995, Burak proposed the following vision for the public service:

To transform and downsize the OPS to match the government's vision of a reduced role for government in the economy. This transformation would be achieved while maintaining:

- Efficient service to the public
- Probity/integrity/accountability
- Non-partisan/professional public service
- Valuing staff/merit principle

And this process would set a new quality standard for the transformation and downsizing which will be recognized internationally.[107]

The task was substantial. Under Burak, the Cabinet Office would acquire the necessary capacity to provide the support needed to lead a transformation of this magnitude. From 1995 to 2000, the Ontario public service was reduced by about 20 per cent, and, at the same time, it developed or implemented a number of restructuring initiatives, such as corporate standards for customer service; a shared-services bureau responsible for 'backroom' operations, common to all ministries, such as payroll; the establishment of Government of Ontario Information Centres; regional delivery; an information-technology strategy; and corporate-wide systems for human resources and finance as well as alternative service delivery. In 1998 this modernization agenda was recognized by the Commonwealth Association of Public Administration and Management, which awarded the Ontario public service its first gold medal for innovation.

This was to be a paradoxical reorientation under which the Cabinet Office was both shrunk and strengthened. Between 1996–7 and 1999–2000, the Cabinet Office budget grew from $10 million to $17.5 million (the Ontario Jobs Investment Board accounted for one-third of the 1998–9 and 1999–2000 budget allocation),[108] and in 1996–7 Burak restructured the Cabinet Office and downsized its staff complement. The Cabinet Office expanded the number of senior executives from five to ten persons with assistant-deputy-minister, deputy-minister, or associate-secretary rank. In addition, a Red Tape Secretariat as well as a Voluntary Sector Initiatives unit, which was to support the government's interest in more effectively harnessing the voluntary sector, were established. The assistant-deputy minister responsible for policy coordination presided over a growing internal policy capacity as three policy-field units were established with six staff each. In 1997–8, in a move that augmented the leadership capacity already established, a deputy minister responsible for public-service restructuring was appointed and was in turn supported by two assistant-deputy ministers. All in all, these were the components of Burak's machinery and to make it all work, she understood, it must function as a team.

In the early months of the Conservative government, David Lindsay, then principal secretary to the premier, commented that 'communications of the key messages the government is trying to get out is critical, and this has had marginal success, and input into how better to do it is welcome.'[109] The Conservative agenda amounted to something approaching a revolution and, as Guy Crittenden wrote in the *Globe and Mail* on 1 November 1997, 'revolutions depend on good propaganda.' Consequently, in 1998–9, and indicative of the need at the centre for greater alignment with respect to the government's messaging, a new position of deputy minister of communications and associate secretary of the cabinet was established. Three assistant-deputy ministers responsible for 'strategic communications' were appointed as well.

In 1999–2000, Burak's final year as secretary, the centre began to turn its attention towards increasing policy capacity. In an 'Executive Dialogue' in 2000, Burak said, 'We currently have an opportunity to build on our policy capacity in the OPS. At both the political and civil service levels there is an interest in developing a more strategic, comprehensive and longer-term approach to policy development.'[110] The initiative, first pioneered in 1999 at the Ministry of Community and Social Services, was dubbed Investing in Policy and focused on such questions as: What makes a good policy professional in the Ontario public service? What makes a good policy product? And what are successful practices in good policy research and analysis?[111] The concern with revitalizing policy at the centre, and in the ministries, was reflected in the appointment of a deputy minister and associate secretary of the cabinet responsible for policy. Such a position had not existed since the Davis era, and one could argue persuasively that the new position was substantially different. In addition, there were two policy assistant-deputy ministers: one responsible for social policy and the second for strategic planning and economic/fiscal policy.

Whereas the New Democrats had distrusted the public service's willingness to participate in their project, the Conservatives enlisted the centre as a partner in transformation. While the first Conservative term, in 1995–9, resurrected the politics/administration dichotomy, the second term was very much about employing the apparatus of the state to achieve policy and organizational objectives. In this regard, Burak cautions that the secretary must be flexible with respect to where the focus of any given government may be: 'You also need to understand there will be greater or lesser emphasis on policy and communications – depending on what works for any given Premier. We must remember no one elected us and what they see as the focus ought to be the focus. We must be flexible and agile enough to ebb and flow with the needs of the government.'[112]

Burak's successor was Andromache Karakatsanis, In the twenty-nine months of her term as secretary of the cabinet (30 June 2000 to 20 November 2002), Karakatsanis consolidated the structures and functions established by Burak since 1995. Between 1995 and 2000, the public-service workforce was downsized from 81,300 to 60,337.[113] Business-planning processes were now embedded within each ministry and these were linked to the overall government priorities. There was also some movement towards alternative service delivery and a separation of policy formulation from delivery. Internal administrative processes were re-engineered through such initiatives as the Shared Services Bureau. And performance measurement and monitoring were now, as part of the annual ministry business plans, a key tool in ensuring that budget allocations were attached to outcomes. These innovations were conceived and launched under Burak and so it is not surprising that Karakatsanis would view her term as one of 'continuity and evolution.'[114] Resources for the Cabinet Office expanded from 117 to 155–60 full-time staff and a budget that fluctuated between $17 million and nearly $19 million. The number of senior executives providing leadership roles within the Cabinet Office remained stable at ten. However, what sets the Karakatsanis regime apart from others is her focus on organizational integration. This, too, was a logical extension of what the business-planning process had begun. The fourth 'Framework for Action' document issued in 2000 characterized public-service integration as follows: 'We often picture the OPS as a series of vertical towers (commonly known as silos). An integrated OPS is not just the same towers with walkways between them here and there. An integrated organization is like a structure with interlocking parts. The connections are not decoration; they are not add-ons. The strength of the whole comes from the alignment of each section with the rest, and the support they give each other.'[115]

For Karakatsanis, the provision of quality services was dependent upon an integrated organization, but, more than this, it was a means by which the Ontario state apparatus could adapt to rapidly changing circumstances. As the *Framework for Action 2000* stated, a good reason to integrate was the need to respond to an increasing level of environmental complexity, where public-policy issues require multi-jurisdictional responses.[116] As a means of embedding integration into management practice and culture, Karakatsanis added a section to the deputy ministers' performance agreements which addressed 'corporate contributions.' Her explanation for this: 'I was of the view that we were not fully utilizing the deputy ministers as a corporate resource. I thought of them as a corporate board of directors. I encouraged deputies to raise what they thought to be common challenges for the OPS as a whole. I asked that they run their ministries in a way that is contributing to corporate objectives.'[117]

The project of rebuilding policy capacity, which had begun with Burak, was of central importance to Karakatsanis. A 1999 consultant's report noted: 'One view is that the overall Ministry policy agenda, including a range of possible solutions, has, in recent years, been largely predetermined at the political level. This view holds that there has been little room for alternative approaches and "new" thinking.'[118] The point here is that substantive debate necessitates a full examination of the issues, which may include raising questions that challenge the policy preferences of the governing party.

In other words, something more than 'responsive competence'[119] was required. In Ontario, where the policy agenda was set by the Conservative electoral manifesto, there was little room for extended policy discussion. Consequently, as one senior manager has said, 'we have moved from being architects to being contractors. And I don't think we have many architects left.' Karakatsanis echoes this diagnosis: '[The Conservatives] came in with a detailed policy agenda. This moved the public service into focusing on the implementation of that agenda. There was a sense in the aftermath that we needed to reinvest in policy capacity. This coincided with the Conservatives second term when they began to look to the public service for policy options.'[120] To build on this renewed interest in the policy role of the public service and to reorient senior executives and managers towards a policy-advisory role, Karakatsanis started to use the 'Executive Dialogues' as 'a way to generate ideas and begin a process of culture change where the public service saw itself as playing an important role in offering impartial policy advice. I wanted to create a new culture that was confident in bringing forward new ideas. This was important as we had been so focused on delivery, we now needed to remind ourselves that the main concern is with the public interest.'[121]

While the Karakatsanis term was an expression of continuity with her predecessor, it was also (and perhaps most important) a period of consolidation. All revolutions require a period of normalization wherein the changes that have been brought about have time to settle and become institutionalized in everyday practice. It is at that point that such changes are no longer just technical or managerial innovations, becoming part of the organizational culture. Karakatsanis's achievements, then, amounted not to institution building but rather to consolidation of the most fundamental reforms in the history of the Ontario state. Her work relating to organizational integration was a means of operationalizing this project of consolidation by deepening and embedding what had been learned since 1995.

On 20 November 2002 Tony Dean became Ontario's twelfth secretary of the cabinet, a post he holds to this day. He led a transition from Harris's seven years as premier to the premiership of Ernie Eves and then, in October 2003, the transition to a rather different, Liberal, government, where the public service was seen not as the problem but as part of the solution. There can be little doubt that the more consensus-building philosophy of the new premier, Dalton McGuinty, and government appealed to Dean's labour-relations background. Dean's leadership style and vision, to date, may be characterized as one of both consolidation and institution building. While the Cabinet Office budget actually shrunk from $17.7 million in 2002–3 to $15.3 million in 2004–5, staff has expanded from approximately 185 to about 300 positions. Of course, this growth in staff was a function of Dean's focus on improving the capacity of the centre to manage human resources for an organization of 60,000, and it also reflected the transfer of human-resources management staff from the Management Board Secretariat. Under Dean, the Cabinet Office complement of executives (that is, those of assistant-deputy, deputy-minister, and associate-secretary rank) remained stable at ten positions. Still, Dean had observed gaps in human resources and strategic planning: 'My sense was that the business of thinking through, of visioning, of strategic planning for the OPS as an organization had not received due attention. My strong feeling was that we needed to build capacity to do that.'[122]

To underscore his commitment to building a stronger corporate-management perspective and practice, Dean's first innovation was to take a look at his title: secretary of the cabinet and clerk of the Executive Council. It harkened back to a much less formalized time when the position was not much more than an administrative-support role to the premier and the cabinet. Dean had had an opportunity to observe and reflect on several of his predecessors and their role. His observation was that 'the role was three-pronged – deputy minister to the premier; manager of the cabinet decision-making process; and, thirdly, manager of the machinery of government. It was this third piece that seemed underdeveloped.'[123] Dean insisted that the title be amended to read 'secretary of the cabinet and head of the public service,' identical to the title used at the federal level.

Dean remarks that, while there was a great deal of transformational work being done on the leadership and human-resources front, 'there was no strong sense of coordination and alignment.'[124] To bring a more strategic approach to human-resources management and leadership, he integrated the human-resources functions of Management Board with the Centre for Leadership programs already located within the Cabinet Office. By bringing together the full range of human-resources management functions under one executive head, a critical and strategic area of the public service would be amenable to more coordinated and horizontal management and policy setting. Thus, Dean institutionalized and expanded the scope and capacity at the centre for more strategic thinking and policy on management issues.

Five new assistant-deputy ministers were appointed to support the deputy minister in leading new divisional structures within the Cabinet Office responsible for employee relations, human-resources service delivery, 'Leadership and Learning,' human-resources strategy and policy, and 'Excellence and Innovation' (which replaced the Ontario Public Service Restructuring Secretariat). While these were new positions within the Cabinet Office, they were created by reducing senior management elsewhere in the system so that there was no overall growth in the total number of senior-management positions. However, Carman's vision of building a corporate-management cadre was being provided with the necessary structures.

The second gap identified by Dean was concerned with strategic planning – the capacity of the public service to get out in front of the curve and become more anticipatory, future-oriented, and horizontally managed and integrated. Dean identified two mechanisms for achieving this. In 2004–5 the Results Office emerged, led by a deputy minister. In an interview in 2003, Dean commented that 'building horizontal and integrated organizations is a key element of improving customer service and developing better public policy ... The business planning approach used at the ministry level since 1995 has encouraged ministries to think in an integrated and horizontal way, breaking down internal barriers. That momentum has now been carried over to clusters of ministries and we are seeing the development of business plans at the cluster level.'[125] The emergence of results-based management (RbM) was a logical extension of the re-emergence of policy-field committees of cabinet in 1999–2000 and, at the public-service level, the formation of policy and planning clusters among ministries as a means of achieving greater policy coherence, that is, horizontal alignment with the key priorities of the government. An expression of managerialism and concern with public-sector productivity, RbM was in many respects derivative of the Management by Results movement of the 1970s.

The interest in a 'results' approach to policy development and coordination originated with the new premier and his key policy advisers, who, even while in opposition, were very much influenced by some of the so-called 'Third Way' thinking coming out of the United Kingdom. Premier McGuinty had spent time studying the Prime Ministers Delivery Unit (PMDU), which had been set up in the United Kingdom Cabinet Office under the direction of Michael Barber in June 2001. The overriding mandate of the unit is to 'ensure the delivery of the Prime Minister's top public service priority outcomes.'[126] In Ontario, the Results Office was inspired by the British PMDU model, with a clear focus on providing corporate oversight of the many strategies under way. The McGuinty Liberals have identified health, education, and economic growth as their principal priorities and the Results Office provides secretariat support to a number of Results Team meetings chaired by the premier.

The objective of results-based management is to link these politically determined priorities to policy and program achievements. Results-based management is thus defined as 'a comprehensive, government-wide, approach that informs results-based decision-making, ensuring that all government funded activities are aligned with strategies that contribute to meeting government priorities and serve an important public interest.'[127] RbM is essentially the application of horizontality to an environment of scarcity amidst unlimited wants and demands. Much in the same way that the COGP recommendations required the creation of a Policy and Priorities Board as a mechanism for setting priorities at the cabinet level, the turn to RbM was a 'recognition that increased funding to priority areas – without examining what results we obtain from existing funding – is not sustainable. So it's critical to examine what outcomes can be achieved through a refocusing of our existing funding levels to match priorities.'[128]

The second contribution to building a horizontal corporate-management perspective within the public service is expressed in Dean's attempts to expand the role of deputy ministers as corporate rather than ministry leaders. Dean has identified the 'dual accountabilities' of deputy ministers – to their minister and to the premier through the secretary of the cabinet – as problematic. He says, 'My own sense is that if we are going to transform this organization in the way that we need to it has to become truly horizontal and corporate. Corporate leadership is critical. We need to encourage deputy ministers to step out of their ministerial silos and come together to actively make decisions as corporate leaders – as a CEO management team.'[129]

To operationalize his efforts to create such a corporate-management cadre, Dean looks to the Deputy Ministers' Council (DMC) to take on a more 'board of directors' role for the public service. Rather than being the domain of the central agencies – Management Board, the deputy minister of finance, and the secretary of the cabinet – the DMC will become much more of a decision-making structure respecting business planning, budgets, human-resources strategy, and, indeed, the design of transformation initiatives. In the end, according to Dean, 'these issues are everyone's responsibility and everyone is responsible for marketing and defending those decisions. So, in effect, we are breaking from the traditional idea and role of the central agencies as the centre of corporate planning and leadership. That's a fundamental shift in the work that a deputy minister does.'[130] As an example of the emerging new role, Dean points to the 2004 budget process, where deputy ministers were provided with unprecedented access to information and opportunities to share their ideas, as much as were cabinet ministers.

As secretary of the cabinet, Dean is both consolidator and institution builder, and he is so by having both built upon and retrieved the ideas and initiatives of previous secretaries of the cabinet. Arguably, Dean's most significant contribution to date is the building of 'corporate managerialism' into the public service and, with this, the movement towards a horizontal-management practice and culture, particularly evidenced in his policy-renewal and results-based management projects. In a sense, these journeys were begun with the COGP and were the particular focus of Bob Carman from 1985 to 1989.

## Conclusion

Joseph Schumpeter[131] introduced the idea that changes in institutions, as with technology, are an evolutionary process – both incremental and path dependent.[132] The leadership lessons of Ontario's secretaries of cabinet demonstrate something of a Schumpeterian flavour in that there is a gradual evolution where each succeeding secretary builds upon the legacy of his or her predecessor(s) and is also engaged in a continuous process of adaptation to changing conditions and needs. Thus, there is constraint as well as innovation within the context of that constraint. This is not to say that Ontario's secretaries of cabinet are not 'switchmen' (and women) of history, as Pusey characterizes senior public-service leaders. This small number of individuals has, since 1948, demonstrated, if only by virtue of their location at the apex of the centre, an important leadership role in policy and management. However, while they are substantial actors, they are not autonomous. They innovate in response to political and economic cues, but this, it must be said, is much more of a post-COGP development. The Ontario Cabinet Office has incrementally grown more directive as it constructed the machinery to do so. The post-war long economic boom of 1945 to 1975 provided an unprecedented degree of economic and, consequently, political stability. From the end of Second World War through to 1985, Ontario's secretaries of cabinet worked within a political context continuously dominated by a single political party – the Progressive Conservatives – who had held office since 1943. The political hegemony of the Conservatives began to show strains in the mid- to late 1970s, no doubt as a result of the growing economic instability, and was expressed in two consecutive minority governments (1975–7 and 1977–81).

From a global perspective, the 1980s and 1990s were decades of profound change, and this found expression in an ideological shift wherein Keynesian orthodoxy gave way to an ascendant neo-liberalism inspired by the work of Friedrich von Hayek and Milton Friedman. This was of particular significance in the United Kingdom, Australia, New Zealand, and the United States. In Ontario, the 'paradigm shift' was also under way, but the inevitable coming-to-terms with issues of globalization, competitiveness, and the need to retune the provincial state apparatus was delayed (something that Robert Carman so astutely noted in 1988).

The formative importance of the Committee on Government Productivity in setting a long-term agenda for public-service reform has not been fully appreciated. This was the Ontario state's first attempt to 'get ahead of the curve' and begin to address questions relating to the appropriate role for government in service delivery, and improved policy development, by institutionalizing a more formal and rigorous decision-making apparatus at the cabinet level, which would lend itself to greater horizontality and give consideration to the strategic role of management. Though partially implemented in 1972, and then only with respect to the working of cabinet, it would take until 1995, and the Conservatives' return to government, to begin to pick up on other key themes left untouched, such as service delivery and managerial reform. What is remarkable is how a series of secretaries of cabinet – Robert Carman, Peter Barnes, Rita Burak, Andromache Karakatsanis, and Tony Dean – have all struggled, with some success, in recovering the recommendations of the COGP. Yet this was not so much a deliberate and conscious project on their part (save for, perhaps, Carman) as a response to fiscal and political imperatives.

Moreover, after a period of neo-liberal-inspired restructuring, both in Ontario and throughout the world, the state sector continues to play an important and growing role in leading and adapting to changing environmental (i.e., political and economic) conditions.[133] The emergence of the 'adaptive state' is very much an expression of the efforts of the state, even a subnational state, 'to harness the potential of innovation in other sectors in order to re-equip government.'[134]

## NOTES

1  Dennis Olsen, *The State Elite* (Toronto: McClelland and Stewart, 1980), 10.

2  Michael Pusey, *Economic Rationalism in Canberra: A Nation Building State Changes Its Mind* (New York: Cambridge University Press, 1991), 2.

3  See R.A.W. Rhodes and P. Weller, eds., *The Changing World of Top Officials: Mandarins or Valets?* (Buckingham, U.K., Philadelphia: Open University Press, 2001); and Peter Shergold, 'Lackies, Careerists, Political Stooges? Personal Reflections on the Current State of Public Service Leadership,' *Australian Journal of Public Administration*, 63 (2004): 3–13.

4  Christopher Dunn, 'The Central Executive in Canadian Government: Searching for the Holy Grail,' in Christopher Dunn, ed., *The Handbook of*

*Canadian Public Administration* (Toronto: Oxford University Press, 2002), 311–12.

5   Donald Savoie, *Governing from the Centre: The Concentration of Power in Canadian Politics* (Toronto: University of Toronto Press, 1999), 71–81.

6   The 'president of the executive council' in Ontario was termed 'prime minister' until 1972. At that point 'premier' became the official title of the head of Ontario's government.

7   F.F. Schindeler, *Responsible Government in Ontario* (Toronto: University of Toronto Press, 1969), 42.

8   Cabinet Office, 'History and Role of Policy and Priorities Secretariat,' unpublished paper, Toronto, 30 January 1989, 1.

9   Schindeler, *Responsible* Government, 44.

10   Ibid., 42.

11   Ibid., 45.

12   Graham White, 'Change in the Ontario State 1952–2002' (Toronto: Role of Government Panel, 2002), 36.

13   Ibid., 17.

14   Cabinet Office, *History,* appendix A, 6.

15   Ibid., 3.

16   Ibid.

17   Ibid., 6.

18   Ibid., 5.

19   Peter Barnes, interview with author, Toronto, 27 February 2004.

20   Archives of Ontario, RG 18–257, box Y69, Charles McNaughton, 'Operational Plans II–40' (1969).

21   White, 'Change in the Ontario State,' 15.

22   James Simeon, 'Policy-Making in the Cabinet,' in Donald MacDonald, ed., *Government and Politics of Ontario*, 2nd ed. (Toronto: Van Norstrand Reinhold, 1980), 103.

23   George Szablowski, 'Policy-Making and the Cabinet: Recent Organizational Engineering at Queen's Park,' in Donald MacDonald, ed., *Government and Politics in Ontario* (Toronto: Van Norstrand Reinhold Ltd., 1975), 114.

24   Ibid., 119.

25   Simeon, 'Policy-Making,' 105.

26   White, 'Change in the Ontario State,' 16.

27   Archives of Ontario, RG 18–257, box Y69, Charles McNaughton, 'Operational Plans II–40,' Toronto, 1969.

28   Archives of Ontario, RG 18–527, box Y82, 31–2, Boards and Commissions,

'Agencies, Boards and Commissions: A Discussion Paper,' 25 February 1972.

29  Archives of Ontario, RG 18–527, box Y82, Government of Ontario, 'Organization for Program Delivery (draft),' n.d., File: Ross – Structures of Government, Toronto, 6.

30  David E. Osborne and Ted Gaebler, *Reinventing Government: How the Entrepreneurial Spirit is Transforming the Public Sector* (Reading, Mass.: Addison-Wesley, c. 1992).

31  Ministry of Finance, Ontario Budget, 1974 (Toronto: Queen's Printer, 1974), 1.

32  White, 'Change in the Ontario State,' 123.

33  Ministry of Finance, Ontario Budget, 1975 (Toronto: Queen's Printer, 1975), 16.

34  Ibid., 17.

35  Executive Council of Ontario, 1975, order-in-council 1701/75.

36  Ramesh Mishra, Glenda Laws, and Priscilla Harding, 'Ontario,' in Jaqueline S. Ismael and Yves Vaillancourt, eds., *Privatization and Provincial Social Services in Canada* (Edmonton: University of Alberta Press, 1988), 124. In today's terminology, we would call this 'neo-liberalism.'

37  Special Review Committee, 'The Report of the Special Program Review' (Toronto, November 1975), 20 and 36.

38  Ibid., 1.

39  Ibid., 37.

40  Cabinet Office, *History*, 10.

41  James Fleck, interview with author, Toronto, 12 May 2004.

42  Ibid.

43  Ibid.

44  Ibid.

45  White, 'Change in the Ontario State,' 18.

46  Ministry of Finance, Ontario Budget, 1978, 1970–5 figures (Toronto: Queen's Printer, 1978), 30; Ontario Budget, 1983, 1975–82 figures (Toronto: Queen's Printer, 1983), 84.

47  White, 'Change in the Ontario State,' 36.

48  Ontario Civil Service Commission, *Annual Report 2000–2001* (Toronto: Queen's Printer, 2001), 7.

49  Ministry of Treasury and Economics, Public Accounts 1979–80, 1970/1–1979/80 figures (Toronto: Queen's Printer, 1980), 2–48; Ministry of Treasury and Economics, Public Accounts 1989–90, 1980/81–1989/90 figures (Toronto: Queen's Printer, 1990), 2–54.

50  Ministry of Finance, 1981, 1973–5 figures, A–19; 1979–81 figures, 25.

51 Edward Stewart, interview with author, Toronto, 9 March 2004.
52 Ibid.
53 Cabinet Office, 'The Ontario Public Service in the Year 2000: The Challenge of Renewal' (unpublished paper, prepared for Executive Resources, Toronto, 1988), 1.
54 Carman, 'A Pace-Setting Public Service for a World Class Society' [undated speech], 13–21.
55 Evert Lindquist and Graham White, 'Streams, Springs, and Stones: Ontario Public Service Reform in the 1980s and the 1990s,' *Canadian Public Administration*, 37, no. 2 (1994): 276.
56 Cited in Georgette Gagnon and Dan Rath, *Not without Cause: David Peterson's Fall from Grace* (Toronto: Harper Perennial, 1992), 28.
57 Ibid., 28–9.
58 Robert Carman, interview with author, Toronto, 17 October 2005.
59 White, 'Change in the Ontario State,' 20.
60 Ministry of Finance, Ontario Budget, 1989, 1982–7 figures (Toronto: Queen's Printer, 1989), 66; Ontario Budget, 1997, 1988–96 figures (Toronto: Queen's Printer, 1997), 66.
61 Ontario Civil Service Commission, *Annual Report 1984–1985*, 1984–5 figures (Toronto: Queen's Printer, 1985), 21; *Annual Report 1989–1990*, 1989–90 figures (Toronto: Queen's Printer, 1990), 7.
62 Cabinet Office, *History*, 20–1.
63 Robert Carman, 'Executive Dialogue: Transformation in a Pace Setting OPS' (Toronto: Cabinet Office, 17–18 March 1989).
64 Alexander Kouzmin, Robert Leivesley, and Nada Korac-Kakbadse, 'From Managerialism and Economic Rationalism: Towards "Reinventing" Economic Ideology and Administrative Diversity,' *Administrative Theory and Praxis*, 19, no. 1 (1997): 19.
65 Robert Carman, interview with author, Toronto, 9 March 2004.
66 Ibid.
67 Ontario Public Service Restructuring Secretariat, 'Transforming Public Service for the 21st Century' (Toronto, April 2000), 13.
68 Ibid., 14.
69 Ibid., 13.
70 W.P. Moher, *Managing Human Resources in the Ontario Public Service* (Toronto: Queen's Printer, 1986), 40.
71 Carman interview, 2004.
72 Ibid.
73 Ibid.

74  Ontario Public Service Restructuring Secretariat, 'Transforming Public Service,' 12.
75  Ibid.
76  Ibid.
77  Ministry of Finance, Ontario Budget, 1991, 1990–1 figures (Toronto: Queen's Printer, 1991), 29; Ontario Budget, 1993, 1991–2 figures (Toronto: Queen's Printer, 1993), 55; Ontario Budget, 1995, 1992/93–1994/95 figures (Toronto: Queen's Printer, 1995), 34.
78  Ministry of Finance, Harvey Bradley, Office of Economic Policy, '1981–2000 GDP,' 1981–2000 figures. Correspondence with author, 2005.
79  Ministry of Treasury and Economics 1993, 1990/91–1992/93 figures, 2–60; Ministry of Finance, 1996, 1993/94 figures, 65.
80  Lindquist and White, 'Streams, Springs, and Stones,' 280.
81  Ibid., 281.
82  Gagnon and Rath, Not without Cause, 163.
83  Ibid.
84  Barnes interview, 2004.
85  Ibid.
86  Ibid.
87  Ibid.
88  Lindquist and White, 'Streams, Springs, and Stones,' 283.
89  The Premier's Council was established in 1986 during Premier David Peterson's first term. It was to serve as a forum in which the province's diverse sectoral interests – business, labour, social activists, academics – could exchange policy ideas. In essence, it was a form of proto-capitalist bargaining seeking to construct multipartite consensus around social and economic policy.
90  David Agnew, interview with author, Toronto, 12 March 2004.
91  White, 'Change in the Ontario State,' 23.
92  See ibid., 23, where White states unequivocally that 'the NDP's record of bureaucratic appointments differed little from that of previous governments.' Though this is a valid point, it requires more research to be completely substantiated. Towards the end of the Rae regime, there is anecdotal 'evidence' that a number of NDP staffers were parachuted into managerial positions below the assistant-deputy-minister level throughout the public service. But the point made by White still stands: Is this practice fundamentally different from that of previous regimes?
93  Lindquist and White, 'Streams, Springs, and Stones,' 286.
94  Barnes interview, 2004.
95  Agnew interview, 2004.

96  Christopher Hood and Maurice Wright, ed., *Big Government in Hard Times* (Oxford: Martin Robertson, 1981), vii.

97  Savoie, *Governing from the Centre*, 33.

98  Agnew interview, 2004.

99  Ibid.

100 David Cameron and Graham White, *Cycling into Saigon: The Conservative Transition in Ontario* (Vancouver: University of British Columbia, 2000), 86.

101 Andrew Gamble characterizes Thatcher's project as a 'grand enterprise' in his book *The Free Economy and the Strong State: The Politics of Thatcherism*, 2nd ed. (Durham N.C.: Duke University Press, 1988), 159.

102 David Lindsay, interview with author, Toronto, 8 December 2004.

103 Rita Burak, interview with author, Toronto, 27 February 2004.

104 'How Ontario Will Be Governed: Summary of Proceedings,' Public Policy Forum, Toronto, 7–8 December, 1.

105 Ibid.

106 Burak interview, 2004. Emphasis added.

107 Slide Presentation, Rita Burak, Cabinet Office, 5 September 1995.

108 Cabinet Office, 'Ten Year Comparison of Cabinet Office Allocations and FTE's,' memorandum, Toronto, 24 May 2005.

109 Public Policy Forum 1995, 4.

110 Cabinet Office, Rita Burak, 'Year 2000 Executive Dialogues' (Toronto, n.d.), 19.

111 Ibid., 20.

112 Burak interview, 2004.

113 Ontario Civil Service Commission, *Annual Report 2000–2001* (Toronto: Queen's Printer, 2001), 7.

114 Andromache Karakatsanis, interview with author, Toronto, 30 April 2004.

115 Cabinet Office, *Framework for Action 2000, Working Together: An Integrated Organization* (Toronto: 2000), 4.

116 Ibid., 5.

117 Karakatsanis interview, 2004.

118 Cabinet Office, Executive Resources Group, 'Investing in Policy: Volume 1. Needs Analysis and Strategies for Action' (Toronto, 1999), 15.

119 This refers to Herbert Kaufman's 1956 article 'Emerging Conflicts in the Doctrines of Public Administration,' *American Political Science Review*, 50 (1972): 1057–73. Kaufman states that public-service policy work is characterized by 'neutral competence' – that is, the ability to offer objective and expert advice, free of partisan or political calculation. Savoie observes that this approach came to be seen as providing too much influence to public servants over policy. Instead, politicians came to demand that public ser-

vants demonstrate 'responsive competence,' paying more heed to partisan and political factors.

120  Karakatsanis interview, 2004.
121  Ibid.
122  Cabinet Office, Tony Dean, 'Executive Dialogue Speaking Notes,' 2004.
123  Ibid.
124  Ibid.
125  Paul Crookal, 'Tony Dean: Head of Ontario's Public Service, on Leadership, Horizontal Teams, and the Transformational Journey of the OPS,' *Canadian Government Executive*, no. 4 (2003): 8.
126  United Kingdom, Cabinet Office, 'Prime Minister's Delivery Unit': http://www.cabinetoffice.gov.uk/pmdu/index.asp, accessed 27 May 2005.
127  Cabinet Office, Policy Innovation and Leadership, 'Results-Based Management: Implications for Policy Professionals' (PowerPoint Presentation, Toronto, 2004).
128  Cabinet Office, Tony Dean, 'Executive Dialogue Speaking Notes,' Toronto, 13 May 2004, 6.
129  Tony Dean, interview with author, Toronto, 18 May 2004.
130  Ibid.
131  See *The Theory of Economic Development* (1911); *Business Cycles* (1939); and *Capitalism, Socialism and Democracy* (1942).
132  Leonardo Burlamaqui, Ana Celia Castro, and Ha-Jon Chang, *Institutions and the State* (Cheltenham, U.K.: Edward Elgar, 2000), xi.
133  See, for example, the special issue of *The Economist*, 'The Visible Hand,' 27 September 1997, 6–48.
134  Tom Bentley and James Wilsdon, eds., *The Adaptive State: Strategies for Personalising the Public Realm* (London: Demos, 2003), 17.

# 5 The Secretary to the Cabinet in Saskatchewan: Evolution of the Role, 1944–2006

GREGORY P. MARCHILDON

While much has been written about the history of the position of secretary to the cabinet, as well as the individuals who occupied it, at the federal level, relatively little is known about the evolution of the position in the provinces. This chapter reconstructs the evolution of the post of secretary to the cabinet in Saskatchewan since the Second World War. Its reference point is the secretary to the cabinet in the federal government because of the abundance of published information on the topic relative to provincial secretaries to the cabinet.[1] For this reason, it is useful to start with a definition of secretary to the cabinet that is rooted in the experience of the federal government.

In the Canadian Privy Council Office's operational definition of the full responsibilities of secretary to the cabinet, three distinct, yet presumably connected, roles are identified.[2] The first role is overseeing secretariat and policy support to cabinet and cabinet committees as head of the cabinet secretariat. The second role is managing the entire public service on behalf of the prime minister and cabinet as the head of the public service. The third role providing policy advice and administrative support, as well as advice on changes to the machinery of government, to the prime minister. When all three functions are combined in a single position, I refer to this position as the *secretary to the cabinet*, in italics, to separate it from its constituent functions, particularly the more narrowly defined position of cabinet secretary (the head of the cabinet secretariat) which exists in a number of provinces, including Saskatchewan, today. This role, though, is restricted to the narrower function of 'cabinet secretary,' in contrast to the broad role that has come to be assumed by the secretary of the cabinet in the government of Canada and a number of other provinces (including Saskatchewan, in the recent past).

At the federal level, the *secretary to the cabinet* position was 'grafted' on to the position of clerk of the Privy Council, a position that encompassed rather formal and historic functions since Confederation.[3] The statutory function included preparing, recording, and keeping all orders-in-council passed by the Executive Council (cabinet) pursuant to the authority given by Parliament.[4] As replicated in the provinces, and in Ottawa, the role has also included clerical functions such as maintaining formal records on behalf of cabinet and ceremonial functions such as the swearing in of ministers. Similarly, in a few provinces such as Manitoba, the *secretary to the cabinet* position was also grafted on to the position of clerk of the Executive Council.

In Saskatchewan this was not the case. Initially, the narrow cabinet secretary function was grafted on to the position of executive assistant to the premier, laying the groundwork for the emergence of the full *secretary to the cabinet* position. At times, in the late 1950s and 1960s and the very recent past, the narrow version of the position of cabinet secretary and the post of clerk of the Executive Council were combined, but, contrary to the practice in Ottawa and provinces such as Manitoba, the position of deputy minister to the premier has never been combined with clerk of the Executive Council in Saskatchewan.

In addition, while the clerk of the Executive Council has had a formal legislative basis since the province was first created in 1905, the role has always been extremely limited compared to the position of *secretary to the cabinet* or the individual positions of cabinet secretary and deputy minister to the premier when they have been separated. It is also interesting to note that the position of cabinet secretary remained informal until the new Executive Council Act of 1972 – twenty-two years after the office was permanently established.[5] In contrast, the position of deputy minister to the premier was given a legislative basis a mere two years after its actual establishment in 1977.[6]

### Tim Lee: The First Permanent Cabinet Secretary

In 1944 the first socialist government in North America was elected in Saskatchewan. The Co-operative Commonwealth Federation (CCF), led by Tommy Douglas, came into office with one of the most detailed set of policy initiatives ever designed by a political party in Canada. To implement the CCF's detailed program, the new government required sophisticated planning, committed bureaucratic talent, and a visionary premier to convince the population of the desirability of major change.[7]

In response to these new demands, the machinery of government would be fundamentally reshaped within a few years. Most marked among these changes was the advent of a troika of cabinet committees and related central agencies that would become a permanent feature of the administrative machinery and style in Saskatchewan. By 1947, these cabinet committees – supported by a corps of brilliant civil servants – were providing a steady stream of analysis that both systematized and improved decision making while also permitting multi-year planning on a scale never before achieved by a provincial government.[8]

In contrast, cabinet functioned largely as it had since the province's creation in 1905. This was despite the fact that the secretariat for the powerful Economic Advisory and Planning Board (EAPB) was located in the Department of Executive Council – the department of government supporting the cabinet in general and the premier in particular. Unlike the EAPB, which mixed cabinet members with civil servants, the cabinet room was reserved for ministers only. Policy items were discussed, generally, at the instigation of line ministers. The occasional memo would be provided by a minister, but usually the discussion, and the decisions flowing from it, occurred without the benefit of written documentation. Like his predecessors, as head of the Executive Council, Douglas would provide a verbal summary of the discussion and decision and the relevant minister would then go off to implement the cabinet's decision.[9]

On occasion, when a cabinet decision required extensive and complex instructions on implementation, Douglas would act as his own cabinet secretary, dictating a memo based upon his own verbal summary in cabinet. This responsibility became so onerous over time that he asked Woodrow Lloyd – a former teacher, who was diligent and systematic in his approach to programs and policies – to act as cabinet's secretary and prepare memos on the more complex decisions.[10] Occasionally, on particularly technical or important matters that required extensive note taking, Douglas directed his executive assistants, first Morris Shumiatcher and later Jim Graham, to come into the cabinet room in order to record the discussions and manage the follow-up, thereby providing 'full-fledged Cabinet secretarial service for that particular instance.'[11] This ad hoc system, though, had serious limitations. Despite Lloyd's best efforts, he could draft only the most cryptic minutes, given his own participation in cabinet. His heavy responsibilities within the government prevented him from developing procedures that would improve the operation of cabinet and cabinet-committee decision making.[12]

Douglas, and the rest of his cabinet, was ready for the change implied by the appointment of a permanent cabinet secretary. In November 1950 Douglas hired Tim Lee as his executive assistant when Graham left the government to return to a private practice in law. Unaware at the time that Graham (and before him Shumiatcher) had entered the cabinet room only occasionally, Lee would explain years later how he became the government's first permanent cabinet secretary: 'I thought [Shumiatcher and Graham] were full-fledged cabinet secretaries and so I conducted myself in the way in which I thought a cabinet secretary ought to act. The Premier didn't change that in any way, so, from the day of my first appointment, I attended all of the cabinet meetings. That was the first time any outsider had done so.'[13]

Tim Lee was then twenty-seven years old and had come into the government to work as a research economist for the Economic Advisory and Planning Board. He had met the head of the EAPB, George Cadbury, in Vancouver while doing graduate studies in economics at the University of British Columbia. Cadbury encouraged Lee to apply for a position with the EAPB. Lee soon found himself working for Tom McLeod, the secretary of the EAPB, and Thomas K. Shoyama, a more senior economist who would soon become the secretary of the EAPB. Lee was also interested in politics, both as an analyst and as a supporter of the CCF, and it was his analysis of the results of the 1948 provincial election – political work that was done on his own time, away from the EAPB – that likely brought Lee to the attention of Douglas.[14]

Lee's new responsibilities included generating the cabinet agenda by collecting items from the ministers chairing the cabinet committees – the only individuals authorized to put items on the cabinet agenda. In addition, Lee obtained orders-in-council prepared by John Telford, the clerk of the Executive Council, so that they could be included as part of the cabinet docket. Appointed in 1944, Telford was the fifth clerk of the Executive Council, since 1905, and was largely responsible for preparing orders-in-council and administering the oath at the swearing-in ceremonies for new ministers. According to Lee, this formal role never overlapped with the cabinet secretary.[15] In fact, in 1956, when Telford retired from government, Lee was appointed clerk of the Executive Council, taking on the extra responsibility without any reduction in his existing duties (or any increase in salary). This practice continued through the 1960s, during the Lloyd and Thatcher governments.

The Douglas government held cabinet twice a week, Tuesdays and Fridays, from 10:00 a.m. to 1:00 p.m. The first items on the agenda were the orders-in-council, followed by the Treasury Board recommendations that required cabinet approval. This was followed by the substantive decision items from individual ministers, generally presented on a 'first come first served' basis, though Douglas sometimes reshuffled items, just before cabinet, by urgency or importance. Generally, a memorandum from the minister accompanied any item. As time went on, more of these memoranda were circulated in advance by Lee's office – sometimes upon Lee's suggestion to a minister that advance notice improved chances of a favourable decision. Lee, however, had no authority to delay any item or provide any documentation 'on top' of the item itself.

Lee's role as cabinet secretary was limited to the narrow definition of the office. At no time did he act as Premier Douglas's chief adviser on policy or the machinery of government. For policy advice, Douglas relied upon the secretariat supporting the EAPB, the cabinet's main policy committee, and the individual civil servants who headed up the EAPB secretariat. In its first years of operation, the key individual was George Cadbury, a prominent Fabian socialist from Britain, as well as Thomas McLeod.[16] Cadbury and McLeod were eventually succeeded by Tommy Shoyama, the secretary of the EAPB from 1950 until 1964. For advice on the machinery of government, Douglas relied upon the central agency supporting Treasury Board and, in particular, A.W. (Al) Johnson, who was the secretary of Treasury Board from 1952 until 1964.[17]

In his fourteen-year tenure as cabinet secretary, Lee was never considered the head of the public service. Indeed, no civil servant played such a role during the Douglas era. Instead, the formal lines of accountability were directly from the deputy ministers to their respective ministers, with no real connection to the premier or his department of Executive Council. While the premier was consulted on some deputy-minister appointments, most were decided by ministers themselves, at a time when the tenure of both ministers and deputy ministers was very long by contemporary standards. Collegiality and collective responsibility were encouraged through the cabinet-committee structure, but the deputy ministers reported solely to their ministers, not to the premier or any single high-ranking official within the premier's department.

Nor did Lee manage ministers on behalf of the premier. However, after the passage of many years, Lee did begin to instruct new ministers on their collective responsibilities as members of cabinet and their individual responsibilities for their department so that they 'did not have to depend upon a deputy minister' to learn how to be a cabinet minister. With these ministers, according to Lee, he was able to 'go through in considerable detail the cabinet routine and the whole sequence of events that occurred over the period of the year: the way in which proposed legislation ought to come to the cabinet, and what they ought to do with the legislation, once cabinet approval is obtained; remind them of their responsibility (if they needed any reminding at all, which was rarely) to the caucus; and to inform them as to what legislation was forthcoming.'[18]

In 1961, when Tommy Douglas left the office of premier to become the first federal leader of the New Democratic Party (NDP), Lee continued in the position as cabinet secretary. Under the new premier, Lee's work expanded since Woodrow Lloyd 'was more precise than Douglas' and therefore preferred more formal preparation for cabinet, including memoranda written in advance and more systematic liaison with Treasury Board before cabinet meetings. This emphasis on documentation and process was necessary, because, in Lee's words, Lloyd 'sought crisper discussion and sharper decisions' as well as 'faster decisions,' though the decision-making approach, and the cabinet processes that supported it, remained rooted in the Douglas system.[19]

By 1963, however, Lloyd remained dissatisfied enough with the cabinet process status quo that he established a temporary Cabinet Committee on Cabinet Procedure. In addition to three ministers, four officials were assigned to the committee: Tim Lee, EAPB Secretary Tommy Shoyama, Deputy Provincial Treasurer Al Johnson, and Lloyd's executive assistant, Wes Bolstad. Following the cabinet committee's recommendations, the premier ordered that, henceforth, all agenda items forwarded to the cabinet secretary would be accompanied by a supporting summary of the item as well as a draft cabinet minute. In addition, a new process on legislation was inaugurated to ensure that the detailed review was done by the Department of Justice, leaving the issues of principle for cabinet discussion. In addition, a cabinet committee on orders-in-council was established so that they could be vetted before meeting, preserving more time for substantive discussion in cabinet.[20] These reforms barely had time to become an established part of the system when the CCF government, under Lloyd, was defeated at the polls by Ross Thatcher's Liberals.

## The Thatcher Era, 1964–71

Tim Lee was one of a number of civil servants who left Saskatchewan following the 1964 defeat of the CCF and the election of the Liberals.[21] He moved to Toronto to become an academic and administrator at York University.[22] The new premier, Ross Thatcher, was light years removed from both Douglas and Lloyd in terms of leadership style and approach to government, although a detailed study of this era has been hampered by a lack of documentation. Virtually every file or paper relating to the Premier's Office or the operations of cabinet, during the Thatcher era, was destroyed. Numerous verbal accounts, however, make it clear that Thatcher was impatient with process and reluctant to delegate and that he insisted on dealing with the civil service in a direct and personal way. He was hostile to what he perceived as 'socialist planning' and may have made some of the government's most important decisions without the input of his cabinet.[23]

Despite the paucity of documentation from the Thatcher era, one scholar has suggested that, 'aside from the lack of minutes,' the actual procedures in the Thatcher cabinet were 'not that different from the procedures in the Lloyd cabinet.'[24] Yet, given Thatcher's singular control over government and his reluctance to delegate key administrative functions to his ministers or the bureaucracy, it is unlikely that the position of *secretary to the cabinet* could have emerged under his premiership.[25]

Except for his first and short-lived cabinet secretary, Ed Odishaw, Thatcher carried on the practice of combining the roles of cabinet secretary and clerk of the Executive Council, and it appears that he observed little distinction between the two offices. Appointed in October 1964, J.R. (Ron) Parrott was Thatcher's first clerk-cabinet secretary.[26] Parrott seems to have provided Thatcher with policy advice on a range of issues. Lack of documentation, however, makes it almost impossible to discern whether he gave advice informally to incoming members of cabinet, in a manner similar to that of Lee under Douglas and Lloyd. In any case, as with Lee, Parrott's duties did not include giving advice on the machinery of government. This was the responsibility of a small 'Organization and Management' unit within the Budget Bureau in the Department of Provincial Treasury, where it had been operating since the late 1940s. It remained separate from the office of the premier and the Department of Executive Council until at least the 1980s.[27]

Towards the end of 1967, Parrott left his position, which was then filled by Michael Wood, who would remain in the job for little more than a year and a half before he was succeeded by Michael Rosenroll, Thatcher's last cabinet secretary.[28] Both Wood and Rosenroll were Liberal partisans and close political advisers to Thatcher.[29] As a consequence, it appears that they both focused on the more political matters of cabinet and house management, rather than planning, public policy, or the machinery of government.

## Blakeney and the Establishment of a Deputy Minister to the Premier

Before he became premier, in 1971, Allan Blakeney had served a long apprenticeship in the Douglas government as a civil servant. By 1960, he had become an elected politician. His quick intelligence, as well as his intimate understanding of the machinery of government, and the civil servants who ran it, quickly made him one of Woodrow Lloyd's most senior and trusted ministers. In 1970 he beat out Roy Romanow, in a close race, to become leader of the NDP. One year later, he led his party to victory in the general election and remained premier until 1982.[30]

While Blakeney quickly reintroduced elements of the Douglas-Lloyd model that he knew so well, he also gradually introduced permanent changes that would establish the position of deputy minister to the premier, for the first time. These changes included a shift to a more premier-centred system that included a head of the public service responsible for hiring and firing deputy ministers, as well as a deputy minister to the premier responsible for managing both policy and advice on the machinery of government. These changes were accompanied by a major expansion of, and specialization within, the Department of Executive Council.

When first elected, Blakeney had an executive assistant who did double duty as his cabinet secretary.[31] As had been the case before 1956, a separate individual occupied the relatively clerical function of clerk of the Executive Council. Thatcher cabinet members having eliminated any trace of cabinet documentation, Blakeney temporarily brought back Tim Lee as a consultant to help him re-establish cabinet processes based upon his memory of the Douglas and Lloyd administrations. He also set up an Advisory Committee on Organization for Policy, Planning and Program Development, dominated by civil servants who had experience in the Douglas-Lloyd era: Grant C. Mitchell (chair), Wes Bolstad, and Roy Lloyd, as well as Keith Saddlemyer, a civil servant with extensive experience in law and public administration, who was on secondment from the federal government.[32] All of these individuals would go on to play key roles in the Blakeney administration, with three eventually taking their turns as cabinet secretaries and one, Wes Bolstad, also becoming the province's first deputy minister to the premier.

This 'organization' committee recommended strengthening planning units within all government departments, as well as a reorganization of cabinet committees to improve overall government planning. At the same time, permanent changes were made to cabinet processes. Blakeney required that cabinet agendas, as well as cabinet memoranda and cabinet-committee minutes, be circulated to ministers in advance.[33]

In 1972 the Department of Executive Council was reorganized. A new Executive Council Act was passed, giving the cabinet secretariat a legal basis within the Department of Executive Council for the first time.[34] The legislation made it clear that the cabinet secretariat would be headed up by the cabinet secretary, but that it would also include the clerk of the Executive Council who, in effect, reported to the cabinet secretary.[35] In May 1972 the Blakeney government's cabinet secretary was Keith Saddlemyer,[36] then on leave of absence from the federal Department of Regional Economic Expansion. Saddlemyer's chief responsibility was to ensure proper coordination between cabinet and the cabinet committees and central agencies serving cabinet.[37]

In 1973, upon becoming provincial deputy minister of industry and commerce, Saddlemyer was replaced in the position of cabinet secretary by Wes Bolstad. After growing up in small-town Saskatchewan, Bolstad had moved on to do a bachelor of commerce degree at the University of Saskatchewan and, eventually, a master of public administration degree at Harvard. From 1953 until 1961, he had worked in the innovative incubator of the Budget Bureau. During that time, he was responsible for a number of studies on subjects ranging from local government to medical-care insurance. From 1961 until 1964, he served as executive assistant to Premier Lloyd. After the Lloyd government's defeat, he became an assistant professor in the College of Commerce at the University of

Saskatchewan. Two years later, Bolstad moved to the Regina campus of
the University of Saskatchewan, where he was instrumental in establishing the School (later Faculty) of Administration, becoming its first
dean.[38] Although he would stay in the post of cabinet secretary for only
six years, Bolstad had a profound impact on the management of processes and people in the Blakeney government.[39]

In 1976 Blakeney created the new position of deputy minister to the
premier and moved Bolstad into the job. Although the position was not
given a legislative basis until three years later, Bolstad became, in effect,
the first real head of the public service.[40] His job was to advise Blakeney
on the hiring, firing, and shuffling of deputy ministers. By this time, it
had become clear that the premier, as opposed to individual cabinet
ministers, was ultimately responsible for the selection of the most
senior bureaucrats within the government.

This was a major shift from the very first years of the Blakeney
administration, when the government's initial group of cabinet ministers made the decision whether to keep their Thatcher-era deputy ministers or select new ones. In the years immediately following the 1971
election, Blakeney ensured that new deputy ministers were 'jointly'
selected by himself and the responsible minister to minimize the
reshuffling of deputies upon every ministerial shuffle.[41] Although
Tommy Douglas had rarely changed ministers, and both ministers and
their respective deputies often served very long terms together, Woodrow Lloyd had been more prepared to change ministers, particularly
when their performance did not meet his exacting standards.

Blakeney went further. He not only changed ministers but introduced
the practice of wholesale cabinet shuffles, a practice that was continued
by subsequent administrations. The cabinet shuffles also allowed Blakeney to arrange personnel so that ministers weak in administrative and
policy skills, but important to the government for other reasons, were
bolstered by strong deputy ministers.[42] In addition, Blakeney believed
in the utility of comprehensive shuffles of deputy ministers and other
senior administrative personnel. In one such shuffle, involving personnel in fourteen different ministries, Blakeney explained that such civil-
service shuffles ensured 'continued infusion of new energies and new
ideas' while maintaining 'a core of senior personnel with a broad experience that avoids departmental parochialism,' thereby 'providing better government-wide policy and administrative development.'[43]

It was Bolstad's job, as deputy minister to the premier, to ensure that
the right deputy ministers were selected, as well as to intervene when

relationships between the deputies and their respective ministers did not gel after the major shuffles.[44] As head of the public service, the deputy minister to the premier became responsible to the premier – and, through the premier, to cabinet – for the performance of deputy ministers, a responsibility that had never existed before in the provincial government. In contrast, the cabinet secretary, a position always occupied by a different individual during the Blakeney administration, continued to be responsible for cabinet processes, including ensuring the implementation of cabinet directives by the bureaucracy. During Bolstad's tenure as deputy minister to the premier, that position was occupied by John Scratch.

In 1979, upon Scratch's resignation, Blakeney returned Bolstad to the position of cabinet secretary and appointed Murray Wallace to the position of deputy minister to the premier.[45] Blakeney had come to the conclusion that the role of cabinet secretary was to be an 'enforcer,' since that individual had to make sure the administration was working effectively and this sometimes required 'knocking heads together.' On the other hand, the cabinet secretary had to be a 'super-diplomat,' in terms of dealing with cabinet ministers, and a 'super-expediter' of cabinet direction, in terms of the public service. Coming from the Department of Finance, Murray Wallace had the former characteristics, while Bolstad, both in experience and in temperament, had the latter ones.[46]

In March 1980 Wallace left the post of deputy minister to the premier to become chief financial officer and, within a short time, president of Saskatchewan Government Insurance (SGI) – a large provincial Crown corporation. He was replaced by John Sinclair, who remained in this position until after the Blakeney government was defeated, in the 1982 election. Sinclair was an academic with a PhD in political science and had taught at the University of Texas in Austin. He left university life to join the Budget Bureau in 1975 and became the director of the unit within three years.[47]

After Bolstad left the position of cabinet secretary to become executive director of the Meewasin Valley Authority in Saskatoon, Blakeney would appoint Grant C. Mitchell as cabinet secretary. Mitchell was a veteran public servant, having joined the provincial government in 1949. Raised on a farm near Weyburn, Saskatchewan, Mitchell served with the Royal Canadian Air Force in the Second World War, later graduating with a bachelor of science in agriculture, alongside a host of fellow veterans, from the University of Saskatchewan. He then immediately joined the provincial government, where he would remain for the rest of his career. From May 1972 until his appointment as cabinet secretary in October 1979, Mitchell was deputy minister of the Department of Environment. He remained in this position until February 1981, when he became deputy minister of the Department of Co-operation and Co-operative Development. In his stead, Florence Wilkie became the first woman cabinet secretary in the province and (perhaps) the country. She had gradually worked her way up the bureaucracy from the position of secretary in the 1950s. By 1974, she was a special assistant to the premier, by 1978 the clerk of the Executive Council, and by 1979 the duties of assistant cabinet secretary had been added to her continuing position as clerk.[48]

### Devine and the First Full-Fledged Secretary to the Cabinet

In the general election of 1982, the Blakeney government was defeated by the reinvigorated Progressive Conservatives. As the new premier, Grant Devine fused the positions of deputy minister to the premier and cabinet secretary, while adding the third role of chief adviser on policy and the machinery of government into the provincial version of the *secretary to the cabinet* position that had, by this time, become entrenched in the federal government.[49] The reason for creating the fused position, at least initially, may have had more to do with the personalities than with any game plan based upon a change in managerial or policy direction..

Devine and his new cabinet believed that the senior public service inherited from Allan Blakeney was politically aligned with the NDP and could not be trusted.[50] However, it was easier to fire civil servants than to find experienced individuals to take their place, in particular to find the appropriate deputy minister to the premier. After consulting with other Conservative premiers in the country, Devine chose Derek Bedson for the new position.[51]

With some fifteen years of experience working as a full-fledged *secretary to the cabinet*, Bedson would not likely have accepted any watered-down or divided role. The former clerk of the Executive Council in Manitoba, Bedson had performed the tripartite role of cabinet secretary, head of the public service, and deputy minister to the premier for four successive premiers of Manitoba. After he was fired by NDP government in Manitoba led by Howard Pawley, Bedson was hired by Ontario Conservative Premier William Davis to become the province's agent-general in London. When asked by Devine, Davis agreed to allow Bedson to step down and move to Regina in order to help establish his new government.[52] Bedson, for his part, undertook to stay in Saskatchewan for two years.[53]

While the combination of experience and perceived political alignment may have smoothed Bedson's entry into Saskatchewan, it did not guarantee smooth sailing afterwards. One of the most critical elements determining the effectiveness of the full-fledged *secretary to the cabinet* is the nature of his/her relationship with the sitting premier/prime minister. Complete trust is essential, as well as a profound respect for, and understanding of, the respective roles and responsibilities of both offices. This requires that both individuals feel comfortable enough to exchange hard truths about the people, policy directions, and machinery of government. Bedson clearly had that relationship with successive Manitoba premiers, but he and Devine were not able to 'bond' in the same way. The two could not 'speak the same language' and the relationship simply did not work. As a consequence, Bedson left Saskatchewan after little more than a year.[54]

Since there was no one then in the province that Devine wanted in this post, Grenville Smith-Windsor, the assistant cabinet secretary and clerk of the Executive Council, was appointed acting deputy minister to the premier and cabinet secretary until a suitable person could be found.[55] In the fall of 1983, however, Devine met Normal Riddell. Riddell, who had grown up in the same part of rural Saskatchewan and had gone to grade school with Devine, had eventually joined the Canadian foreign service and happened to be stationed in Brazil when Devine visited on a business trip. In addition to having a PhD from Stanford University, Riddell had extensive experience in the federal government, including some time working for Michael Pitfield in the Privy Council Office. A couple of months after the visit from Devine, Riddell was asked to become associate-deputy minister responsible for intergovernmental affairs in the Department of Executive Council by his old classmate. He agreed and arranged an extended leave of absence from the government of Canada.[56]

In July, six months after his arrival, Devine asked Riddell to become the deputy minister to the premier, leaving Smith-Windsor in the position of cabinet secretary. Although the official news release for the appointment set out a rationale for the division of positions based upon Devine's 'dual functions as premier and chairman of Cabinet,' the separation of the positions would not endure.[57] Smith-Windsor knew that the arrangement was only transitional.[58] And, for his part, Riddell had arrived in his position only to discover an undisciplined set of cabinet processes. This situation had also created havoc in the bureaucracy: decisions were continually being made and unmade by cabinet and its committees. Not being able to fulfil his functions of head of the public service and deputy minister to the premier, without first fixing the cabinet processes, Riddell soon took over the job as cabinet secretary as well. He thereby became the second (after Derek Bedson) full-fledged *secretary to the cabinet* in Saskatchewan.[59]

Remaining in this position until 1988, Riddell would become the most influential civil servant within the Devine government. In a government characterized by loose cabinet process – at least in comparison to the Blakeney government – he imposed considerable discipline and structure. For those ministers not inclined to take cabinet solidarity very seriously, he tried to exert collective discipline in their departments through their respective deputy ministers. For cabinet ministers who were used to having considerable autonomy before Riddell's arrival, the transition was difficult; in particular, there was considerable conflict between Riddell and Eric Bernston, Devine's deputy premier.

As head of the public service, Riddell put great emphasis on hiring capable individuals as deputy ministers, despite the fact that Saskatchewan had gained a notorious reputation among senior executives for its bloody transitions.[60] In Riddell's view, this challenge could be addressed by assuring some length of tenure through the creation of contracts between deputy ministers and his office, guaranteeing a given length of tenure in lieu of which a generous payment would be made. These contracts also made it clear that, in addition to their respective ministers, deputy ministers reported to the premier via the *secretary to the cabinet* and that their performance would be evaluated by the latter. Through this security of tenure, as well as clarification of reporting authority, Riddell hoped that deputy ministers would be able to do 'the right thing' on behalf of the government as a whole, whatever the position of their respective minister. Finally, Riddell relied more upon competitions than direct appointments to recruit new deputy ministers.[61]

Towards the end of 1987, Riddell was asked by Premier Robert Bourassa to leave Regina in order to become a deputy minister in Quebec as the associate secretary to the cabinet responsible for intergovernmental affairs. Riddell was attracted to the position. He also felt that his usefulness in Saskatchewan had run its course, given the difficult relationship he had with certain members of cabinet. The move was timed to ensure as little disruption to the Devine government as possible. Riddell would be succeeded as *secretary to the cabinet* by two individuals,

Larry Martin and Stan Sojonky.[62] Both would serve, in succession, a little less than two years in the same position at a time when the Devine
government was plummeting in popularity as it grappled with a wors-
ening economic and fiscal situation.[63]

## Romanow and Entrenchment of the Secretary to the Cabinet Position

The unpopularity of the Devine government led to the election of the
NDP, under the leadership of Roy Romanow. In a move similar to Blakeney's decision to bring in Tim Lee from the Douglas-Lloyd government to assist in the 1971 transition, Romanow brought in Wes Bolstad
as a transitional adviser and acting deputy minister to the premier and
cabinet secretary.

For the permanent *secretary to the cabinet* position, Bolstad recommended Ronald S. Clark, a Harvard-trained specialist in public administration who was then the chief administrative officer for the regional
municipality of Ottawa-Carleton. Clark had been a community planner
in the Blakeney government as well as director of planning for the city
of Regina between 1976 and 1980 and a senior Treasury Board analyst
in the provincial Department of Finance from 1980 until 1984.[64] His
influence in the position was limited by the fact that he left in less than
two years in order to become the president of a major provincial Crown
corporation, SaskEnergy.[65]

In 1994 Clark was succeeded by Frank Bogdasavich, a career public
servant who had been a deputy minister in the Blakeney government
and who was well known to Romanow. Bogdasavich had more than
twenty years of experience as a civil servant. He had been a deputy
minister during the Blakeney administration and had gone on to senior
posts within the federal government after 1982. As a result of budget
cuts during the latter part of the Devine administration and the first
two years of the Romanow government, the policy capacity of the
Saskatchewan government was at a low point when Bogadasavich
became *secretary to the cabinet*. He attempted to increase the central
planning and policy capability within Executive Council while encouraging line departments to increase their own policy capacity.[66]

At the end of 1996, I succeeded Bogdasavich in large part because I
had worked closely with Premier Romanow as his deputy minister of
intergovernmental affairs.[67] I remained in the position until mid-Sep-
tember 2000.[68] Many of the following observations and conclusions
concerning the evolution of the *secretary to the cabinet* position during

the Romanow years is derived from my personal experience during this period.

Romanow's decision to keep the full-fledged *secretary to the cabinet* position, as it had developed in the Devine government, as well as in Ottawa, and not return to the Blakeney model of a divided position, had much to do with his own personality and mode of governing. Unlike Blakeney, he preferred to have as small a senior staff as possible within the Department of Executive Council directly advising and reporting to him. He wanted one main political adviser as his chief of staff and one principal adviser from the civil service as his deputy minister. He desired cooperation and collaboration between his main political and bureaucratic advisers but also wanted his regular meetings among his chief advisers to be as brief as possible, which in turn required that the meetings involve as few individuals as possible. In the cabinet room, he expected both his chief of staff and his deputy minister to be present, along with the clerk of the Executive Council, who took the detailed notes from which the cabinet minutes were drawn. Cabinet minutes were sent to relevant cabinet ministers, officially approved, and signed by the deputy minister to the premier as *secretary to the cabinet*.

The three roles encompassed by the full-fledged *secretary to the cabinet* are comparatively easy to identify in the Romanow period. As head of the cabinet secretariat, the *secretary to the cabinet* was responsible for supporting all cabinet meetings and cabinet retreats as well as for the issuing of cabinet decisions and ensuring implementation of cabinet direction by the government as a whole. In 1997 a number of changes were implemented to improve cabinet processes, including: 1) the regularization of pre-cabinet briefings between the *secretary to the cabinet* and the premier; 2) the issuing of cabinet minutes to the deputy ministers of departments directly implicated in the particular cabinet minute;[69] and 3) the establishment of Monday morning meetings of cabinet-committee secretaries and central-agency deputy ministers, chaired by the *secretary to the cabinet*, in an effort to coordinate more effectively the business of cabinet and cabinet committees.

As the head of the public service, the *secretary to the cabinet* was ultimately responsible for hiring, firing, promoting, and demoting the permanent heads of all departments as well as associate-deputy ministers who, unlike assistant-deputy ministers, were appointed through orders-in-council, rather than through the Public Service Commission process. This role involved an annual performance review of individual deputy ministers by the *secretary to the cabinet*. Beginning in 1997, open competitions for new deputy-minister jobs were encouraged, with approximately two existing deputy ministers serving on a hiring panel chaired by the *secretary to the cabinet*.

As chief adviser on the machinery of government and policy, the *secretary to the cabinet* was responsible for all recommendations to the premier concerning changes in government departments and agencies. In 1997 a senior position on the machinery of government was created in the deputy minister's office of the Executive Council in order to provide more continuous and systematic advice to the premier.[70] As chief policy adviser to the premier, the *secretary to the cabinet* was closely associated with the Executive Council's Priorities and Planning Unit. Made up of senior policy advisers, and headed by the associate-deputy minister to the premier, this unit was enlarged, repositioned, and renamed the Cabinet Planning Unit in 1997. The research and advisory role of the Cabinet Planning Unit was also extended beyond social policy to economic policy, including the Crown corporations. The unit became the key source of advice to the premier on all major policy items, as well as a key instrument in dealing with administrative and policy crises within government.

### The Calvert Government: Return to the Split Position

In February 2001 Lorne Calvert took over as leader of the NDP and head of government. One of his first decisions was to separate the position of deputy minister to the premier from that of cabinet secretary. Prior to this, Marianne Weston, the veteran associate-deputy minister to the premier and head of the Cabinet Planning Unit within the Department of Executive Council, had occupied the full-fledged *secretary to the cabinet* position in an acting capacity after my departure from the government, in September 2000. The individual permanently appointed to the position of deputy minister to the premier was Dan Perrins, a thirty-year veteran of the Saskatchewan public service, who had started his career as a front-line social worker. The person appointed to the position of cabinet secretary was Judy Samuelson, former chief of staff to Roy Romanow, who also assumed the position of clerk of the Executive Council.[71]

Under Calvert, the position of deputy minister to the premier involved two of the three roles inherent to *secretary to the cabinet*, including that of head of the public service and chief adviser on policy and the machinery of government. In contrast, the position of cabinet secretary was restricted to its historic role of overseeing secretariat support to cabinet and at least some of its committees. To support this structure, the Cabinet Planning Unit (and its head) reported to the cabinet secretary for the purpose of supporting cabinet and the Cabinet Committee on Planning and Priorities, as well as to the deputy minister to the premier for the purposes of managing crises and issues directly of relevance and importance to the premier and his deputy minister.

There were both advantages and disadvantages associated with the splitting of the *secretary to the cabinet* roles. The main advantage is that it divided the workload and responsibility of what had become an increasingly large and complex job. The chief disadvantage was the conceptual and practical difficulties of separating the functions, in particular, the job of being the government's chief adviser on policy and the machinery of government and the job of supporting cabinet and its committees. This was seen most graphically in the need to have the Cabinet Planning Unit report to both positions in the Calvert government.

### Conclusion

The evolution of the *secretary to the cabinet* position in Saskatchewan shares some important similarities to the evolution of the position in the federal government. Both governments, in the 1940s, required an individual who could coordinate and support an increasingly institutionalized cabinet. This 'cabinet secretary' role was grafted on existing positions within both systems – the clerk of the Privy Council position in the federal government and the executive assistant to the premier position in the provincial government.

It was not until the 1970s that the function of head of the public service emerged in both governments with the increase in power of first ministers in directing cabinet and government. In Saskatchewan, in 1976, this was recognized in the creation of the position of deputy minister to the premier, by Premier Allan Blakeney. Wes Bolstad's appointment to this position took place only one year after Michael Pitfield had been appointed clerk by Prime Minister Pierre Trudeau, and reflected a fundamental shift in the focus of the position from cabinet to the prime minister. This was soon followed by the inclusion of a third role – the premier's chief adviser on policy and the machinery of government – as had become evident by the time of the Devine government.

There are also some differences with the federal government. One is that the role of 'head of the public service' in Ottawa was associated with the clerk of the Privy Council from at least the 1940s, while in Saskatchewan there is little evidence to suggest that it became part of the *secretary to the cabinet's* role until the 1970s. Finally, and most important, the three roles associated with the federal *secretary to the cabinet*, once assumed, have never since been split as they have been in Saskatchewan during the Blakeney and Calvert administrations.

The periodic dividing of the role in Saskatchewan bears some interesting resemblance to the history of the position in Newfoundland. In 1994 Premier Clyde Wells split the position because of his concern that the individual occupying it had become too much like a 'civil service Premier,' or, as I would put it, the chief executive officer of the government. In 1996 the roles were rejoined in a single position and individual by Liberal Premier Brian Tobin, only to be split again by Conservative Premier Danny Williams.[72] Whether this formed part of Premier Lorne Calvert's reasoning in splitting the roles into two different positions is open to conjecture, but it is not hard to imagine a future prime minister of Canada deciding to hive off at least one of the current roles assumed by the clerk of the Privy Council for identical reasons. On the other hand, the Saskatchewan Party government under Premier Brad Wall (elected in 2007) returned to the single position of *secretary to the cabinet*.

## NOTES

1 Twenty-five of these publications, articles as well as key extracts from monographs, were collated by the machinery of government secretary of the Privy Council Office in *The Roles and Responsibilities of the Clerk of the Privy Council and Secretary to the Cabinet* (Ottawa: Privy Council Office, 1999).

2 Quoted in Donald J. Savoie, *Governing from the Centre: The Concentration of Power in Canadian Politics* (Toronto: University of Toronto Press, 1999), 113. In 2005 the three roles of the clerk of the Privy Council were entitled: 1) deputy minister to the prime minister; 2) secretary to the cabinet; and 3) head of the public service. Clerk of the Privy Council's website, http://www.pco-bcp.gc.ca/default.asp?Page=Clerk&Language=E&Sub=aboutclerk, accessed on 19 December 2005.

3 Gordon Robertson, 'The Changing Role of the Privy Council Office,' *Canadian Public Administration*, 14, no. 4 (1971): 487.

4  Gordon Robertson, *Memoirs of a Very Civil Servant: Mackenzie King to Pierre Trudeau* (Toronto: University of Toronto Press, 2000), 302–4.

5  *Statutes of Saskatchewan*, 1972, cap. 40.

6  Executive Council Act, *Statutes of Saskatchewan*, 1979, cap. L-11.1.

7  A.W. Johnson, *Dream No Little Dreams: A Biography of the Douglas Government of Saskatchewan, 1944–1961* (Toronto: University of Toronto Press, 2004); Thomas H. McLeod and Ian McLeod, *Tommy Douglas: The Road to Jerusalem* (Edmonton: Hurtig, 1987).

8  Ken Rasmussen and Gregory P. Marchildon, 'Saskatchewan's Executive Decision-Making Style: The Centrality of Planning,' in Luc Bernier, Keith Brownsey, and Michael Howlett, eds., *Executive Styles in Canada: Cabinet Structures and Leadership Practices in Canadian Government* (Toronto: Institute of Public Administration of Canada and University of Toronto Press, 2005), 184–207.

9  Saskatchewan Archives Board, Regina (SAB), R-8433 to R-8435, transcript of Jean Larmour's interview with H.S. (Tim) Lee, Toronto, 20 January 1982.

10  Dianne Lloyd, *Woodrow: A Biography of W.S. Lloyd* (Woodrow Lloyd Memorial Fund, 1979). Diane Norton, 'Woodrow S. Lloyd,' in Gordon L. Barnhart, ed., *Saskatchewan Premiers of the Twentieth Century* (Regina: Canadian Plains Research Centre, 2004), 213–36.

11  SAB, transcript of Lee interview, 9.

12  Johnson, *Dream No Little Dreams*, 106.

13  SAB, transcript of Lee interview, 9.

14  Ibid.

15  Indeed, Lee described the clerk's role as 'complementary' to his own: ibid., 11.

16  On George Cadbury's role, see Robert I. McLaren, 'George Woodall Cadbury: The Fabian Catalyst in Saskatchewan's "Good Public Administration,"' *Canadian Public Administration*, 38 (1995): 471–80; and Gregory P. Marchildon, 'George Woodall Cadbury,' in Brett Quiring, ed., *Saskatchewan Politicians: Lives Past and Present* (Regina: Canadian Plains Research Centre, 2004), 36–7.

17  Rasmussen and Marchildon, 'Saskatchewan's Executive Decision-Making Style.'

18  SAB, transcript of Lee interview, 25.

19  Ibid., 33.

20  Jamesina G.L. Jamieson, 'The Evolution of Executive Power in Saskatchewan, 1944 to 1982,' LL.M thesis, University of Ottawa, 1989, 136–8.

21  This 'Saskatchewan Diaspora' is described in the Foreword of Johnson,

*Dream No Little Dreams*, xxi–xxii. For conflicting views on the Lloyd-Thatcher transition, see Norman Ward, 'Changing the Guard at Regina,' *Canadian Forum*, 44 (September 1964): 127–8; and Meyer Brownstone, 'Another View on the Saskatchewan Government,' *Canadian Forum*, 44 (December 1964): 198–200. Gregory P. Marchildon, entry for 'Saskatchewan Mafia' in the *Encyclopedia of Saskatchewan* (Regina: Canadian Plains Research Center, 2005), 813.

22  Johnson, *Dream No Little Dreams*, 123.

23  On Thatcher's governing style, see Dale Eisler, *Rumours of Glory: Saskatchewan and the Thatcher Years* (Edmonton: Hurtig Publishers, 1987); David E. Smith, *Prairie Liberalism: The Liberal Party in Saskatchewan, 1905–1971* (Toronto: University of Toronto Press, 1975); and Evelyn Eager, *Saskatchewan Government: Politics and Pragmatism* (Saskatoon: Western Producer Prairie Books, 1980).

24  Jamieson, 'Evolution of Executive Power,' 166.

25  *Saskatchewan Executive and Legislative Directory: Supplement, 1964–1971* (Regina and Saskatoon: Saskatchewan Archives Board, 1978), listing of clerks of the Executive Council, 28.

26  Jamieson, 'Evolution of Executive Power,' 164–5; SAB, *Saskatchewan Government Directory, 1965–66* . While the position of 'Cabinet Secretary' is mentioned for the first time in 1965, no individual is identified as occupying the post.

27  SAB, R-331, 2.1, press releases: Premier W. Ross Thatcher press release, 22 June 1965; and memo from J.R. Parrott to Thatcher, 18 May 1966. On the Organization and Management Unit in the Budget Bureau, see A.W. Johnson, 'The Treasury Board in Saskatchewan,' *Proceedings of the Annual Conference of the Institute of Public Administration of Canada* (1955); and Johnson, *Dream No Little Dreams*, xvii.

28  SAB, Government of Saskatchewan yearly directories, 1965–71.

29  Dale Eisler, telephone interview with author, 14 October 2005.

30  Dennis Gruending, *Promises to Keep: A Political Biography of Allan Blakeney* (Saskatoon: Western Producer Prairie Books, 1990).

31  This transitional figure was Gerry Wilson, who was executive assistant to Premier Blakeney as well as cabinet secretary. In May 1972 Wilson was appointed executive assistant to Health Minister Walter Smishek: SAB, R-1183, III, 10D, Premier's Office press release, 26 May 1972.

32  SAB, R-1183, 10C, Government of Saskatchewan press release, 27 October 1971.

33  Allan E. Blakeney, interview with author, Saskatoon, 21 October 2005.

34  *Statutes of Saskatchewan*, 1972, cap. 40.

35  Jamieson, 'Evolution of Executive Power,' 205. This legislation came thirty-two years after similar federal legislation creating the position of cabinet secretary, although the position of the clerk of the Privy Council was 'rolled' into the position of cabinet secretary at that time. See A.D.P. Heeney, *The Things That Are Caesar's: Memoirs of a Canadian Public Servant* (Toronto: University of Toronto Press, 1972), 74.

36  SAB, *Government of Saskatchewan Directory*, 1972–3.

37  SAB, R-1183, IV, 10D, Premier's Office press release, 26 May 1972.

38  SAB, R-1183, III, 10E, Premier's Office press release, 29 August 1973.

39  Ken Rasmussen, 'Super Diplomat and Super Expediter: Wes Bolstad as Cabinet Secretary in Saskatchewan, 1973–9,' chapter 6 of this volume.

40  The Legislative Assembly and Executive Council Act, *Statutes of Saskatchewan*, 1979, cap. L-11.1. See Jamieson, 'Evolution of Executive Power,' 206–7.

41  Blakeney interview, 2005.

42  Allan Blakeney and Sandford Borins, *Political Management in Canada: Second Edition* (Toronto: University of Toronto Press, 1998), 20. Strong deputy ministers were also useful in reining in capable but head-strong ministers who might chaff at the collective discipline of cabinet.

43  SAB, R-1094, IV, 12D, Blakeney quoted in Executive Council news release 79–664, 29 August 1979.

44  Blakeney interview, 2005.

45  There is little evidence on the role of cabinet secretary during this time. In early March 1979 Scratch was moved to the Department of the Attorney General to become coordinator of policy and legislative programs: SAB, R-1094, IV, 12C, Executive Council news release 79–159, 5 March 1979.

46  Rasmussen, 'Super Diplomat and Super Expediter'; Blakeney interview, 2005.

47  SAB, R-1094, IV, 12F, Executive Council news release, 7 March 1980.

48  SAB, R-1094, IV, 10H, Executive Council news release 81–029, 14 January 1981, plus biographical notes.

49  The only difference between the two positions lay in the fact that the narrow job of 'clerk,' in terms of issuing and recording orders-in-council, remained in the hands of a separate clerk of the Executive Council in Saskatchewan, while the 'clerk' in Ottawa has remained formally responsible for this function as well.

50  On this difficult transition, see H.J. Michelmann and J.S. Steeves, 'The 1982 Transition in Power in Saskatchewan: The Progressive Conservatives and the Public Service,' *Canadian Public Administration*, 28, no. 1 (1985): 1–23.

51  Norman Riddell, telephone interview with author, 19 December 2005.

52 Howard Pawley and C. Lloyd Brown-John, 'Transitions: The New Democrats in Manitoba,' in Donald J. Savoie, ed., *Managing Governments in Transitions* (Ottawa: Institute of Public Administration of Canada and Canadian Centre for Management Development, 1993), 193.

53 Government of Saskatchewan news release (Executive Council 82–284), 10 May 1982: 'The premier also expressed his appreciation to Ontario Premier Bill Davis for releasing Bedson form his commitment there so he could quickly move into his new position in Regina. Bedson will remain in his post for two years.'

54 Grenville Smith-Windsor, interview with author, Saskatoon, 9 April 2005; Riddell interview, 2005.

55 Government of Saskatchewan news release (Executive Council 83–443), 30 June 1983.

56 Riddell interview, 2005.

57 Government of Saskatchewan news release (Executive Council 84–602), 16 July 1984.

58 Smith-Windsor interview, 2005.

59 Riddell interview, 2005.

60 See, for example, Michelmann and Steeves, 'The 1982 Transition in Power in Saskatchewan.'

61 Riddell interview, 2005.

62 Government of Saskatchewan news releases (Executive Council 88–430 and 89–742), 5 August 1988 and 17 November 1989.

63 James Pitsula and Ken Rasmussen, *Privatizing a Province: The New Right in Saskatchewan* (Vancouver: New Star Books, 1990); James M. Pitsula, 'Grant Devine,' in Barnhart, ed., *Saskatchewan Premiers of the Twentieth Century* .

64 Government of Saskatchewan news release (Executive Council 92–002), 3 January 1992. Entry for Ronald Stewart Clarke in *Canadian Who's Who, 2001* (Toronto: University of Toronto Press, 2001), 248.

65 Government of Saskatchewan news release (Executive Council 94–326), 24 June 1994.

66 Government of Saskatchewan news release (Executive Council 96–502), 17 October 1996.

67 Government of Saskatchewan news release (Executive Council 96–595), 23 December 1996.

68 Government of Saskatchewan news release (Executive Council 2000–558), 15 September 2000.

69 In the Devine administration, Norman Riddell had begun the informal practice of distributing extracts of cabinet minutes to relevant deputy ministers but they were not formally 'carbon copied' on the cabinet minutes.

70  The corporate 'machinery of government' unit in the Department of Finance had disappeared by the 1980s.

71  Government of Saskatchewan news release (Executive Council 2001–065), 8 February 2001.

72  Christopher Dunn, 'The Persistence of the Institutionalized Cabinet: The Central Executive in Newfoundland and Labrador,' in Bernier, Brownsey, and Howlett, eds., *Executive Styles in Canada*, 47–74.

# PART THREE

Leaders in Action

# 6 'Super Diplomat and Super Expediter': Wes Bolstad as Cabinet Secretary in Saskatchewan, 1973–9

KEN RASMUSSEN

Allan Blakeney's New Democratic Party (NDP) government, in the 1970s, has earned its place in public-administration lore as one in a long series of innovative Saskatchewan governments.[1] This reputation is based on many factors, including a strong history of policy planning and effective recruitment into the senior ranks of the public service.[2] Yet, despite this reputation for both policy and bureaucratic innovation, there is virtually no discussion of the nature of the leadership role played by the public servants who helped bring about these innovations. Indeed, the innovations are seen to be a result of the instruments of management that were already in place, combined with the strong and effective leadership of Allan Blakeney and other leading politicians who came into office with a clear and strong set of objectives.[3] While a number of individual public servants had strong reputations within government as good managers, and were seen as effective in coordinating government processes through central agencies, their leadership skills have been ignored. True, they are regarded as entrepreneurial and innovative, but they are not discussed in terms of leadership ability.

This group of entrepreneurial public servants in Saskatchewan has been known mostly for its ability to successfully develop Crown-run enterprises that engaged in aggressive resource development.[4] These efforts began with the creation of a small exploration company called the Saskatchewan Oil and Gas Exploration Company (SaskOil) in 1973, followed the next year by the Saskatchewan Mining Development Corporation (SMDC), which was set up to tap into the potential of hard-rock minerals in northern Saskatchewan – particularly uranium and gold. In 1976 the Potash Corporation of Saskatchewan was created, and it quickly purchased 50 per cent of the capacity of the provincial potash industry.[5] By the end of the 1980s, Saskatchewan had created its so-called family of Crown corporations, which included some of the largest resource producers in the province as well as all major utilities, and plans for aggressive expansion were well under way. It had also passed much innovative social legislation.[6]

Given the tremendous policy and organizational innovations and developments that took place in Saskatchewan between 1971 and 1982, it is difficult to conceive a situation in which no leadership was exercised by public servants. This chapter is an examination of one of the overlooked public service leaders during this era. Wesley ('Wes') Bolstad was cabinet secretary and deputy minister to Premier Allan Blakeney in Saskatchewan during the most tumultuous period in the mid-1970s. Through an examination of his career, it is possible to recover the qualities, attributes, behaviours, and self-assessments associated with public-sector leadership in a Canadian province that was experiencing a great deal of change and perhaps the richest and most robust policy agenda of any provincial government at that time or since.[7] While it is a truism to note that leadership is required during times of rapid change, and management skills are more urgent in times of stability, it is an important truism all the same.[8] Watching an individual during a period of tremendous change allows us to begin to identify the leadership characteristics that allowed him or her to thrive.

For a variety of reasons, leadership has been ignored in most examinations of the behaviour of public servants in Canada. Even though it is hard to imagine that individuals in charge of organizations with thousands of employees and billion-dollar budgets would not be considered leaders, senior civil servants have nevertheless generally been viewed as managers not leaders. This is partly because administrative leadership is always something associated with private-sector organizations. More important than this, however, is the fact that the organizational and efficiency problems confronting public-sector organizations have traditionally been defined as managerial and organizational in nature and not as products of ineffective leadership.

Administrative reform for the past century has been predicated upon the belief that issues such as organizational form, reporting relationships, and control are the keys to improving the operation of government. The leadership skills of senior public servants are rarely a target of reform, and the notion that public-sector management is mostly a technical activity, rather than a moral or social commitment, has dominated discourse for the past forty years.[9] This chapter tries to reverse this view with an examination of the professional leadership style of

Wes Bolstad. From this case study, we can develop some more general understandings and draw lessons about the nature of leadership in the public sector.

The use of biography to understand administrative leadership is not something that has a strong tradition in Canada, but it has had a place in the study of public administration in both the United States and the United Kingdom.[10] It is a tool that should not be ignored and has in fact been employed to great success in the business- administration literature. What are some of the things we can hope to accomplish in this chapter through the use of a brief biography sketch? The first is to discover the ways in which leadership can and has been exercised in the Saskatchewan civil service. Also, this approach allows us to analyse the opportunities for, and constraints on, bureaucratic leadership in a political setting, and to observe over time the changes to the character of the bureaucratic-political system in Canada.[11]

While studies generally support the view that leadership matters to overall organizational performance, it is less clear how leadership in a public-sector context is defined. Indeed, many of the tales of public-administration leadership are case studies of extraordinary individual leaders.[12] Though this is often useful, it reduces our ability to develop more general findings or lessons for all public managers. Thus, the task of this chapter is to try and determine why one leader, Wes Bolstad, was particularly successful in his role as cabinet secretary and to develop lessons from this case study. To understand Bolstad in the context of leadership theory, he must be seen as belonging to the school of individuals who lead by personal qualities. Like many such leaders, he was unaware of the reasons for his own effectiveness. Nevertheless, Bolstad intuitively understood that leadership was a social process in which he, as leader of the bureaucracy, had to find ways to enlist others in the common task of government. In this vital task, he performed brilliantly, helping to create an atmosphere that encouraged creativity and flexibility. His style of leadership was the opposite of the autocratic leader; instead, he worked with people to outline what the premier expected from them and encouraged them to meet their goals while also devising ways to make that possible. In this sense, his leadership style has been best described as that of both a diplomat and an expediter.

## Wes Bolstad: 'A Super Diplomat and Super Expediter with the Soft Sell'

When the Blakeney government came to office, it found that it had inherited a public service that had grown demoralized and tired under the autocratic Liberal Premier Ross Thatcher.[13] There had been little program innovation, to speak of, in the last years of the Thatcher government, and many public servants were not prepared or able to help the new government implement its ambitious program. Blakeney knew from long experience as a public servant and cabinet minister in the T.C. Douglas government that the public service would need to be a fully engaged partner in the process of innovation if the promises made in the NDP's ambitious election platform were to be effectively turned into programs that citizens would value.

The structures of effective public administration in the Saskatchewan tradition had been maintained for the most part during the Thatcher era, but they were not used to their greatest effect.[14] Still, most of the central agencies in Saskatchewan, but especially the Budget Bureau of the Department of Finance, had a strong tradition of recruiting from across the country, and they developed these individuals into the best and brightest.[15] This was a non-partisan process and the preference was for people who were not politically active but strong academically. In many ways, Bolstad was the ultimate product of this program, and he moved steadily up the hierarchy, from a junior position in the Department of Education to the position of cabinet secretary and deputy minister to the premier.

Bolstad began working for the government of Saskatchewan immediately upon graduation, in the mid-1950s, after leaving the University of Saskatchewan with a bachelor of commerce degree. During this period he was one of those fortunate individuals who were invited to participate in the renowned Budget Bureau Training Program, run by the Department of Finance. This program had begun in the late 1940s and included weekend seminars on public administration, discussions, readings, and mentorship programs for young public servants and has been described as being, at that time, the best graduate program on public administration in the country. Bolstad was spotted early and, after only a few years in the Saskatchewan public service, was given the opportunity to take part in this program. Under it, employees were encouraged to participate in, and contribute to, the Institute of Public Administration of Canada, which Bolstad did, and the civil service worked hard to create a culture of pride and high expectations, with a strong reference to past traditions of excellence, as well as skill in building new programs.

The government did other things to create a strong leadership cadre in the public service. In particular, it sent a number of the most promising individuals to Harvard University to pursue a master of public administration degree in the Graduate School of Public Administration. Bolstad followed luminaries such as A.W. Johnson and Tommy McLeod in this program, graduating in 1961. He had his salary paid while he was away, and, after finishing his studies in one 'extremely gruelling year,' he was back in Saskatchewan working at the Department of Education in its Organizational Studies Division. There, he had an opportunity to meet, and work with, the minister of education at the time, Woodrow Lloyd. When Lloyd became premier of Saskatchewan, he asked Bolstad to consider becoming his executive assistant. While there was no position at the time called 'deputy minister to the premier,' clearly his role was more akin to this than a conventional executive assistant.

As a result of his obvious connections with the premier, and the politicized nature of a government that had been in power for twenty years, Bolstad found himself out of a job with the arrival of Ross Thatcher's Liberal government. (Saskatchewan has a rather weak tradition of public-service neutrality, especially at the senior ranks, and, like most other provinces, a weak version of a public-service commission. The Executive Council, or cabinet, retains a great deal of ability to appoint outsiders as deputies who have a particular political orientation.) During the Thatcher era, Bolstad began an academic career, first teaching at the University of Saskatchewan and then going to Queen's to begin his PhD. He eventually returned to Regina to become the first dean of the newly created Faculty of Administration at the University of Regina. With the return to power of the NDP under Allan Blakeney in 1972, Bolstad was recruited by the premier; he quickly became an indispensable component of the leader's group. As Blakeney noted: 'I was sure that I wanted Wes in my government, but I did not know exactly what role I wanted him to play.'[16] The role he soon settled upon was that of cabinet secretary.

The role of cabinet secretary in Saskatchewan has undergone a good deal of evolution, but it has never really been the fulcrum of policy in the province, given that policy advice traditionally has come from a variety of other sources: for example, planning boards, the Crown Investments Corporation, special committees, line departments, and traditional central agencies. The strong push towards planning, both bureaucratic and political, since the arrival of the Co-operative Commonwealth Federation (CCF) government in 1944, has meant that the cabinet secretary is not the funnel through which all policy decisions are made, as is true in other governments.[17] Nonetheless, it is often the case that the cabinet secretary, in Saskatchewan as elsewhere, is the person who controls the agenda of cabinet.

The premier was well aware of Wes Bolstad, whom he described as extremely intelligent, hardworking, and possessed of the substantive skills that would be an asset to the kind of activist government that Blakeney had promised to the people of Saskatchewan in his election platform. Once in office, Blakeney was pleased to discover that he would have the financial resources to promote the new government's agenda, and that the central-agency system, while ignored by the previous premier, was still around and could be quickly made operational. Thus, the first thing that the premier did was to find excellent bureaucratic talent, personified by a trio of gifted public servants: Wes Bolstad, Murray Wallace, and Garry Beatty. All were teaching at the University of Regina at the time and would become core components of the Blakeney team both in the Executive Council and in the Department of Finance.

There was little question who was in charge of the government when Blakeney was premier. He had developed an enviable reputation as someone who understood both the political and administrative realities of government and would ensure that both ministers and their deputies remembered that they worked for him.[18] As premier, Blakeney had a complex structure of government and, at any one time, four or five individuals at the level of deputy minister reporting directly to him. During most of his period in office, three individuals held the rank of his deputy, and one of these worked exclusively as the cabinet secretary. Blakeney realized that the role of deputy minister to the premier was of a different sort and that those two positions should be held by different individuals.[19] He was also not concerned by the fact that federally, and in many provinces, the cabinet secretary and the deputy minister to the prime minister or premier were the same individual and operated in a hierarchical manner, with only one senior bureaucrat reporting to the first minister. Blakeney intuitively understood that, for him, the skills required of a cabinet secretary and a deputy minister to the premier were so different that it would be wrong to combine the positions.[20] He also recognized, though, that he needed to build the government around the available people, and their skills, fitting the organization around them – rather than fitting people into a pre-existing organization.

What Blakeney wanted were individuals who would compensate for his weaknesses. By his own admission, Blakeney was not a natural politician with great people skills and so needed help in this regard. In particular, he required someone around him who was – to use his term – a 'schmoozer': someone able to tell people they were doing a good job or convey the impression that the premier was pleased with how things were going. These were different from the skills required of the deputy minister to the premier, who was considered to be, to borrow another Blakeney expression, a 'rammer': someone who would ride herd on the public service and push things when they needed to be pushed. These two skills, in Blakeney's judgment, were rarely found in the same person. Two people, at least, were needed – and a third to act as what Blakeney liked to call the 'political' deputy.

It is equally important to note that the cabinet secretary in Saskatchewan was part of the Premier's Office. As such, he was appointed directly by the premier. This was different from the situation in Manitoba, for example, where at the same time there was a tradition of a 'neutral' cabinet secretary who could work for whatever party was in power. During this period, Manitoba had Derek Bedson, who worked as cabinet secretary for Walter Weir, Ed Schreyer, and Sterling Lyon. The position of cabinet secretary in Saskatchewan was more politicized, in that it changed with incoming governments, since the office was created in the post-war era. This was something that Blakeney was adamant about; he could not imagine having a cabinet secretary who was not someone whom he personally trusted and had selected. Indeed, he was dismayed with other NDP premiers who retained incumbents in this sensitive position who had worked for other governments.[21] In his view, the cabinet secretary was accountable directly and personally to the premier and him alone.

Bolstad brought many skills to the job – a lot of them emerging from his understanding of, and respect for, the work of civil servants. Other deputies from that time note an important element in Bolstad's leadership style: he liked civil servants, enjoyed being around them, and loved the idea of public service. He conveyed his strong opinion about both the importance and the worthiness of the public servants' work to those in the service.[22] His skills in this area are described by Blakeney as those of a 'super diplomat and super expeditor with the soft sell,' which meant, among other things, that Bolstad was able to referee diplomatically between ministers and deputies. The relationship between deputies and ministers can often become strained, particularly when the deputies' loyalties are focused on the premier, who in Saskatchewan appointed all deputies and judged their effectiveness. Thus, it was crucial for the cabinet secretary to maintain cordial relations between the two groups, which do not have a direct employer-employee relationship. The cabinet secretary had to maintain the 'appropriate relationship' between the deputies and ministers. In this, Bolstad was a master.

Likewise, his relationship with individual deputy ministers required a great deal of subtlety. Since cabinet is a consensus-based institution, the cabinet secretary has to be careful in explaining disagreements among cabinet ministers to deputies, and does this on a strict 'need to know' basis. While cabinet decisions often require someone to act, Bolstad was able to convey exactly what needed to be done without compromising cabinet secrecy. He did not circulate copies of cabinet's minutes, and those minutes were terse in the extreme. Cabinet meetings have no movers and seconders, nor the other protocols of parliamentary procedure; rather, the cabinet secretary must interpret the consensus. During a meeting, Blakeney would occasionally say to Bolstad: 'I think cabinet has decided the following ... ' However, since minutes were not circulated, it fell to Bolstad to communicate what went on. He had to relay part of the proceedings to the people who needed to know. This required a fair bit of judgment when deputies asked him what it was that cabinet did not like about a proposal. He might also tell a deputy how to reshape an idea that had been rejected by cabinet, or he might tell the deputy that the idea was dead and that he or she should move on – cabinet had no further interest in it.

One of the biggest issues, then, for Bolstad was trust: both the trust that he inspired and the trust that he could offer to others. If Bolstad felt he could trust deputies, he would tell them a great deal, but otherwise he told them only what they needed to know. The ability to determine 'who needs to know' and 'who needs to know what' was one of the main reasons for the success that Bolstad enjoyed as cabinet secretary in Saskatchewan. Throughout, he was also careful not to reveal which cabinet ministers put up what sort of resistance.

In addition, Bolstad played a central role in the shuffle of deputies and would consult with the premier to ensure a smooth match between deputies and ministers. He made it his business to know about the relationships between ministers and deputies and to promote harmonious ones. This was something that Blakeney encouraged and that Bolstad was good at. If there was real unhappiness between a deputy and a minister, Blakeney always retained the right to have the final say on appointments. He found out which deputies were getting burnt out and losing interest in the job. When there was a shuffle, Bolstad was instrumental in the process: his close working knowledge of both the deputy and the minister ensured the most productive match. The system relied heavily on the knowledge and judgment of Bolstad, who did this without access to any committee of senior officials or to systems common in other jurisdictions.

When judging the success of a cabinet secretary in Saskatchewan, it is important to remember that there is no particular tradition in the province of this being a civil- service position in the sense that it is in either the federal or the United Kingdom government, or even some other provinces in Canada.[23] From the point of view of Blakeney, the premier and ministers needed to be completely certain that cabinet confidence would be maintained. The cabinet secretary was expected to convey what was necessary to deputies to ensure proper implementation without breaking any confidence; to ensure that deputies were happy, and if not, to know why not; and to ensure that ministers had a comfortable shoulder to cry on when necessary, while also keeping the minister out of the details of his/her department's administrative affairs. Bolstad excelled at all of this. If a minister was unhappy, Bolstad let the premier know. Ministers might be reluctant to discuss their displeasure with the premier, but Bolstad was a sympathetic figure who would convey this sentiment to the premier. These were staff functions in the classic sense of that term.

Bolstad always recognized his responsibilities for ensuring that the machinery of government was effectively working, and, to this end, he created the Executive Development Program, which was headed by Mel Derrek, a former Saskatchewan deputy minister of health. This program grew out of Bolstad's strong interest in public administration and was also based on his own experiences. The program was designed to identify 'high flyers' and to ensure that they got the training and development that was needed to help them, eventually, advance to the assistant-deputy and deputy ranks. Bolstad was keen on this sort of process and promoted it throughout the public service whenever he had the opportunity.

Bolstad's leadership, then, never resembled the iron hand in the iron glove. Rather, he was what could be described as the 'quality operator' of the machine of government. He was someone who did not look to accumulate power or ensure that the spotlight was focused on him. He was probably not even the most powerful public servant in government at the time, but he was someone whom everyone turned to when they needed good advice on how to move the machinery forward and get a decision out of the government. It is important, of course, not to lose sight of the fact that Bolstad worked for an amazingly energetic premier, who had a strong agenda and a decisive set of advisers and deputies. Bolstad was well aware of the need to heed the advice of the premier and experienced deputies.

While Bolstad was not officially the head of the public service when he was cabinet secretary, spending most of his time on his cabinet-secretary duties, he did perform some of that function, if only informally, in providing advice on senior appointments. He was clear about the need for all public servants to serve ministers loyally, but he made sure that public servants were not asked to do anything compromising, partisan, or illegal. Bolstad was a cautious and careful cabinet secretary, one who loved procedures and precedents, ensuring that those involved on all sides of a decision-making process 'followed the book.'

Like most senior officials, then or now, Bolstad was comfortable with the shroud of secrecy that surrounded government decision making. Well aware that government in a fishbowl was not compatible with sound decision making or good management, he exercised a form of leadership concerned with increasing the capacity of organizations to implement the priorities of government effectively, helping to bring about some culture changes, and dealing productively with difficult and emerging issues. Not only was he the kind of leader who could create a high-trust situation, he thrived in such an environment. His leadership challenges were harnessing and integrating the knowledge and expertise of various individuals and groups to make explicit, and criticize, underlying assumptions, while building common ground and momentum for change. These were challenges that Wes Bolstad rose to constantly.

**Leadership Lessons from Wes Bolstad**

The important point to note again about the leadership of cabinet secretaries is that it is based often on example, advice, and communication. Cabinet secretaries do not give orders to many people, and they spend much of their time assisting ministers and deputies in the administration of their duties. Likewise, the role of mentor is clearly an important aspect of the position, and, in Bolstad's case, he became aware that newly appointed deputies often did not have experience in dealing with ministers. They needed coaching in the nature of the appropriate relationship, particularly in the distinct Blakeney style, which, while very traditional, also required individuals to understand and respect the various roles and responsibilities. For example, as already noted, Bolstad occasionally reminded ministers not to interfere with the administrative activities of a department, something about which, he emphasizes, Blakeney had a zero-tolerance policy.

The cabinet secretary, while formally a representative of the premier, of course, could never afford to be too soft on the premier himself. He had to tell the premier whom he needed to meet, whom he could not avoid, and he could not afford the luxury of being overly polite about it all the time. He needed to be able to provide the premier with 'frank and fearless advice' and never become a 'yes man.' He was a mandarin – not a valet![24]

The position of cabinet secretary, almost by definition, creates an idiosyncratic relationship for which no single set of characteristics can establish the tone. One thing that was clear in Blakeney's mind was that the cabinet secretary must fill in the deficiencies of the premier while also being an extension of the premier's leadership and power. There can be no room for principal-agent misunderstandings between the premier and the cabinet secretary. A great capacity was needed to deal, sympathetically and empathetically, with other ministers and deputy ministers. Ultimately, though, the cabinet secretary represented the premier and, in the end, Bolstad was on one side only – the premier's – in any dispute.

As mentioned above, the cabinet secretary was not the head of the public service in Saskatchewan under Blakeney, and, as a consequence, the job of cabinet secretary was focused on the management of cabinet and deputies as a collective. Bolstad was the general manager of government. He found a way to make ministers and deputies work together effectively and harmoniously. Mostly, however, he facilitated the relationship between the two groups by both his calm demeanour and his seeming detachment – in addition to his intellectual gifts.

In the end, the biggest factor in Bolstad's success was that he was the most trusted official in the government. He was, in the words of Blakeney, 'trusted by more people at more levels than anyone else in the Government of Saskatchewan.' To use Blakeney's description again, he was a 'super diplomat and super expediter with the soft-sell.' Blakeney knew what he wanted to get done while he was premier, and Bolstad was the key figure in getting it done. Bolstad had the skills that Blakeney lacked for 'greasing' the machine, and he had the trust of both cabinet and the public service. What made it work was the fact that he was an extension of Blakeney, but also an addition to him.

Bolstad never sought personal attention. He was generally obscure to the media and respected the public-service tradition of anonymity. While he believed in personal leadership, he was less content with the notion of exposure and visibility. He represented the old-style public servant. Yet this sort of leadership position, in the end, became frustrating for him, and, after all the new policies had been developed, the nationalizations completed, and much of the agenda implemented, he asked for a new job with real management responsibilities. He got his wish when he became the founding director of the Mewassin Valley Authority, in Saskatoon, which had authority over vast tracts of land that were to be developed as recreational, commercial, and heritage property. This was Bolstad's first real management job. Though he had been a civil servant, he was a classic 'Super Bureaucrat' – knowledgeable about, and adept at, the workings of the system. Still, he craved the opportunity to manage an actual agency, and, while not a government department, the Meewasan Authority was an agency set up under provincial legislation and infused with public purpose. And so it makes a great deal of sense that a public servant of Bolstad's character would eventually tire of a strictly staff function and desire to actually manage.

## Wes Bolstad: Managerial Leadership

By examining the leadership lessons of Wes Bolstad, one may think more broadly about what constitutes good public-service leadership. The beginning of this chapter noted a general lack of leadership orientation in Canadian public administration. The leadership of a deputy minister or a cabinet secretary appears tentative when so much is shared with the political leadership, not to mention the numerous control agencies that regulate and supervise the public service. In this context, leadership can often raise difficult questions about accountability and responsibility, as seen with the Gomery Commission on the sponsorship program. These factors, when combined with the risk-adverse nature of public management and the tight control that is often exercised within the system over public servants, make it difficult to find the space for a discussion of effective public-sector leadership.

Yet, as we have seen, in examining the leadership of Wes Bolstad, it is possible to examine managerial leadership within a political context and draw useful conclusions. In Bolstad's case, it is clear that the political and the managerial should not be separated when analysing public-service leadership. Indeed, there is now an increased, and long overdue, interest in how public servants can most effectively exercise leadership in a political context – particularly in the United States and the United Kingdom.[25] Part of this is based on both the successes of 'New Public Management' (NPM) reforms and the need to re-examine the role of public servants in light of the success of these reforms. For some, the NPM reforms have resulted in a more politicized public service through a process of intimidation and overall decline in willingness to provide 'frank and fearless advice.' As a result of the attempt to restore political leadership over the bureaucracy, the public service – particularly those senior officials who are in charge of government organizations – has been unfairly characterized as 'lackeys, careerists, and political stooges.'[26] It may be that public servants are not 'fearless' in the sense associated with the old mandarin class of public servants, but it is still possible to be a professional public servant while operating in a politicized environment.[27]

It appears that the boundaries between political and managerial leadership are not as straightforward as these characterizations would have us believe. They are actually quite blurry: politicians probably need to learn to manage politically their organizations, ensuring some general leadership of services; bureaucrats need to develop political skills. Though the analysis of Blakeney and Bolstad's working relationship might lead to the view that leadership can be undertaken only by exceptional individuals, during exceptional times, this would be a mistaken conclusion. Rather, there is a need to ensure – through education, training, and socialization – that potential managers understand the necessary leadership skills and behaviours that will allow them to flourish in a political, though not partisan, environment at the top of the hierarchy.

What the relationship between Blakeney and Bolstad reveals is that public-sector leadership differs from that of almost all other sectors. Leaders in other sectors, including the non-profit sector, have much more ownership of the visions, values, and directions of their organizations than do senior public servants. It is important to recognize the need for political and managerial leadership, and how to realize their coexistence; the legacy of the past is the failed notion that these forms of leadership are distinct. One, it is thought, consists of policy leadership, exercised by politicians, and the other consists of the responsibilities of public servants for implementation of those policies. This case study has demonstrated the capacity to have a productive engagement between a politically driven policy agenda, such as the NDP's 'New Deal for People,' and the capacity of the public service to respond with creative implementation while not losing sight of the government's policy objectives. The leadership challenge is to facilitate the alignment of the public-service leadership of senior civil servants and the politician-driven policy dimension.

To overcome this dichotomy, it is necessary to move way from the focus on management that has recently been reasserted by the popularity of NPM, and begin the process of thinking about the role of leadership in conjunction with the leadership role of both public servants and politicians. One emerging view suggests that public servants not only have a right to engage in leadership, but also an actual obligation to become leaders. They are part and parcel of the constitutional system of government and, as such, they have a duty to ensure that some of the imperfections in any system of governance are overcome.[28]

According to Robert Behn, a leading advocate of this view, public servants need to exercise leadership, because narrow interests can capture government; citizens often lack the necessary knowledge and information to act; the executive can focus only on a few bureaucratic agencies; legislation is frequently vague and confusing; and the judicial branch is more interested in process than in achieving broad public purposes.[29] Owing to the various failures of existing democratic intuitions, public servants have not only a right but a positive obligation to exercise leadership.

Such a view, however, seems too compartmentalized and even too confrontational. It lacks the degree of trust that is essential for public servants to act as leaders. Once again, the experiences of Wes Bolstad suggest a more conciliatory approach. For public servants, leadership must be based not on their assertion of constitutional rights, or bureaucratic position, but rather on the trust that exists between themselves and their political counterparts. The question of trust is, of course, key: cabinet secretaries have no direct managerial responsibilities like those associated with line-department deputies; they do not have to engage in any of the dualities associated with being both managers and leaders, as is the case with many others in the public sector. Cabinet secretaries, therefore, represent a form of 'pure leadership' in the public sector, but a form dependent on their relationship with the first minister.

Complicating the leadership role of all senior public servants is the fact that there is no guarantee that anyone will actually follow them.

Here, again, trust is the key. To lead, they need to engage and have 'buy-in' from key allies in the organization, such as line deputies and other senior officials. Implementing a government's dynamic agenda for change requires not only a leader, or leaders, but also people who will follow those in leadership positions. People, ultimately, need to feel that they are being treated fairly if they are going to follow. If they don't, there are countless ways that public servants, at any level, can thwart an agenda for change.

To a great extent, the role of cabinet secretary in Saskatchewan fits the profile of what Joel Aberbach, Robert Putnam, and Bert Rockman have famously described as the Image IV bureaucrat.[30] This model is based on the fact that some public servants, at the highest levels, do develop and employ a full range of political skills and passionately commit themselves to assuring specific policy outcomes. While this seems to cross certain lines in terms of the formal neutrality of public servants, even one of Canada's most traditionally minded public servants, Gordon Robertson, has stated: 'The secretary to the cabinet was and is the senior deputy minister in the public service: the prime minister's own deputy minister and important link between an always-busy prime minister and his ministers, and a bridge between the political level of government and the public service.'[31] The secretary to the cabinet is not a politician, Robertson goes on to note; the fundamental qualities of a cabinet secretary are: 'good judgement, a temperament compatible with the Prime Minister and complete reliability.'[32] This is a compelling description of the skills possessed by Wes Bolstad, skills that made him so valuable to Allan Blakeney during a period of unprecedented change and controversy.


NOTES

1 Dale Poel, 'The Diffusion of Legislation among the Canadian Provinces: A Statistical Analysis,' *Canadian Journal of Political Science*, 9, no. 4 (1976): 605–26; Eleanor D. Glor, ed., *Policy Innovation in the Saskatchewan Public Sector, 1971–82* (Toronto: Captus Press, 1997).

2 A.W. Johnson, *Dream No Little Dreams: A Biography of the Douglas Government of Saskatchewan, 1944–1961* (Toronto: University of Toronto Press, 2004).

3 Dennis Gruending, *Promises to Keep: A Political Biography of Allan Blakeney* (Saskatoon; Western Producer Prairie Books, 1990).

4  Jeanne Kirk Laux and Maureen Appel Molot, *State Capitalism, Public Enterprise in Canada* (Ithica, N.Y.: Cornell University Press, 1988); John Richards and Larry Pratt, *Prairie Capitalism: Power and Influence in the New West* (Toronto: McClelland and Stewart, 1979).

5  Maureen Appel Molot and Jeanne Kirk Laux, 'The Politics of Nationalization,' *Canadian Journal of Political Science*, 12 (June 1979): 227–58.

6  Jim Harding, ed., *Social Policy and Social Justice: The NDP Government in Saskatchewan during the Blakeney Years* (Waterloo, Ont.: Wilfrid Laurier Press, 1995).

7  Glor, ed., *Policy Innovation*.

8  John P. Kotter, 'What Leaders Really Do,' *Harvard Business Review*, May/June 1990, 1–23.

9  Amanda Sinclair, 'Leadership in Administration: Rediscovering a Lost Discourse,' in Glyn Davis and Patrick Weller, eds., *New Ideas, Better Government* (Brisbane, Australia: Allen and Unwin, 1996), 229–44.

10  Kevin Theakston, *Leadership in Whitehall* (London: Macmillan Press, 1990).

11  Kevin Theakston, 'Comparative Biography and Leadership in Whitehall,' *Public Administration*, 75 (winter 1997): 651–67 (652).

12  Robert Caro, *The Power Broker: Robert Moses and the Fall of New York City* (New York: Knopf, 1974).

13  Dale Eisler, *Rumours of Glory: Saskatchewan and the Thatcher Years* (Edmonton: Hurtig, 1987).

14  Christopher Dunn, *The Institutionalized Cabinet: Governing the Western Provinces* (Toronto: University of Toronto Press, 1995).

15  Robert McLaren, 'George Woodall Cadbury: The Fabian Catalyst in Saskatchewan's "Good Public Administration,"' *Canadian Public Administration*, 38 (fall 1995): 471–80.

16  Allan Blakeney, interview with author, Saskatoon, 7 February 2005.

17  Ken Rasmussen and Gregory P. Marchildon, 'Saskatchewan's Executive Decision-Making Style: The Centrality of Planning,' in Luc Bernier, Keith Brownsey, and Michael Howlett, eds., *Executive Styles in Canada* (Toronto: University of Toronto Press, 2005).

18  Allan Blakeney and Sanford Borins, *Political Management in Canada* (Toronto: McGraw-Hill, 1992).

19  Allan Blakeney, 'The Relationship between Provincial Ministers and Their Deputy Minister," *Canadian Public Administration*, 15 (spring 1972): 42–5.

20  Allan Blakeney, interview with author, Regina, 17 February 2005.

21  Blakeney interview, 7 February 2005.

22  Doug McArthur, interview with author, Regina, 13 January 2006. McArthur

was a deputy minister of agriculture in Saskatchewan and a cabinet secretary in British Columbia.

23 Peter Hennessy, *Whitehall* (Toronto: Harper Collins Canada, 1990).

24 R.A.W. Rhodes and P. Weller, eds., *The Changing World of Top Officials: Mandarins or Valets* (Buckingham, U.K.: Open University Press, 2001).

25 Eileen Milner and Paul Joyce, *Lessons in Leadership: Meeting the Challenges of Public Service Management* (London: Routledge, 2005); Larry D. Terry, *Leadership of Public Bureaucracies: The Administrator as Conservator* (Thousand Oaks, Calif.: Sage, 1995).

26 Peter Shergold, '"Lackeys, Careerists, Political Stooges"? Personal Reflections on the Current State of Public Service Leadership,' *Australian Journal of Public Administration*, 63 (December 2004): 3–13.

27 Jack Granatstein, *The Ottawa Men: The Civil Service Mandarins, 1935–57* (Toronto: Oxford University Press, 1982).

28 Lorne Sossin, 'Defining Boundaries: The Constitutional Argument for Bureaucratic Independence and Its Implications for the Accountability of the Public Service,' *Restoring Accountability,* Research Studies, volume 2 (Ottawa: Public Works and Government Services Canada, 2006).

29 Robert Behn, 'What Right Do Public Managers Have to Lead?' *Public Administration Review* 58, no. 3 (1998): 209–24.

30 Joel Aberbach, Robert D. Putnam, and Bert Rockman, *Bureaucrats and Politicians in Western Democracies* (Cambridge, Mass.: Harvard University Press, 1981).

31 Gordon Robertson, *Memoirs of a Very Civil Servant: Mackenzie King to Pierre Trudeau* (Toronto: University of Toronto Press, 2000), 77.

32 Ibid., 215.

# 7 Leviathan Awakes: Harry Hobbs and the Rise of Alberta

KEITH BROWNSEY

The Alberta provincial election of August 1971 was a turning point in the province's history. An urban, business-oriented Progressive Conservative Party with an energetic, youthful leader replaced an aging, rural-based Social Credit government led by a farmer, Harry Strom. The new premier, Peter Lougheed, spoke to the concerns and interests of a new urban middle class. While Social Credit was focused on cooperatives and community, the Progressive Conservative government promoted an ideology of free markets and economic growth. The democratic ideals of earlier populist movements were replaced by a concern with rational decision making and corporate governance. An activist, pragmatic style became the self-identified administrative model of the Lougheed government.[1]

The new approach to governance was apparent in several institutional changes. The Executive Council was transformed from a weekly gathering of cabinet ministers into an elaborate decision-making body,[2] and the unstructured and informal executive was replaced by a more collegial, rational organization. This institutionalized cabinet reflected the Progressive Conservative government's business orientation. While the new premier, Peter Lougheed, was the principal architect of this administrative style, other individuals played crucial roles in its design and operation. One of these individuals was Harry Hobbs. As the province's first deputy minister of the Executive Council, Hobbs initiated and managed the institutionalization of executive decision making, the expansion of the public service, and the centralization of authority in the office of the premier. An individual cannot be credited or blamed for all the actions of a government, but Hobbs was a central figure in the evolution of the provincial state in Alberta.

## Leadership Styles in the Alberta Public Service

A focus on the career of Harry Hobbs as deputy minister of the Executive Council reveals a great deal about the subject of administrative leadership. James MacGregor Burns defines leadership as a type of power. Leadership, he states, is exercised when persons with motives mobilize, in competition with others, institutional, political, psychological, and other resources to engage and satisfy the motives of followers.[3] The 1971 election signalled Alberta's transformation from a rural, agricultural backwater into an urban, capitalist society within the Canadian state. The old Social Credit regime could not meet the demands of the new urban middle class. Lougheed was the face of this new Alberta. He promised to expand the influence of the province both within Canada and with the various transnational oil and gas companies that dominated the Alberta economy. Lougheed wanted to deliver public goods such as education, health care, culture, and social services within a political context favourable to economic development. In this way, Lougheed and his supporters believed that they could ensure Alberta's future prosperity and meet the needs of an emerging middle class based in the cities.

After the 1971 election, Lougheed turned to a small group of long-time friends and associates for advice and support. Sharing a common background in education, business, and politics, this group included Ted Mills, Jim Seymour, Harold Milliken, and Harry Hobbs. They had attended high school and university together and had, in some cases, been business associates. Their view of the world had been formed on the playing fields of the Canadian Football League, at law school, and in the private sector. While Lougheed had worked for the Mannix Corporation, others in his circle had been self-employed consultants, engineers, lawyers, or entrepreneurs. They were the leadership group that set about to fulfil the promises made by Lougheed and his Progressive Conservative Party.

As with most concepts in political science, leadership can be interpreted in a number of ways. Burns categorizes leadership under two headings: 'transactional' and 'transformative.' Transactional leadership refers to some type of exchange: a politician, for example, will offer some benefit (public or private) for votes, contributions, or labour. The other type of leadership is transformational. It recognizes a need or demand within society; then, an individual or group identifies this need and undertakes to satisfy it. There is a sense in which mutual aspirations and values are engaged by the leader and those who follow. In order for the transformation to succeed, individuals must have the capacity to choose among alternative programs. Voters must be aware of, and understand, that there are other possibilities; they must make a choice among several different strategies and outcomes. If there are no choices to be made, transformative leadership cannot be said to exist. Finally, transformative leaders must take responsibility for their actions. If they promise change, they are accountable to those who supported them.[4]

The categories of transactional and transformative leadership help explain the evolution of the executive decision-making process in Alberta. In the case of deputy ministers to cabinet and their predecessors, secretaries to cabinet, two distinct types are apparent. First, there are the transformative deputies. These were individuals who oversaw fundamental change in executive decision making or the civil service. John D. Hunt, clerk of the Executive Council, 1917–34, under both Liberal and United Farmer governments, presided over the creation of a merit-based civil service. He can be described as a transformative leader in that he was instrumental in altering the system of governance in Alberta.

On the other hand, during the years of Social Credit hegemony, there were a number of deputy ministers, secretaries, or clerks of the Executive Council in Alberta who were something other than transformative. Though they were very good in their role – whatever that role was at a particular moment in the province's history – context did not allow them the same opportunity to act in a transformative manner as those earlier individuals who had altered the province's model of governance. Senior civil-service positions with governments that have been in office for decades are not a natural environment for transformative leadership. This does not mean that the deputies, secretaries, and clerks of the Executive Council under Social Credit governments in Alberta were not leaders in the sense that they failed to instil the bureaucracy with core values and an institutional myth or to maintain the integrity of the executive decision-making process. On the contrary, they managed to protect and transmit the values of the profession – sometimes under difficult circumstances, but, instead of transformation, the conservative model of leadership that they exercised provided 'stability and continuity rather than innovation.'[5] Theirs was a style of guardianship, characterized by a desire to maintain the capabilities of the state through its institutions, processes, and staff. Nor was Alberta unique in this respect. In 1942, for example, senior Ontario civil servants kept the government operating after Premier Mitch Hepburn became increas-. ingly absent from Queen's Park.[6] Without leadership in the senior levels of the civil service, the government of Ontario would have ceased to operate during the height of the Second World War. These individuals played an important leadership role in the maintenance of the state, but they were not transformative.

Many senior civil servants in Alberta, such as the secretary of the Executive Council, have not been leaders in a transformative way. Rather, they have been managers, who maintained the integrity of the public service and who ably served the government of the day. The opportunity for transformative leadership arises either in a crisis or when there is a change of government. Change of government has been infrequent in Alberta – it has happened only three times in the history of the province: the United Farmers defeated the Liberals in 1921, Social Credit was elected with an overwhelming majority in 1935, and the Progressive Conservatives swept to power in 1971. An argument can be made that when the governing party selects a new leader, the context allows for a different and possibly transformative style of leadership. The recent evidence for this, though, is slim. When the Social Credit League chose Harry Strom to replace Ernest Manning as party leader and premier in 1968, there was little or no change in the senior levels of the Alberta public service. The same situation occurred in 1985, after Peter Lougheed stepped down. The new premier, Don Getty, did little to encourage change in the civil service. Only when Ralph Klein became Progressive Conservative Party leader and premier in 1992 was reform of the public service undertaken.

In the early 1970s, circumstances permitted a transformation of the administrative style of Alberta. A new premier, Peter Lougheed, and a new party, the Progressive Conservatives, came to power. Appointed the first deputy minister of the Executive Council in 1974, Harry Hobbs was assigned the task of institutionalizing the decision-making processes of cabinet and establishing a civil service capable of administering an urban, industrial state. Hobbs was given the opportunity to be a transformational leader at a critical juncture in the evolution of Alberta. Although his role in events was out of public view, he was a necessary part of the effort to bring a new style of administration to the province. His ideology, personality, and ability – combined with the reformist agenda of the government – provided him with opportunities seldom presented to his predecessors or successors. The mix of personality, organization, and context made Harry Hobbs a transformative leader in the rise of the Alberta state.

## Styles, Administration, and the Deputy Minister of the Executive Council

Much has been written in recent years about the concentration of power in the hands of the prime minister and a few key advisers at the national level in Canada. Donald Savoie's *Governing from the Centre* and Jeffrey Simpson's *Friendly Dictatorship* are two of the better-known studies of the increasing power of the prime minister and federal cabinet. The growth in the authority of the central executive has come as a surprise and is a concern to many observers of Canadian political life. Power has shifted, Savoie argues, from the legislature to the cabinet committees, cabinet and the prime minister, and a few senior advisers. This style of management, at the core of the Canadian state, is unique. It is a mix of the Westminster parliamentary model and the efforts of the political executive, since the late 1960s, to rationalize and coordinate an increasingly complex state structure. The centralization of authority in the Prime Minister's Office and the cabinet secretariat, the Privy Council Office, has been described as a reflection of the personal styles of the individuals who have held the office of prime minister.

In several Canadian provinces also, power has moved towards the centre. The factors promoting cabinet institutionalization – and in some cases cabinet de-institutionalization – in a province are a melange of history, ideology, individuals, and politics.[7] (This is, simply put, the historical and institutional context of governance.) In Alberta, for example, politics and governance have been dominated by a history of right-wing populism and strong premiers who determined the policy agenda. A variety of influences have played a part in the development of the particular style of Alberta cabinets; the province's history of near-autocratic leadership (both political and bureaucratic) has been key in determining outcomes despite institutional arrangements. As well, there has been the almost constant conflict with the federal government over control of natural resources and any number of issues from gun control to the Canada Wheat Board. The result has been a provincial government able to portray itself as the defender of Alberta's interests against a distant, alien national government. It is within this context of perceived external threat that power has come to reside in the Executive Council, and especially the office of the premier.

While institutions do not determine outcomes, they do 'provide an enabling, restricting, or stimulating context for individual or corporate action.'[8] Alberta proceeded along a path similar to that taken by the other provinces and the federal government in institutionalizing cabinet committees, the position of a deputy to cabinet, and a cabinet secretariat, but there were certain features unique to the province. In particular, the process of de-institutionalization of the cabinet in Alberta has recently set the province apart. The adaptation of the institutionalized cabinet to Alberta followed what March and Olsen have described as the 'logic of appropriateness.' The tradition of centralized, premier-centred decision making structured the process of cabinet 'by affecting not only the strategies, but also the preferences of the relevant actors.'[9] Consequently, though the Lougheed and Getty governments of the 1970s and 1980s adopted the features of the institutionalized cabinet, the new structures were deeply affected by the existing style of decision making within the cabinet and by the individuals involved in the process. The relative success of the new institutionalized cabinet of the 1970s demonstrates the importance of individual actors in the process of institution building and design.

The development of the Alberta cabinet system has followed the logic of appropriateness. That is to say, there has been change within the system rather than change of the system. The reorganization of cabinet, after the Progressive Conservatives came to office in 1971, fell within the parameters of the existing style established years before under Social Credit premiers William Aberhart and Ernest Manning. Nevertheless, the unaided premier-centred decision making of Aberhart and Manning was replaced with a system of cabinet committees, the creation of the position of deputy minister of the Executive Council, and the formation of a cabinet secretariat. These changes were effected within the particular institutional context of Alberta political life. It was only in the late 1980s and early 1990s, when Premier Don Getty disengaged from the traditional role of premier, that the cabinet decision process was seen to be distant, over bureaucratized, and ineffective.

One of Ralph Klein's first acts as premier, in December 1992, was to reorganize the cabinet decision-making structure. He reverted to an earlier, pre-institutionalized, model of cabinet, which closely resembled the type of decision-making structure he had used when he was mayor of Calgary in the 1980s.[10] The Getty government's cabinet committee system was replaced by a fusion of caucus and cabinet committees, with a small committee – Agenda and Priorities, chaired by the premier – at the centre of the system.[11] This post-institutionalized cabinet system of Ralph Klein represented a return to the tradition of strong premier-centred governance in the province. Klein's new system of standing policy committees blurred the lines between the cabinet and caucus. While this reorganization may have given the backbench government member a sense of participating in decision making, power was further concentrated with the premier through the Agenda and Priorities Committee and the Executive Council Office.

Yet there was also a measure of continuity between the system devised by Klein and that established by Lougheed. When he was elected to government in 1971, Lougheed appointed friends and associates to key positions in the Premier's Office and in the Executive Council Office. This group of senior advisers remained with Lougheed throughout his time in office. While a formal distinction between the two offices was maintained on paper, both were involved with political and administrative decisions. Located directly across the corridor from one another in the provincial Legislative Building, the two groups in-tertwined politics and policy into a seamless web. Lougheed, in fact, never made a distinction between the political and administrative; he saw the Executive Council Office and the role of deputy minister as political. Problems arising on either side of the political/administrative divide were dealt with by the two offices. After thirty-six years in office, the Social Credit government had grown tired. A new ambitious agenda was put in place that required a more elaborate decision- making structure, with an emphasis on rapid response to emergent issues, bold initiatives, and agenda control.[12]

This pattern of renewal and activism was also apparent in the early years of the Klein government in the 1990s. The executive director of the Premier's Office, Rod Love, believed that the key to successful governance was to manage the media, which, it was thought, had the power to sway an increasingly volatile electorate. The only way to achieve this was through the coordination of the Premier's Office with Executive Council staff. Greater flexibility, Love thought, was needed in the cabinet process in order to cope with growing electoral instability.[13] The result was a highly politicized decision-making process, with a focus on the premier and the Executive Council, which became a defining feature of the administrative style of senior bureaucratic leadership in Alberta.

Klein also expanded the role of deputy minister to cabinet. His first deputy, Vance MacNichol (who also held the title of secretary to cabinet), followed the new premier from the Department of the Environment. Yet, although they had worked together, they were not friends. Unlike the Lougheed, government, whose appointment of trusted political associates to the posts of cabinet secretary and deputy minister to cabinet occurred as a matter of routine, that of Klein saw to it that Mac-Nichol underwent a formal interview. Both John (Jack) Davies (1997–9) and Julian Nowicki (1999–2004) underwent a formal hiring process too. Nowicki was also appointed clerk of the Executive Council. This produced a further centralization of power in a small group of advisers surrounding the premier. The most important criteria in choosing a deputy were the individual's knowledge of the Alberta government and his ability to work with the executive director in the Premier's Office.[14] 'There could be no light between the two positions.'[15]

While the Lougheed and Klein governments followed the historical pattern of strong premiers, there were significant differences between their governance styles. Lougheed had sought to rationalize and coordinate the decision-making process at the executive level. Klein, on the other hand, dismantled the cabinet committee and policy process created by Lougheed and replaced it with a much more politically sensitive model of governance. Lougheed was a manager who sought practical solutions to issues. Klein, on the other hand, was a right-wing populist who wanted to broaden the appeal for his government and its programs through a series of organizational changes within the Executive Council and caucus. Lougheed was able to surround himself with individuals he knew and trusted. Klein lacked Lougheed's business and political connections and, instead, relied on the civil service to fill senior positions. But it was in the practice of policy making that the two premiers differed most.

### Hobbs and the Provincial State

The 1971 provincial election was a turning point in Alberta's history. Not only did the Progressive Conservatives defeat the Social Credit government – one of the longest- ruling governments in Canadian history – they set out on a course of reform that updated and altered much of the traditional character of Alberta political life. Not the least among these changes were the innovations to cabinet. When Peter Lougheed arrived at the legislature, he did not find what he expected. There was no cabinet secretariat, staff assistance, or central policy coordination.[16] As one former Conservative member of the Legislative Assembly has stated, 'there was nothing there.'[17] Along with the statutory cabinet committee, Treasury Board, Lougheed established four policy committees: Agenda and Priorities, Economic Planning, Social Planning, and Intergovernmental Relations. As well, Lougheed appointed Ted Mills – a political ally who had run the Progressive Conservative Party office – as secretary to cabinet. Mills began the practice of attending meetings of the full cabinet as well as its various committees. He also put in place secretarial and research assistance for all committees, including the various ad hoc or special committees organized to meet specific, time-sensitive tasks. Minutes of all cabinet meetings were now kept and a record was made of all votes. Other changes occurred in the Executive Council Office. Using a model adopted from business, the government separated administrative and political functions – a key feature of the process of institutionalization. Lougheed gave responsibility for political duties to the Premier's Office staff while allocating central-agency functions to the Executive Council Office. The same process had occurred at the federal level under Pierre Trudeau, several years earlier, but Lougheed denies using this as a model for his reforms.[18]

In the last years of Lougheed's government, the cabinet secretariat became in fact – if not title – a cabinet-planning secretariat. Cabinet design in this period reflected coordination between specialized political and policy functions, but also their separation. The structure put in place by Lougheed remained largely unchanged until Ralph Klein succeeded Don Getty as premier in December 1992. Whereas Getty modified the decision-making structure from time to time but kept the essential features of the Lougheed model, Klein replaced it with a more centralized structure which emphasized the role of the Agenda and Priorities Committee as the central planning and coordinating agency of government.

The secretary of cabinet was now responsible for hiring and firing of staff, allocating resources to various cabinet committees, and responding to the various policy initiatives of cabinet. Most important, cabinet agendas were now formalized. As with the clerk of the Privy Council in Ottawa, Mills was the secretary to cabinet. The secretary was also assigned the task of preparing an agenda for cabinet meetings as well as the various standing and ad hoc committees. The two divisions under the direction of the secretary were the Cabinet Secretariat and the Administrative Services Centre. Lougheed also established the position of executive director – chief of staff – in the Premier's Office. This position is best described as a political deputy minister. The executive director was responsible for the Legislative Affairs Branch, the Communications Office, the Correspondence Unit, and the Southern Alberta Office of the Premier.

In October 1973, though, the world changed. The Organization of Petroleum Exporting Countries (OPEC) instituted an oil embargo on Western Europe and North America, in response to their support of Israel during the Yom Kippur War, which dramatically altered the provincial government's agenda. As the level of government responsible for oil and natural gas, the new Conservative cabinet confronted a situation that would define its focus for generations. With oil prices increasing in price from around $3 (US) a barrel to more than $12 a barrel, almost overnight, the provincial government was faced with a new set of problems. Suddenly the federal government took great interest in Alberta's oil and gas reserves. Moreover, after years of neglect, multinational oil and gas companies began to re-enter the Alberta oil patch. These events threw the agenda of the Lougheed government into turmoil. After two years in office, the Progressive Conservatives now faced a very different policy environment. One response to these changed circumstances was reorganization at the top levels of the bureaucracy.[19]

In July 1974 Harry Hobbs was appointed the first deputy minister of the Executive Council. He was given the task of coordinating policy and administration between the various departments as well as within the executive. Hobbs was not a civil servant: he had no experience with the provincial bureaucracy other than his two years as executive director in the Premier's Office. He did not undergo a formal hiring process – for example, there was no interview. He was a close friend of Lougheed's: someone Lougheed trusted, who thought much like the premier, and who understood how complex business organizations worked.

Hobbs and Lougheed had attended high school together in Calgary, as well as the University of Alberta, in the 1950s. After graduation from the University of Alberta, Lougheed went on to earn a law degree from the same university and a master's of business administration from Harvard. For his part, Hobbs entered business after graduating from university, but he maintained a personal and professional relationship with Lougheed. In 1965 he worked on Lougheed's campaign for the leadership of the Progressive Conservative Party and was responsible for all seventeen Edmonton ridings in the 1971 provincial general election. Because of these close political and personal connections, Lougheed asked Hobbs to become executive director in the Premier's

Office.[20] Two years later, he agreed to take on the responsibilities of running a reorganized cabinet. Then, in 1974 came his appointment as appointed deputy minister of the Executive Council, a position he held for ten years.[21]

Hobbs took the job to serve the premier and, through the premier, the cabinet, legislature, and people of Alberta.[22] As the province's senior public servant, he had day-to-day responsibility for the deputy ministers, for the establishment and administration of a cabinet secretariat, and for the operation of the various offices associated with the Executive Council, including the Public Affairs Bureau. Mills remained as secretary to cabinet but now reported to Hobbs. With Hobbs's appointment as deputy minister of the Executive Council, the position of secretary to cabinet was renamed the assistant secretary to Cabinet.

The role of deputy minister of the Executive Council, as constructed by Hobbs, consisted of three parts. First, there was the role of deputy minister to the premier. Hobbs saw the position as that of a political adviser. He consulted the premier on issues ranging from the appointment of deputy ministers to relations with the federal government. Second, there was the role of secretary to cabinet. While Mills was the deputy secretary to cabinet, Hobbs was responsible for the cabinet's agenda and for supporting its work. He attended all cabinet meetings, ensuring that decisions of the Executive Council were communicated to the bureaucracy, and coordinated policy implementation among the various departments. He also attended meetings of the new Agenda and Priorities Committee, which vetted all decisions of the other cabinet committees before presentation to the full Executive Council. This was a dramatic change from past practice, where, under the three Social Credit premiers –Aberhart, Manning, and Strom – no staff member sat in on cabinet meetings. Third, Hobbs was responsible for the administration of the provincial bureaucracy. While much of the day-to-day administration of the growing Alberta public service rested with Alan Craig, the civil service commissioner, Hobbs chaired the committee that set the pay for deputies and ministerial executive assistants. As well, he was central to the hiring, promotion, and assignment of deputy ministers. Choosing from a list of three candidates, a search committee of senior civil servants and a private citizen was struck to interview the candidates and make recommendations to the premier and secretary to cabinet. Hobbs and Lougheed made the appointment based on the selection committee's recommendation. It was understood that the deputy minister needed to have the confidence of the minister and the government.[23] This meant that the deputy had to be ideologically compatible with the government.

After having loyally served a Social Credit government that had been in office for thirty-six years, many of the top-ranking civil servants found the transition to the Progressive Conservative government difficult.[24] Lougheed and Hobbs's approach to government reflected their experience in the business community. They were, moreover, faced with a variety of issues – from the 1973 oil crisis to constitutional negotiations – that demanded a more informed and prepared response than that of the former Social Credit governments. Hobbs and Lougheed wanted to ensure that their senior administrators were loyal and that they would be ideologically compatible with the new activist agenda. As a result, they recruited individuals known from the business community to fill the senior ranks of the civil service. This was viewed as politically and administratively appropriate.

Hobbs felt that no civil servant could be completely neutral and, as with any management change in the private sector, a new team had to be assembled. In order to ensure coordination and loyalty, he quickly ended the practice of deputy ministers regularly meeting together. He was sure there were senior members of the civil service who wanted to frustrate the government's plans. From this point on, only the premier or Hobbs could call a meeting of deputies. Lougheed did this once a year, at Government House, where, in a meeting of all deputies and heads of Crown corporations, he would outline the government's agenda. It was not left to the deputies to coordinate government policy; this was the function of the Executive Council Secretariat and the Treasury Board. In contrast, the Saskatchewan New Democratic Party government of Allan Blakeney left policy coordination to deputy ministers; only occasionally did Blakeney, or the cabinet secretary, have to intervene.[25] While Blakeney thought a decentralized decision-making structure worked for his province, Lougheed reinforced the premier-centred style of Alberta political life.

The deputy minister of the Executive Council also provided support to those ministers who found themselves in political difficulty or who strayed too far from the government's stated program. Under Hobbs's direction, the Executive Council office would intervene in an effort to correct a politically or administratively difficult situation. It was made clear, though, who initiated policy. Under Lougheed-Hobbs, policy had three sources: the caucus, the premier, and several senior advisers. Civil servants were administrators who wrote regulations, implemented the decisions of cabinet, and administered programs.[26] This contrasts with the Blakeney government in Saskatchewan, where policy ideas came mainly from the caucus and premier but also from the party and bureaucracy.[27]

This new model for cabinet organization originated in the business-management practices of the late 1960s and early 1970s. Hobbs claims that Lougheed brought in this private-sector style of organization. It was a style that conflicted with the more traditional approach to decision making found in Ottawa – under the Trudeau government in the late 1960s and early 1970s – with its division between the Privy Council Office and the Prime Minister's Office. At the highest level, the Lougheed-Hobbs approach to public administration did not reflect the political-administrative division of the institutionalized cabinet emerging in the other provinces and Ottawa at this time. Instead, the position of deputy minister of the Executive Council in Alberta was closely modelled on the role of a corporate chief executive officer. With Hobbs as the province's chief executive officer, and Lougheed as the chairman of the board, they set out to implement the Conservative's policy agenda. Neither Hobbs nor Lougheed had an understanding of traditional public administration. Instead, they relied on their friendship and business experience to design Alberta's new governance structure.

Before the appointment of Hobbs in July 1974, there had never been a deputy minister of the Executive Council. From the time Alberta was established in 1905, there had been thirteen clerks or secretaries of Executive Council.[28] The job was limited in scope. The clerk/secretary was an executive assistant who provided some administrative support to cabinet and the premier. For example, during Manning's twenty-five years in the Premier's Office, the clerk/secretary typed the agenda for the weekly cabinet meeting after it was compiled by the premier. Other duties included writing memoranda for the premier, booking rooms for meetings, and performing traditional secretarial and administrative functions. Moreover, there was no research support or coordination of policy provided by the Cabinet Office. This informal system reflected the limited scope of state activity, as well as Manning's distaste for formalized decision making and routinized activity.[29]

As the first deputy minister of the Executive Council, Hobbs was able to define a new role and reform established institutions within the context of Alberta political life. Influenced in his new job by his friendship with Lougheed and his private-sector experience, he perceived himself to be a manager, coordinating the different departments to ensure that they followed government policy.[30] His role, though, was also political – he was not a neutral civil servant. In his own role, Hobbs made no distinction between politics and administration. Moreover, his close relationship with the premier only increased his authority with cabinet and the senior ranks of the bureaucracy. Hobbs believed that, to be of value, he needed political access. He sought, too, the advice of the various deputy ministers involved with the implementation of policy. If they had problems with a particular directive, he would take their concerns to the premier. Deputy ministers would not, he claimed, have the same trust in a career civil servant. As he puts it: 'My appointment was political. I was not a bureaucrat. I was a political person. I was there to serve the premier, also the cabinet, but, primarily, the premier. He was something special. Familiarity did not breed contempt: a great man. I was committed to him. Others were committed as well. When he was through, we would be through.'[31]

In defining the parameters of the new position of deputy minister of the Executive Council, Hobbs had only one piece of legislation to guide him, the Government Organization Act. This is a broad piece of legislation that sets out the basic institutions of the provincial executive and the various departments of the government. It allows for a great deal of discretion within those boundaries. Since his position was created by an order-in-council, Hobbs simply 'went ahead and did it.' The job was what he made it. The new government, he claims, was made up of neophytes, a situation that caused numerous problems for the career public service.[32]

With a history of premier-centred government in Alberta, the expansion of the role, and increase in size, of the Executive Council staff contributed to the authority of both the cabinet and the premier. Hobbs spent much of his time dealing with various crises. There was, he says, little time to think. He was, he claims, a perfectionist, who brought a business perspective, rather than the rural-agricultural perspective of the previous Social Credit government, to the issues at hand.

Many of the changes that occurred in the structure and process of the Executive Council, and the civil service, would have happened without Harry Hobbs. The problems facing Alberta, and the rest of the country, could not have been ignored and would have demanded some solution. It was Hobbs, though, who – with Peter Lougheed – formed Alberta's response to two fundamental questions facing the province and country. The first concerned the oil-price shock of 1973–4. As the cost of a barrel of oil quadrupled as a result of the OPEC oil embargo, the resource revenues flowing into the Alberta treasury increased likewise, from approximately $500 million to $1.5 billion a year. While the rest of the country was scrambling to cope with the sudden increase in energy prices, Alberta was enjoying the benefits of its unique geology.

There was another aspect to the increase in petroleum revenues that had a great impact on Alberta. This was the federal government's response to the oil crisis. Almost immediately after the declaration of the OPEC embargo, the federal government announced a series of policies designed to regulate the production and distribution of petroleum resources. The federal initiatives had four purposes: 1) to ensure a secure supply of energy; 2) to obtain an accurate assessment of the oil-and-gas industry; 3) to increase the federal share of the ever-increasing revenues; and 4) to offset the negative economic impact of the substantial rise in the cost of a barrel of oil. While the sudden and steep increase in the cost of energy was a national issue, the constitutional distribution of powers in the British North America Act gave the provinces jurisdiction over natural resources such as petroleum. As Canada's largest producer of oil and gas, Alberta felt the impact of the federal energy programs more than the other province.

The provincial government's reaction to federal energy policy was dramatic – especially after the introduction of Ottawa's National Energy Program in October 1982.[33] The Lougheed government resented the federal intrusions into its jurisdiction and proceeded to negotiate, threaten, and litigate. In order to achieve their objectives of sovereignty over natural resources, Lougheed and Hobbs recognized the need to increase the policy capacity of the provincial civil service. In the process, Alberta nearly doubled the size of its public service. Within a few years, the Alberta civil service became one of the most efficient and effective public sectors in Canadian history. It was under Hobbs's direction that the contemporary Alberta civil service took shape.

A second crisis engulfed the Lougheed government at the same time as the energy battles. The Liberal government of Pierre Trudeau was committed to some form of constitutional renewal. While the Alberta government was not opposed to such an initiative, it did want to protect what it saw as its interests in several areas, including natural resources. Again, the province built a capacity to match that of the federal government in the area of constitutional law. A massive recruiting campaign was launched, which saw hundreds of new hires by the provincial public service. It was this policy capacity, according to Hobbs, that gave the

Progressive Conservative government the ability to negotiate constitutional renewal with the federal government.

## Conclusion: The Lessons of Hobbsian Leadership

The twenty individuals who have served in the capacity of clerk of the Executive Council, secretary of the Executive Council, and deputy minister of the Executive Council have all demonstrated a capacity for leadership. However, few have had the opportunity to implement dramatic change. The first clerk, John MacDonald, set a pattern for public administration in the province that lasted for a generation. Other former clerks, like John Hunt, implemented reforms such as the merit system for hiring and promotion. Then there was Harry Hobbs, who established an institutional framework capable of managing a complex political and administrative environment. What set these individuals apart from the others were the historical circumstances in which they found themselves. Hobbs was deputy minister of the Executive Council at a time when the Alberta state was expanding its scope in terms of social, cultural, and economic polices. It faced perceived threats from what its political and administrative elites considered to be an intrusive federal government. Hobbs was capable of improvization within a fluid political environment, but it was this context that allowed him to make choices from imperfect information. Circumstance combined with personality and ability to make Hobbs a transformative leader. If any of these three components had been missing, the situation may have been quite different.[34]

Leadership in the public service is a difficult concept. Civil servants work under different conditions than those found in the private sector; they make their 'contributions not in one single indelible endeavour but in manifold and innumerable inputs to the policies and practices of government.'[35] A senior bureaucrat may face a situation in which the state confronts a variety of external and internal pressures. As a result, the appropriate task may be the maintenance of the status quo. In this circumstance, senior officials in the public service are often classified as managers, rather than the entrepreneurial, heroic leader common in the private sector. Still, while not transformative leaders, these individuals may play just as important a role in the public sector as a reformer or instigator of change does in the private sector. What differentiates them from their more radical counterparts is context. Context dictates their role as that of a conservator. Their task is to transmit the values of public service and protect the integrity of government institutions. This may not be particularly glamorous, but it is essential to the maintenance of the state.

By his own admission, Harry Hobbs is a reserved individual who avoids public recognition. He did not set out to remake the Alberta public service or the cabinet decision-making structure. He worked within the logic of appropriateness or context of Alberta politics. Without a fundamental shift in existing patterns of political and administrative life, there was little else he could do. He saw his role as background to that of his political masters, bringing to his job a number of skills learned in the private sector. Nevertheless, he was central to the province-building project of the Lougheed government.

Although much of what Hobbs accomplished responded to circumstances beyond his control, without his management background, his close relationship to the premier, and his capacity for adaptation to change, the many successes of the Lougheed years would have been diminished in their scope. Personal factors can be strengths or weaknesses. It was Hobbs's management skills that allowed him to initiate a series of institutional reforms that had a dramatic impact not only on Alberta but on Canada as a whole. This reticent individual was able to grasp the historical opportunity for major change and became one of the transformative leaders in Alberta's political and administrative history. Simply put, he was a tenant of time and context, whose training and personality allowed him to construct a state apparatus capable of meeting the political, social, and economic challenges of the last twenty-five years of the twentieth century.

NOTES

1 Peter Lougheed, interview with author, Calgary, 6 September 2007.
2 Peter Lougheed, interview with author, Calgary, 19 August 2005.
3 James MacGregor Burns, *Leadership* (New York: Harper and Row, 1978), 4, 18.
4 Ibid., 18–19.
5 Kevin Theakston, 'Comparative Biography and Leadership in Whitehall,' *Public Administration*, 75 (winter 1997): 651–67.
6 Neil McKenty, *Mitch Hepburn* (Toronto: McClelland and Stewart, 1967), 244.
7 Christopher Dunn, *The Institutionalized Cabinet: Governing the Western Provinces* (Toronto: University of Toronto Press, 1995), 5.

8 Christoph Knill, 'European Policies: The Impact of National Administrative Traditions,' *Journal of Public Policy*, 18, no. 1 (1998): 1–28.

9 Ibid., 3.

10 Julian Nowicki, interview with author, Edmonton, 4 May 2005.

11 Rod Love, lecture at Mount Royal College, Calgary, 1 March 1999.

12 Peter Lougheed, interview with author, Calgary, 19 August 2005.

13 Mark Crawford, 'Co-ordination of Communications and Policy Functions' (paper presented to the British Columbia Political Science Association, Victoria, May 2000), 7.

14 Nowicki interview, 2005.

15 Harry Hobbs, interview with author, Edmonton, 4 May 2005.

16 Lougheed interview, 19 August 2005.

17 Ron Ghitter, interview with author, Calgary, 6 June 2002.

18 Lougheed interview, 19 August 2005.

19 Ibid.

20 Most executive directors in the Premier's Office in Alberta refer to their role/ position as chief of staff.

21 Harry Hobbs, interview with author, Edmonton, 3 May 2005.

22 Ibid..

23 Peter Lougheed, interview with author, Calgary, 19 August 2005.

24 Ibid.

25 Allan Blakeney and Sanford Borins, *Political Management in Canada*, 2nd. ed. (Toronto: University of Toronto Press, 1998), 82–8.

26 Lougheed interview, 19 August 2005.

27 Blakeney and Borins, *Political Management in Canada*, 91–101.

28 This information was compiled by the Executive Council Office of Alberta.

29 Frank Dabbs, *Preston Manning: The Roots of Reform* (Vancouver: Greystone Books, 1997).

30 Ibid.

31 Hobbs interview, 4 May 2005.

32 Ibid.

33 For an overview of the Ottawa-Edmonton energy battles of the 1970s and 1980s, see Bruce Doern and Glen Toner, *The Politics of Energy* (Toronto: Methuen, 1985).

34 Michael Ignatieff, 'Getting Iraq Wrong,' *New York Times Magazine*, 5 August 2007.

35 Theakston, 'Leadership in Whitehall,' 654.

# 8 Leadership and Province Building: Guy Coulombe in Quebec*

LUC BERNIER

While it is commonly agreed that the modern Quebec state was born after the death of Maurice Duplessis in 1959, little has been written about the public servants who helped make it happen. The Quiet Revolution, which was set in motion by the Liberal government of Jean Lesage in 1960, has acquired such a mythical status that, forty years later, Quebec governments are reluctant to change its institutions. It is true that some of the most important institutions of the modern Quebec state were created during the 1960s, but it is also important to note that these institutions did not become comprehensive and operational wholes until the 1970s.[1] If, from a political viewpoint, the Quiet Revolution took place in the period 1960–6, the administrative quiet revolution happened in the 1970s. There were thirty-four government departments and agencies created over the 1960s in Quebec and sixty-four over the following decade.[2] During the 1970s, it became necessary to coordinate the initiatives developed in the state apparatus. This decade was characterized by the entrepreneurial spirit of senior public servants who worked in a budgetary climate that was favourable to expansion and intervention. Certainly, political leadership made its mark. More important, however, was administrative leadership. State building owes much to civil servants and among them is Guy Coulombe, who transformed the core of the systems that made possible the management of an expanding state apparatus.

The state grew in mass and in function during the Quiet Revolution. Major Crown corporations, like Hydro-Québec and the Caisse de dépôt, ventured into new fields and began to require a greater degree of coordination in the 1970s.[3] Simultaneously, the departments in the Quebec government also spread their tentacles, creating new tensions between

Ottawa and Quebec City.[4] As long as Quebec did not fully occupy areas of provincial jurisdiction, there was little conflict with the federal government, but the situation would quickly change during the 1970s.[5]

The modern Quebec state was the product of a creative consensus between the political and the administrative. However, while some Quebec premiers have left an easily identifiable legacy, the same cannot be easily said of the public-sector executives who worked in their shadow.[6] Their work was indispensable once a decision had been made or a piece of legislation passed, but it was more discreet and, for students of administration, it is much more difficult to document in the Westminster tradition of parliamentary government.[7] Among the senior public servants who contributed to the construction of the Quebec state, Guy Coulombe stands as one of the most influential. He undoubtedly had one of the most successful careers among Quebec public servants of his generation. He has been honoured with many awards, including the prestigious Georges Vanier Medal of the Institute of Public Administration of Canada. Over his long career, he was appointed secretary to the Treasury Board and then secretary general of the cabinet (Executive Council) before becoming chief executive officer of two of the most important Quebec government corporations, the Société générale de financement and Hydro-Québec.

The role of the secretary to cabinet in Quebec, in which Coulombe's career is especially telling, has not been well analysed. This is equally true of the relationship between the political and the administrative leadership of the Quebec government. Some of those involved have left personal accounts.[8] Others have provided broader analyses.[9] Inevitably, the accounts left by secretaries general are coloured by their closeness to the premier they served. Coulombe has often been urged to write his memoirs but has chosen not to do so.

Coulombe's work as secretary to cabinet (known in Quebec as *secrétaire général du conseil exécutif*, but, for purposes of clarity, I will continue to refer to the post as secretary to cabinet) and the vision that informed it during the years of development of the Quebec state provides interesting insights into the evolution of the role and its place in a rapidly changing bureaucracy. Coulombe worked with two premiers – first with Robert Bourassa during the last years of his first period in office (1975–6), then with René Lévesque during the early years of his government (1976–8). Having been chosen by one premier, Coulombe won the trust of a radically different successor who had watched his work for many years from the opposition benches.

This chapter is divided into four sections. The first describes Coulombe's career path. The second examines his contribution to transforming the role of the secretary to cabinet. The third studies the role of secretary in light of the issue of non-partisanship. The fourth is concerned with the power of the secretary general relative to that of elected officials. According to Philip Selznick, 'the leader is an agent of institutionalization, offering a guiding hand to a process that would otherwise occur more haphazardly, more readily subject to the accidents of circumstance and history.'[10] My argument is that this was Coulombe's role in Quebec.

**Career Overview**

Guy Coulombe was born in Quebec City in 1936, into a comfortable upper-middle-class family. He studied with the Jesuits in Quebec City and then spent three years at the Trois-Rivières seminary. His education took a radically different turn as he entered his twenties, with his decision to start studies in social science at Laval University. Within a few years, he had enrolled in the PhD program in economic development at the University of Chicago.

Former federal cabinet minister Gérard Pelletier remembered the 1950s as 'Years of Impatience.' They were the same for Coulombe, who belongs to the generation that waited for things to change in Quebec. The beginnings of the Quiet Revolution lured him back to Quebec City with a number of jobs in economic development and as a result he did not complete his doctorate. His career began in 1963 at the Bureau d'aménagement de l'Est du Québec (roughly translated as the Eastern Quebec Development Bureau). From 1966 to 1969, he worked as director of regional development at the Office de planification et de développement du Québec (roughly translated as Quebec Planning and Development Bureau). The Quiet Revolution was tested in those days, and Coulombe was disappointed with the agenda of the Union Nationale government of Jean-Jacques Bertrand. He left for Ottawa to take up the post of assistant-deputy minister of supply and services in 1969–70. In 1970 he returned to work for the government of Quebec, first as assistant secretary of the Treasury Board and then, from 1973 to 1975, as the board's secretary. He was thirty-nine years old when he was promoted to secretary to cabinet later that year, a position he held until 1978, when he was appointed chief executive officer of the Société générale de financement. From 1982 to 1988, he was chief executive officer of Hydro-Québec.

Coulombe then left the public sector to become president and chief operating officer of Consolidated Bathurst. Between 1990 and 1995, he took on a number of different assignments: he was given the responsibility for setting up Montréal International, became president of TV5–Canada, was charged with leading negotiations with the Montagnais, headed the committee charged with creating the Centre hospitalier de l'Université de Montréal (CHUM), and was chief executive officer of the Société du centre des conférences internationales de Montréal. In 1996 he became director general of the Sûreté du Québec (the provincial police) and then, from 1999 to 2003, director general of the city of Montreal. In 2003–4 he was appointed chairman of the commission of inquiry into the management of Quebec's public forests. He sums up this varied career as mandarin, diplomat, health administrator, security chief, city manager, and inquiry commissioner as the product of pure luck, but it is clear that Coulombe's many leadership talents were sought in all corners of the province.

His career path raises the question of career management in the upper ranks of the public service in Quebec. Certainly, other public servants in Canada who have held senior posts have left the public service to work for public corporations and private companies. However, unlike, say, its British counterpart, where officials stay in the same position sometimes for decades, the Quebec public service has consistently lost some of its most effective executives fairly quickly. Indeed, Coulombe has worked for three decades after the ending of his tenure as secretary general of the Executive Council. Moreover, in what is an usual pattern in Canada, he was a leader in the public sector and became one in the private sector later in his career. He has served in the municipal, provincial, and federal civil service. Throughout, he has been a man of new systems of management, the leader who institutes order in chaotic organizational structures.

## Modernizing the Quebec Cabinet Office

Coulombe himself has argued that the organization of the Quebec state was not as advanced as that of the federal government in the 1960s and early 1970s. His ambition was to develop structures in Quebec City that would not entail excessive bureaucracy and red tape. Yet it was thought that the growth in government activities required the establishment of a modern system comparable to what was being done in Ottawa during the Trudeau regime. In Quebec City, files were routinely sent to cabinet with little briefing; it was the task of the representing minister to make his case. Robert Bourassa had little enthusiasm for the idea, but Coulombe established a system of ministerial committees that would allow cabinet some comfort in making decisions in context and laid the foundations for a modern management system. It was also during this period that the concept of program-planning budgeting systems (PPBS) was introduced. In Coulombe's view, one of the key duties of the secretary general was to make sure that the Executive Council did not become a bottleneck and that public policy was as cohesive as possible.

Cabinet committees were one thing; Coulombe came to the conclusion that the relationship between the premier and the cabinet secretary had to change also. In 1975, when Bourassa asked Coulombe to succeed Julien Chouinard, the position of secretary general had been in existence for only five years; it originated with the reform of the Financial Administration Act of 1969–70, legislation that was to change the core of the Quebec state and give birth to modern structures. Previously, Chouinard had acted strictly as clerk of the Executive Council, a role that was entirely different from that of secretary general but that Chouinard interpreted in a very legalistic, legislative manner. At the same time, he enjoyed considerable moral authority since he had been in the job since Jean Lesage was premier. That personal relationship had a strange effect on cabinet proceedings. Coulombe, who often attended cabinet meetings in his capacity as deputy secretary of Treasury Board (reporting to Michel Bélanger) or as deputy clerk (reporting to Chouinard), was often surprised to see Bourassa and Chouinard engaged in serious exchanges with each other during Executive Council meetings, virtually ignoring what others were saying.

Chouinard was a person of influence. He was always close to Jean Lesage, who exerted influence over the young Premier Bourassa, so nothing happened in the government without their consent. Coulombe sought to introduce more consistency and rigour to the collective approach of cabinet. In the estimation of Louis Bernard, who succeeded Coulombe as secretary to cabinet, Coulombe should be considered the first modern secretary to cabinet. Under his regime, files could move forward only if they were consistent with government policy. For a file to be submitted to the Executive Council, not only had it to be thoroughly prepared in terms of what it proposed, it also had to show that it had been constructed with an eye to the context so that it would not contradict other files. Coulombe convinced Bourassa, a few ministers, and senior public servants to establish an order of priority for economic files, in which the 'government was always involved in one way or another.' Certainly, there were limits to the extent to which he could formalize the decision-making process. Neither Bourassa nor Lévesque was enthusiastic about rigorous processes.[11]

Coulombe himself was concerned that, while rigour was required at meetings of the Executive Council, he did not want to make the system too rigid. The key was to stimulate the process so that the major development files could progress in a way that maintained a level of flexibility and was open to innovation. 'Too many structures and too much institutionalization cause a system to freeze,' he observes.[12] He had learned how a formalization process could go too far. (At the federal Department of Supply and Services, he worked with four directors general who were former army officers.) Finally, Coulombe also recognized that the era of limited institutionalization could not go on forever. Complex systems could not stay in a equilibrium. 'The mindset changed, and people got to know one another less as the government grew in size,' he notes. 'The era of entrepreneurship had given way to the era of bureaucratization.'

The secretary general must have a broad perspective unencumbered with details. Since he cannot anticipate everything, he must make decisions in a context of relative uncertainty. Policy coordination can become very complicated. The main thing is to move files along: 'I have always believed that you shouldn't try too hard to cover everything, to attempt to resolve all aspects of every problem. I have always been an advocate of what I call creative ambiguity -launching a process and relying on those involved to carry it through. The results can be surprisingly good.' He believes that waiting for all the answers leads only to indecisiveness: 'I have seen so many failures and so many files botched by an obsession with planning down to the tiniest detail.' He came up with a doctrine to counteract this tendency: 'Too much planning and anticipating is counter-productive. You need to have some core principles and place your trust in some competent subordinates.' This was the reasoning he applied when hiring deputy ministers. In interviews for the most senior positions, he would look for individuals who were able to differentiate between what was really important and what was secondary.

At the same time as he was formalizing all the processes, Coulombe played a significant role in orchestrating cabinet meetings. He drafted memoranda and constructed the agenda with the premier to ensure that the files submitted to the ministers were as complete and accurate as possible. He established a mechanism for screening proposals to the

Executive Council and created a preparatory agenda. Emergencies and urgent matters had to be dealt with. To ensure that memoranda submitted to cabinet were thorough, he introduced ministerial committees. In some instances, he would send the files back to ministers and senior officials for revisions. In the more difficult cases, he would ask the premier to intervene.

Coordination of the senior ranks was a key responsibility. One of the contributory factors in the success of public management during his career was what management experts have called a 'third place,' a neutral, informal setting where a group of individuals can meet to discuss a variety of issues. The place in Quebec City that served this purpose in Coulombe's time has assumed legendary status – the bar-restaurant of the George V Hotel on the Grande Allée. According to Coulombe, the 1970s saw the emergence of a solid core of senior officials committed to development. There were eight to ten deputy ministers in the group, the dean of which was Arthur Tremblay, and they would get together to 'change the world.' These informal gatherings were in addition to the formal monthly meetings of deputy ministers, at which the major issues and files were discussed.

Coulombe was secretary to cabinet at a time when the state was seen as a solution, not a problem. It was during this period that the Quebec education system was transformed, its health-care system established, and its infrastructure fortified. What Coulombe liked the most about his position in such a context was that he was involved in all facets of the development of Quebec at a time when that development was in the hands of the state alone – a large-scale francophone private sector did not yet exist. It was before Margaret Thatcher and Ronald Reagan came to power and the failures of the welfare state caused the tide to turn.

Another important duty of the secretary general is to help select deputy ministers. Sometimes, the people proposed by the secretary general, by the premier, or by ministers turned out to be bad choices. Lévesque had experience with such matters and took it all with a grain of salt. There is no officially established procedure, but at the time three methods were in use. In the first instance, an influential minister like Claude Castonguay would choose his own deputy. In some cases, a minister would complain to the premier about his deputy and the matter would be referred to the secretary general. The minister would explain the problem to Coulombe and, if necessary, a lateral transfer could be arranged. In some cases, after the issue was aired, the deputy minister concerned would stay in his position. Finally, there was the case of one deputy minister who told the new minister, a woman, that he was not interested in 'having a woman for a boss.' He was replaced in short order.

Today, appointments to senior positions are handled by a large team. In Coulombe's day, however, there was initially only one person doing the work. Nobody knew how many senior managers there were in the government; there was just an undifferentiated list of names. At the Treasury Board during his time as secretary, Coulombe recounts that appointments were handled in a peculiar fashion. Julien Chouinard and he would set salaries for each person on the list. At one point, his secretary informed him that they had missed five senior officials, to which he retorted: 'What do you mean, I missed five? Who are these people?' Once he became secretary general, he launched a process of rotating deputy ministers that would gather steam over time. According to him, some deputies who had been around for twenty or thirty years were wasting their own time and that of the administration. In addition, over the years, they had become friends with their subordinates, and so they could not make tough decisions. Moving six or seven deputy ministers at the same time was considered revolutionary. It also signalled the start of a proper process for appointing and supervising senior Quebec government officials, and the core of an appointments-coordination team was set up at this point.

As the chief public servant, Coulombe routinely managed specific problems as they arose – for example, situations where a minister could no longer work with the deputy minister or where a deputy minister was in difficulty. The work of the secretary general involved solving problems delegated to him by the premier. As Bourassa would say, the first step was always to 'talk to Coulombe.' Under the government that followed, the wording might be a little different: a minister would say, 'Lévesque told me that you would solve the problem.' In many situations, the secretary general's challenge was to reconcile what politicians wanted with the realities of public administration.

To improve the internal coordination of files within the Cabinet Office (or the Executive Council), Coulombe appointed a few assistant secretaries general to support council subcommittees. They did not have the rank of deputy minister, but they formed the core of a well-oiled coordination team, and his reforms would have a lasting impact. Amidst all the emergencies and problems, Coulombe worked on specific files that he considered to be priorities, such as the agricultural-zoning project. In so doing, he led by example. He managed difficult operational and policy files while simultaneously managing cabinet matters, the demands of the Premier's Office, and the never-ending crises of managing the senior ranks of bureaucracy.

André Trudeau, another celebrated senior official in the Quebec bureaucracy, said that Coulombe was the very definition of the 'boss.' Indeed, Coulombe was the boss of generations of public servants both before and after serving as secretary general. He embodied the calm demeanour of the great ship captain who reassures his crew when it is time to sail though a storm. It was he who organized the Quebec state at a time when doing so was of little interest to Quebec's premiers.

One more lesson can be learned from this mandarin, and it relates to work habits. It has been said and written that the workaholic Jacques Parizeau showed no compunction about phoning his political staff or officials in the middle of the night. Ministers and deputy ministers seemed to consider it a matter of principle to ask for reports on Friday evenings – reports that would be diligently prepared by subordinates over the weekend, and yet that neither the minister nor the deputy minister would consider on Monday morning. Coulombe famously resisted this habit and never made such requests except in times of major crisis. His record of accomplishment suggests that his management approach succeeded in creating commitment among the people around him.

After his departure, the Parti Québécois (PQ) government further complicated the structure of cabinet by establishing a number of 'super-ministries' or ministries of state. The super-ministries replaced the ministerial committees that Coulombe had established under Bourassa. Coulombe believed that appointing full-time ministers with no budget or clear authority would inevitably lead to infighting, counterproductive fiefdoms, and power struggles. The same results would follow from promoting assistant deputies to the rank of deputy minister. That being said, he considers that this type of structure was warranted for a time because the PQ was planning major reforms to the Election Act and legislation on the French language.

## Coulombe and Non-partisanship

Coulombe personified the politically neutral senior public-service official dedicated to serving the state, an official very different from the kind of figure who existed before 1960 and after Coulombe's time in government. As secretary general, he worked with both Robert Bourassa and René Lévesque. He saw no problem with this, since, as far as he was concerned, he, the premier, and the latter's political staff shared the same perspective: 'With respect to the political role, I had my own ways of dealing with the premiers. I was from an apolitical generation, but the situation is different today. Who the political boss was did not matter to me. He had been democratically elected. If he was completely incompetent, I could always quit.' In November 1976 he prepared the briefing books so that the new Parti Québécois government could quickly assume the mantle of government. The incoming ministers, it is said, looked forward to working with him.[13]

In order for the secretary to cabinet to perform his duties effectively, the premier's trust is critical. Coulombe enjoyed Bourassa's confidence. He had to earn Lévesque's, but he feels that, six months after the change in government, he had the same relationship with Lévesque as he had had with Bourassa. For six years, the PQ had watched all the senior officials working with the Liberal government. The new government was by no means convinced that these officials would be sympathetic to its cause, and in some cases it was right to be suspicious. In addition, it was taking power with a substantial agenda and plans to introduce major changes. At the same time, the new Lévesque government needed to draw on some experience – experience that only the senior officials who had worked for the outgoing government could provide.[14] In fact, they not only gave the PQ government the benefit of their experience but also supplied the files that were being prepared. For example, the Agricultural Zoning Act and the Automobile Insurance Act were popular reform measures introduced by the first Lévesque government, and both had been in preparation before it came to power.

As well as enjoying the premier's trust, the secretary general must be able to work with the premier's chief of staff. Coulombe found it relatively easy to adapt to Lévesque's arrival in the Premier's Office because he had forged friendships with Louis Bernard, Jean-Roch Boivin, and Mario Bertrand. Bernard had been a senior public servant in the 1960s but changed the trajectory of his career to work for the Parti Québécois when it was in opposition. Upon becoming premier, Lévesque made him his first chief of staff.[15] According to Coulombe, it was quickly agreed that Bernard would soon return to the public sector and succeed him as secretary to cabinet.

Coulombe chose to stay out of politics and says that he gave the same advice to each of the premiers with whom he worked. He and Bourassa had an unspoken code. At the end of Executive Council meetings, when the time came to talk politics, Bourassa would turn to him and say: 'I'm not going to offer you something to drink, I know your principles.' This was the signal that the secretary general's presence was no longer required. Coulombe, for his part, would say to Lévesque, 'Don't get me involved in the sovereignty file; you've got plenty of people working on it, like Louis Bernard. If it is OK with you, I won't attend meetings on this file.' Lévesque agreed. Coulombe was not always in total agreement with what the elected officials wanted to do, but he says that, in the final analysis, problems of conscience were few and far between, and that reports of conflict between ministers and senior officials in the early days of the PQ government were exaggerated. He adds that, while some files were more important to Bourassa, such as those relating to social order, and others, such as electoral reform, were more important to Lévesque, they were alike in their approach and their careful decision making. He also notes that Quebec society is highly consensus-based and that governments tend to continue the policies of their predecessors. The main problem for a deputy minister is not facing a moral dilemma but ending up with a minister who is not up to the challenge and with whom there is a clash of personalities.

One explanation for the neutrality of senior public servants during the late 1960s and early 1970s is that they were going through their second transition in six years. After the 1966 election, they continued under Daniel Johnson the work started under Jean Lesage, but they also experienced tougher times during the government of Jean-Jacques Bertrand. Three different parties exercised power within a six-year span. This situation was, if not unprecedented in Canada, at least very unusual.

## Managing Files

The secretary's work was focused on building and maintaining the machinery of government. This probably explains why, unless there was a crisis, Coulombe spoke with the premier only two or three times a week. He once told the premier: 'If I don't call you, it means that there are no files important enough for you to spend time on right now.' Even during the centralized collective-bargaining process, he rarely got involved. Similarly, he had only occasional contacts with private companies. He felt that the secretary general should keep his distance from lobbyists. He recounts a conversation he had with an executive who told him: 'I invite you to go hunting, you're not interested; I invite you to come and play golf, you're not interested; I invite you to Florida, you're not interested. What on earth do you do with your time?' Coulombe's answer was short and sweet: 'Don't you worry about what I do with my time.' He jokes that it was easy for him to preserve his virtue since he was never offered a bribe!

In the British parliamentary tradition, government officials play a discrete, faceless role. The institutions based on that tradition – institutions that Quebec did not choose – are the result more of a long period of historical development than of codified rules.[16] Convention requires that ministers be in the spotlight when the time comes to announce some good news. Senior public 'entrepreneurs' enjoy a lower profile than in the U.S. system, where high-ranking government managers like Robert Moses and David Lilienthal have become minor celebrities.[17] Officials make policies, but these policies bear their ministers' names. It is difficult to make officials who have been conditioned to work within such a model admit that they have played an entrepreneurial role. In fact, however, their impact is significant and far-reaching.[18]

In Coulombe's tenure, public-service executives took the lead on three critical issues: accelerating the works on the Olympic facilities in time for the 1976 summer Olympics in Montreal, the Land Use Planning and Development Act, and the Agricultural Zoning Act. The Olympic Games venture almost ended in catastrophe. Legislation had to be pushed through quickly to take over control from the city of Montreal, reorganize financing, and ensure execution. More generally speaking, such situations need a decisive politician with firm resolve. Coulombe gives the example of the zones d'exploitation contrôllée reform, which brought an end to private hunting and fishing clubs; in this instance, one minister's determination was a crucial factor. In the case of the Olympic facilities, Bourassa's trust was total. This was not to say that the public-service executives elbowed out the political. But, in Coulombe's opinion, there must always be two ball carriers to ensure rapid and sustainable progress: a minister who sets out a policy and a team of senior officials who draft and implement it.

This capacity for action and entrepreneurship existed because, in the 1970s, government budgets provided wide margins for manoeuvre. Another reason explaining the capacity for action, argues Coulombe, was the fact that structures were not yet fixed and ambitions faced few restrictions. Coulombe was a builder because he engineered the creation of modern decision-making structures for the Quebec state that were based on a formalization of procedures and, to a certain degree, a marginalization of the Department of Finance and the Treasury Board.

## Conclusion

Guy Coulombe defines the secretary general's role in a context of social and economic development, in addition to the legislative thrust of the position. It was the context of vibrant economic expansion that shaped him, from his earliest position at the Bureau d'aménagement de l'Est du Québec to his most recent job as a commissioner on the future of Quebec forestry. Throughout his career, his role has basically been one of promoting and overseeing social and economic development. Coulombe was the highest-ranking public servant during a period that was crucial for the development and organization of the Quebec state.

Coulombe's career shows that the secretary general of the government must at one and the same time be the premier's deputy minister, act as an expert on public policy, coordinate the efforts of the deputy ministers, and maintain contact with the world of politics while heading up the public service. Also important are Coulombe's views on the Treasury Board and the Department of Finance and on the key factors in hiring senior public servants, his work method, and the enjoyment he clearly derived from his work. While there may be no magic recipe, Guy Coulombe feels that three ingredients are key to the secretary's success: you must get to the heart of the matter, you must surround yourself with good people, and you must have a sense of humour!

The essence of positive leadership is not something obvious in the literature on the topic, as shown elsewhere in this book. It is something that transcends the barriers between the public and private sectors. In Coulombe's case, he has moved back and forth between both. He was a manager almost from the day he left his doctoral studies to become a civil servant. He was also a man of his time, a time when the cabinet had to be institutionalized in part but not entirely.[19] Would he be as suited to heading the civil service in 2007 in a world of horizontal policy making? Probably. When systematization of process was required, he provided it – though it was a subject that was of little interest to the premiers under whom he served. In this, he was doing the right thing at the right time. Today, he is still a respected leader towards whom successive governments turn when they need a problem solver. He is seen as someone who turns complex problems into simple issues.

NOTES

\* This text is based largely on three comprehensive interviews granted to the author by Guy Coulombe on 24 March, 14 April, and 21 April 2005. My thanks to the senior public servants who worked with Coulombe and who commented on previous drafts of this text, and to Michèle Bordeleau for transcribing the interviews. .

1 Luc Bernier, 'The Beleaguered State: Québec at the End of the 1990s,' in Keith Brownsey and Michael Howlett, eds., *The Provincial State in Canada* (Toronto: Broadview Press, 2001), 139–61.

2 See Carolle Simard and Luc Bernier, *L'administration publique* (Montreal: Boréal, 1992), 78.

3 Guy Lachapelle et al., eds., *The Quebec Democracy* (Toronto: McGraw-Hill, Ryerson, 1993); Kenneth McRoberts, *Quebec: Social Change and Political Crisis*, 3rd ed., with postscript (Toronto: McClelland, Stewart, 1993).

4 Jean-Jacques Simard, 'La longue marche des technocrats,' *Recherches sociographiques*, 18 (1977): 93–132.

5 Hubert Guindon, 'The Modernization of Quebec and the Legitimacy of the Canadian State,' in Daniel Glenday, Hubert Guindon, and Allan Turowetz, eds., *Modernization and the Canadian State* (Toronto: Macmillan, 1978), 212–46.

6 Luc Bernier, Keith Brownsey, and Michael Howlett, eds., *Executive Styles in Canada: Cabinet Structures and Leadership Practices in Canadian Government* (Toronto: University of Toronto Press, 2005); Claude Morin, *Mes premiers ministres* (Montreal: Boréal, 1991).

7 John W. Kingdon, *Agendas, Alternatives and Public Policies*, 2nd ed. (New York: Harper, Collins, 1995).

8 Daniel Latouche. 'La culture du pouvoir: le cabinet du premier minister,' in Gladys Symons, ed., *Questions de culture*, no. 14 (1988): 141–74; Morin, *Mes premiers ministres*.

9 Louis Bernard, *Réflexions sur l'art de se gouverner, essai d'un praticien* (Montreal: Québec/Amérique, 1987); Bernier, Brownsey, and Howlett, eds., *Executive Styles in Canada*; Martine Tremblay, *Derrière les portes closes: René Lévesque et l'exercice du pouvoir (1976–1985)* (Montreal: Québec/Amérique, 2006).

10 Philip Selznick, *Leadership in Administration* (Berkeley: University of California Press, 1957), 27.

11 Morin, *Mes premiers ministres*.

12 Interview with Guy Coulombe, Montreal, 14 April 2005.

13 See Tremblay, *Derrière les portes closes*, 67.

14  Graham Fraser, *René Lévesque and the Parti Québécois in Power*, 2nd ed. (Montreal: McGill-Queen's University Press, 2001).
15  On the Parti Québécois government, see ibid.
16  Bernard, *Réflexions sur l'art de se gouverner*, 14–15.
17  Taïeb Hafsi and Luc Bernier, 'Innovation et entrepreneurship dans la réforme du secteur public au Canada,' *Politiques et management public*, 23 (2006): 1–23.
18  Kevin Theakston, 'Comparative Biography and Leadership in Whitehall,' *Public Administration*, 75 (1997): 654.
19  See Luc Bernier, 'Who Governs in Québec? Revolving Premiers and Reforms,' in Bernier, Brownsey, and Howlett, eds., *Executive Styles in Canada*, 130–54.

# Conclusion:
# The Options and Futures of Secretaries
# to Cabinet

PATRICE DUTIL

Secretaries to cabinet seldom make the news much less provide entertainment, but there was a moment in the 1980s when British television viewers were introduced to the role in the form of Sir Humphrey Appleby in the BBC comedy series *Yes, Prime Minister*. Sir Humphrey's mastery of convention, habits, customs, and traditions was deployed to confuse endlessly the prime minister. The prime minister, Jim Hacker, in turn tried his best every week to outwit the secretary, mostly in vain. In one notable episode ('The Key'), however, Hacker suddenly realized that the secretary to cabinet had too much power and access to the Prime Minister's Office. Not satisfied merely to take Sir Humphrey's key to 10 Downing Street, the prime minister mused about removing from the clerk's duties the role of head of the home civil service. Worse than that, he considered giving the role to the dreaded Sir Frank Gordon, the permanent secretary of the Treasury and Sir Humphrey's rival. The panic in Sir Humphrey's eyes had all of Britain laughing (including Margaret Thatcher, the avowed 'number 1' fan of the series).

The fictional Prime Minister Hacker had no research on the secretary to cabinet to consider, only political ruse. But the episode did point to an issue that persists both in the United Kingdom and in Canada, even though it is not often discussed: What exactly is the role of the secretary to cabinet? The Gomery Commission, for the first time in Canada, suggested openly that the job of the secretary to cabinet was not effective and should effectively be split.

The role of secretaries to cabinet has changed dramatically over the past generation, and is likely to change even more in the coming years – but not in the direction Gomery had in mind. This is so for four main reasons. First, the complexities of problems facing the state challenge the rigidity of administrative 'silos' and compel public servants to integrate their efforts. Secondly, as various bureaucracies integrate their functions, a massive learning effort must be sustained in order to improve the management of risk and to fill the many operational and policy gaps that have emerged as governments simultaneously cope with the consequences of the cutbacks of the 1990s that haunt them still. (The massive contracts paid to private-sector consultants eloquently speak to this reality.) Thirdly, there will be a massive transition of authority from one generation of senior bureaucrats to another within a short span of time. Finally, both the public and the political apparatus will continue to demand more cohesion in government response. The office of the cabinet secretary has grown in all jurisdictions to meet these challenges and will continue to grow. In such a context, it is highly unlikely that the combined duties of clerk/secretary/head of the public service will change: most prime ministers will demand to have a cohesive, accountable 'head' of the public service to turn to for advice and to transmit directives.

There is room to debate the leadership role of secretaries to cabinet, however, and much more research needs to be published and discussions must widen. The contributors to this volume have described, dissected, and discussed some of the contexts in which the holders of this office have been able to develop their influence and exercise power. All of them, in some way, have asked if secretaries to cabinet can exercise true leadership on their own, or whether they are merely agents of the elected. All of them have tried to define what makes an effective head of the public service and have devised new ways to find answers to the questions surrounding the issue. What is the deciding factor? Is it personality, behaviour, or the particularities of situations? Is it the nature of the prime minister that is the deciding factor, or do the mood and aptitudes of the senior ranks of the public service make the difference?

All camps of students of leadership will find fodder for their cannons in these pages. What does become clear, however, is that the evolution of Canadian governance cannot be adequately comprehended without a consideration of the consequences (intended and otherwise) that arise from the actions of the men and women who hold the post of secretary to cabinet. Certainly, the features and functions of this position have changed, and these fit awkwardly into the broad business/political literature on leadership that has been created over the past forty years. Yet, taken together, the chapters in this book show that the public service has not been spared by new trends in the business-leadership literature. The

'New Public Management' movement has made demands on public-sector managers to improve productivity and accountability. Leadership traits today continue to place a high value on 'morals,' 'values,' and communication but must also include the ability to challenge the way things were done before, to re-examine existing assumptions critically, and to inspire a vision when unexpected downturns challenge an organization. Recognizing that 'followership' has changed dramatically since the time of Chester Barnard and Philip Selznick, students of leadership today are more concerned about maintaining legitimacy, focusing commitment, and delivering performance.

This book as a whole has probably not done justice to how politicized the office of the secretary to cabinet has become in many parts of the country. Often, the position is seen by party leaders as the representative of the elected to the bureaucracy, not vice-versa. This has become a consistent practice in most provinces, and more than one clerk of the Privy Council has been named in Ottawa because of known political sympathies. Secretaries to cabinet inevitably respond to a variety of impulses but their key tasks are to read political tea leaves. In their search for effective policy making and efficient delivery of operations, they must have a firm grasp of where political wishes intersect with the capacities of the public service. In this they must blend their political aptitudes with their administrative acumen. Increasingly, too, there are new pressures involved, in being an accountable chief executive whose leadership can be accepted, challenged, or simply ignored.

There is another emerging factor that must concern students of public-sector management: the impact of the continued centralization of critical decision making in government machinery. Anecdotal evidence abounds about encroaching central agencies dictating operational measures to departments, leaving seasoned executives merely to implement decisions taken elsewhere. This is where research can and must play a role. It is not clear how the leadership of secretaries to cabinet has been shaped by this new reality. The mysteries of leadership are endless, and, although much progress has been made in understanding how leadership succeeds and fails within the particular constraints of the private sector, the psychology of leadership and followership and the role of particular circumstances in shaping it still require research. The structures of power and hierarchy that have placed secretaries to cabinet in positions of authority are as sensitive as they are complex and often shrouded by conventions of secrecy and tradition.

The chapters in this volume aim to lift part of the veil on this unique form of leadership in the hope that, in doing so, they will lead to closer scrutiny, better understanding, and a deeper appreciation of the role of secretaries to cabinet. The book should be seen as a first step in this direction. Much still needs to be learned and reflected upon. The debates should be based on evidence, and the theory should be grounded in experience. Scholars should see the work of secretaries to cabinet both as significant and as not fully understood. The subject should be an important focus of scholars of public-service management and an ongoing concern for public servants themselves.

Secretaries to cabinet should make efforts at leaving records that reflect on their own lived experience. Certainly this is much to ask, but this form of feedback/learning is essential if a better understanding of their leadership is to be attained. A few clerks (Heeney, Robertson, Pitfield, Tellier) have written a little on their positions and their works are amply cited in this collection. There should be more. There are countless ways in which such records can be left, from recorded interviews to written memoirs (Alan Gotlieb's entertaining and intelligent *Washington Diary* has shown how this device can yield rich insights).[1] At a minimum, it should be required that secretaries to cabinet leave a good set of papers at the archives of their jurisdiction (subject to a suitably long seal). Their records are key ingredients in understanding how they perceived the impulses of the Prime Minister's Office, of cabinet members, and of those who reported to them.

As time shapes perspectives, it is to be hoped that we will gain a better appreciation and understanding of how leadership on the part of secretaries to cabinet was exercised in particular circumstances, that is, of what was done and, just as important, what was not done. In this collection, Brownsey, Bernier, and Rasmussen demonstrate that it is possible to document the works of secretaries to cabinet and from that to deduce some conclusions on the nature of their leadership. Scholars should be encouraged to do more in this area in order to deepen our understanding of how that leadership has evolved in time and place. The interrelationship of leadership and context is vitally important, and studies that take a deliberate historical perspective are likely to yield useful insights. The appendix to this book, listing the names of the secretaries to cabinet in Canadian history, will be a starting point.

The careers of secretaries to cabinet inevitably go through cycles that deserve to be understood and compared. Each secretary reaches heights of influence or power at a different time: the challenge is to identify the timing and circumstances of the high-water marks of authority. The reverse is also true: at points, the work and impact of the secretary to cabinet is of no relevance to the affairs of the state. The exact contours of the particular geography of power of the occupants of the position need to be outlined. By identifying the strengths and career patterns of secretaries to cabinet, we will be able to create a sense of proportion and perspective that should help students of public administration evaluate their performance in shaping the office they occupied and, perhaps more important, how they shaped the leadership that succeeded them. History and the perspective it offers can also offer insights into the leadership qualities each secretary to cabinet possessed. We know next to nothing about the psychology of the public-sector leadership in Canada and how it has evolved through the years.

Leadership is something that takes time to be appreciated and can be understood only if it is sufficiently discussed. Case studies of leadership in action, where secretaries to cabinet can be seen making critical decisions (or not), are imperative if our understanding is to approach anything like completeness. Written without the benefit of long perspectives, but while the topics are still 'alive,' case studies can help public servants to develop a better appreciation of the constraints that present themselves at the interface between the political and the administrative and at the apex of the various government department hierarchies. Studies of secretaries to cabinet as government faces a crisis, as the public-service leadership considers a new organizational strategy, or as new parties assume power (or indeed are about to yield it) will help to distinguish transactional leaders from transformative ones by focusing on particular decisions. Case studies are inevitably difficult to craft in light of cabinet secrecy imperatives, fears of embarrassment, and modesty, but they should be drafted, collected, and used in teaching.

Leadership is exercised; it is also accepted or rejected. It is important in the particular context of the Canadian public service to understand how perceptions of leadership are changing. This is of import in understanding the environment in which secretaries to cabinet operate. As pointed out in chapter 1, some jurisdictions have already begun to measure the 'trust' in leadership, and it is hoped that the courage to undertake such studies will not be discouraged with time. A better understanding of leadership, attained through interviews, focus groups, and questionnaires with all levels of the bureaucracy, will inevitably enrich our understanding of the leadership both of secretaries to cabinet and, obviously, of the bureaucracy as a whole.

The case has been made in the private sector, and indeed in many reaches of the public sector, that leadership matters and that, without it, success in any enterprise is unlikely. Leadership requires autonomy, discretion, and remarkable vision. The search for leadership can be a scholarly pursuit, but, more significantly, it is also a daily activity for individuals who work in Canada's public-service bureaucracies. There is an urgent need to shed better light on the conditions that breed effective leadership and – perhaps more important – on the factors that inhibit its development. In this effort of understanding, politicians, public servants, scholars, students, and journalists must play an active role. The work of secretaries to cabinet illuminates the health of the public service as much as its performance. As such, it is a vital link to a new understanding of the theory and practice of public administration in Canada and promises to be a deep new well of insight. It is hoped that this volume will have struck a rich vein of interest and that many others – scholars and practitioners – will join this most urgent conversation.

NOTE

1 *Washington Diaries, 1981–1989* (Toronto: McClelland and Stewart, 2007).

# Appendix:
# Secretaries to Cabinet, Clerks, and Deputy Ministers

**Government of Canada**
*Clerk of the Privy Council and Secretary to Cabinet*

| | |
|---|---|
| William Henry Lee | (1867–72) |
| William Alfred Himsworth | (1872–80) |
| Joseph-Olivier Côté | (1880–2) |
| John Joseph McGee | (1882–1907) |
| Rodolphe Boudreau | (1907–23) |
| Ernest-Joseph Lemaire | (1923–40) |
| Arnold Danford Patrick Heeney | (1940–9) |
| Norman Alexander Robertson | (1949–52) |
| John Whitney Pickersgill | (1952–3) |
| Robert Broughton Bryce | (1954–63) |
| Robert Gordon Robertson | (1963–75) |
| Peter Michael Pitfield | (1975–9, 1980–2) |
| Marcel Massé | (1979–80) |
| Gordon Francis Osbaldeston | (1982–5) |
| Paul M. Tellier | (1985–92) |
| Glen Scott Shortliffe | (1992–4) |
| Jocelyne Bourgon | (1994–9) |
| Mel Cappe | (1999–2002) |
| Alex Himelfarb | (2002–6) |
| Kevin Lynch | (2006– ) |

## Government of British Columbia*
*Executive Secretary, Cabinet Secretariat, Secretary, Cabinet Committee on Planning and Priorities***

| | | |
|---|---|---|
| David Krasnick | (1979–84) | *Executive Director, Cabinet Operations/ Secretary to Cabinet, Ministry of Inter- governmental Relations* |
| Bert Hick | (1984–7) | *Director, Cabinet Secretariat/Secretary to Cabinet* |
| Kathleen Mayoh | (1987–8) | *Director, Cabinet Secretariat* |
| Ann Newby | (1988–9) | *Deputy Minister and Secretary to the Executive Council* |
| Frank Rhodes | (1989–90) | *Deputy Minister and Secretary to the Executive Council* |
| David Emerson | (1990–1) | *Deputy Minister to the Premier (Responsible for Cabinet Operations, Policy, and Legislation and Intergovern- mental Relations)* |
| David Emerson | (1991) | *Deputy Minister to the Premier and Secretary to the Executive Council* |
| George Ford | (1991–3) | *Deputy Minister to the Premier, Executive Council Operations, and Secretary to the Executive Council with Responsibility for the Cabinet Planning Secretariat* |
| Doug McArthur | (1993–6) | *Deputy Minister to the Premier and Cabinet Secretary* |
| Doug McArthur | (1996–7) | *Secretary to the Executive Council* |
| Eloise Spitzer | (1997–9) | *Secretary to the Executive Council/Cabinet Secretary, Office of the Premier* |
| Joy Illington | (1999–2001) | *Deputy Minister to the Premier and Cabinet Secretary* |
| Ken Dobell | (2001–5) | |
| Jessica McDonald | (2005– ) | |

*Prepared by Nancy Chapman, reference librarian, Government of British Columbia. Thanks also to Sandy Wharf, director, Corporate Priorities and Performance Management, Office of the Deputy Minister to the Premier and Cabinet Secretary.

**In 1979 the Cabinet Secretariat became a division of the new Ministry of Intergovern- mental Relations. In 1982 the position of secretary to cabinet was created in the Office of the Premier and in 1983 the position was transferred to the Ministry of Intergovernmental Relations.

## Government of Alberta
*Deputy Minister of Executive Council, Secretary to Cabinet, Clerk to Executive Council*

| | |
|---|---|
| John Kenneth MacDonald | (1905) |
| Murdock James MacLeod | (1906–10) |
| John A. Reid | (1911) |
| Donald Baker | (1912–17) |
| John D. Hunt | (1917–34) |
| R.A. Andison | (1935–43) |
| C.A Dacre | (1944–53) |
| R. Crenolin | (1954) |
| M.J. Wright | (1954–9) |
| R. Crenolin | (1962–5) |
| G. MacDonald | (1967–71) |
| Darren C. Graves | (1971) |
| Harry Hobbs | (1974–83) |
| George de Rappard | (1983–6) |
| Barry Mellon | (1986–93) |
| Vance MacNichol | (1993–7) |
| John Charles Davies | (1997–9) |
| Julian Nowicki | (1999–2004) |
| Ron Hicks | (2004– ) |

## Government of Saskatchewan*
*Secretaries to the Cabinet***

| | |
|---|---|
| Derek Robert Bedson | (1982–3) |
| [Grenville Smith-Windsor] | (1983–4) |
| Norman Riddell | (1984–8) |
| [Larry Martin] | (1988) |
| Larry Martin | (1988–9) |
| Stan Sojonky | (1989–91) |
| [Wesley Gustav Bolstad] | (1991–2) |
| Ronald S. Clark | (1992–4) |
| Francis Jerome Bogdasavich | (1994–6) |
| [Marianne Weston] | (1996–7) |
| Gregory Marchildon | (1997–2000) |
| [Marianne Weston] | (2000–1) |

*Deputy Ministers to the Premier, 1977–82; 2001–*

| | |
|---|---|
| Wesley Gustav Bolstad | (1977–9) |
| Dennis Murray Wallace | (1979–80) |
| John Earl Sinclair | (1980–2) |
| Dan Perrins | (2001–7) |
| Garvin Garnet | (2007– ) |

*Cabinet Secretaries, 1950–82; 2001–*

| | |
|---|---|
| Horace Stanley (Tim) Lee*** | (1950–64) |
| Joseph Ronald Lindsey (Ron) Parrott *** | (1964–7) |
| Thomas Robert Michael Wood *** | (1967–9) |
| Michael Arthur de Rosenroll *** | (1969–71) |
| Gerry Wilson | (1971–2) |
| K.O. (Keith) Saddlemyer | (1972–3) |
| Wesley Gustav Bolstad | (1973–7) |
| John Scratch | (1977–9) |
| Wesley Gustav (Wes) Bolstad | (1979–80) |
| Grant C. Mitchell | (1980–1) |
| Florence Wilkie | (1981–2) |
| Judy Samuelson*** | (2001– ) |

*Produced by Gregory Marchildon
**Fused position of deputy minister to the premier and cabinet secretary, 1982–2000 (acting in square brackets)
***Individual held position of clerk of the Executive Council simultaneously, except for Tim Lee, who was appointed clerk only on 1 December 1956 but held the position along with the job of cabinet secretary until his departure on 31 August 1964. Unlike the clerk of the Executive Council, the position of cabinet secretary was not a position appointed under legislation and therefore the dates of appointment are not precisely tracked despite the fact that the position of cabinet secretary ranks considerably higher in terms of responsibility than that of clerk of the Executive Council in the Saskatchewan system.

## Government of Manitoba*
*Clerk of Executive Council*

| | |
|---|---|
| Sedley Blanchard | (1871–6) |
| F.G. Becher | (1876–7) |
| Alexander Begg | (1877–8) |

| A Gélinas | (1878) |
|---|---|
| Rice M. Howard | (1878–8?) |
| John McBeth | (188?–4) |
| C.A. Sadlier | (1884–9) |
| Christopher Graburn | (1889–1908) |
| Malcolm McLean | (1909–16) |
| Peter Whimster | (1916–19) |
| Frederick Axford | (1919–33) |
| John Leslie Johnston | (1933–7) |
| Adjutor P. Talbot | (1937–48) |
| Robert E. Moffat | (1948–52) |
| Orville M. Kay | (1952–8) |
| Derek R. Bedson | (1958–81) |
| Michael B. Decter | (1981–6) |
| George H. Ford | (1986–8) |
| Donald Leitch | (1988–99) |
| Jim Eldridge | (1999–2005) |
| Paul Vogt | (2005– ) |

*Produced by Sue Bishop, executive director and legislative librarian, and F.B. Rick MacLowick, head, Reference Services, Legislative Library of Manitoba.

## Government of Ontario
*Secretary to Cabinet*

| Lorne McDonald | (1948–53) |
|---|---|
| William McIntyre | (1953–69) |
| John K. Reynolds | (1969–71) |
| Carl E. Brannan | (1971–3) |
| James D. Fleck | (1974–5) |
| Edward E. Stewart | (1976–85) |
| James D. Fleck | (1974–5) |
| Robert Carman | (1985–9) |
| Peter Barnes | (1989–92) |
| David Agnew | (1992–5) |
| Rita Burak | (1995–2000) |
| Andromache Karakatsanis | (2000–2) |
| Tony Dean | (2002–8) |
| Shelly Jamieson | (2008– ) |

## Government of Quebec*
*General Secretary and Clerk of Executive Council*
*(Secrétaire général et Greffier, Ministère du Conseil exécutif)*

| | |
|---|---|
| Georges Manley Muir | (1867) |
| Félix Fortier | (1867–82) |
| Joseph-Adolphe Defoy | (1882–7) |
| Gustave Grenier | (1887–1912) |
| William Learmonth | (1912–13) |
| Alfred Morriset | (1913–54) |
| Léopold Desilets | (1954–65) |
| Jacques Prémont | (1965–9) |
| Julien Chouinard | (1968–75) |
| Guy Coulombe | (1975–8) |
| Louis Bernard | (1978–85) |
| Roch Bolduc | (1985–6) |
| Benoît Morin | (1986–94) |
| Louis Bernard | (1994–6) |
| Michel Carpentier | (1996–8) |
| Michel Noel de Tilly | (1998–2001) |
| Jean St-Gelais | (2001–3) |
| André Dicaire | (2003–6) |
| Gérard Bibeau | (2006– ) |

*Produced by Jacques Bourgault

## Government of New Brunswick
*Clerks to the Executive Council*

| | |
|---|---|
| John C. Allen | (1851–5) |
| F.A.H. Straton | (1856–1900) |
| Joseph Howe Dickson | (1901–17) |
| Miles B. Dixon | (1918–32) |
| H. Lester Smith | (1933–5) |
| J.B. Dickson | (1936–49) |
| H.W. Hickman | (1950–60) |
| M.M. Hoyt | (1962–78) |
| Harry Nason | (1979–94) |
| Claire Morris | (1995–9) |

| Jean-Guy Finn | (1999–2001) |
| Kevin Malone | (2001–5) |
| Maurice Bernier | (2006–7) |
| David W. Ferguson | (2007– ) |

## Government of Nova Scotia
*Clerk of the Executive Council*

| C.L. Beazley | (1959–66) |
| Innis G. MacLeod | (1966–9) |
| Gordon H. Davidson | (1969–72) |
| H.F.G. Stevens | (1972–91) |
| H.F.G. Stevens | (1972–91) |
| Alison Scott | (1992–4) |
| Alison Scott | (1994) |
| Brenda Shannon | (1994–5) |
| Brenda Shannon | (1995–7) |
| James G. Spurr | (1997–2001) |
| Alison Scott | (2001–4) |
| Paul LaFleche | (2004–7) |
| Robert C. Fowler | (2007– ) |

*Secretary to the Executive Council*

| F.R. Drummie | (1970–2) |
| Innis G. MacLeod | (1972–6) |
| Robert MacKay | (1976) |
| J.H. Clarke | (1979) |
| L. Jerry Redmond | (1985–6) |
| Michael Kontak | (1986–9) |
| G.D. Mendleson | (1989–91) |
| Alison Scott | (1991–3) |
| D. William MacDonald | (1993–5) |
| Robert MacKay | (1995–7) |
| Suzan MacLean | (1997–9) |
| Alison Scott | (1999–2002) |
| Vicki Harnish | (2002–3) |
| Paul LaFleche | (2003–7) |
| Robert C. Fowler | (2007– ) |

## Government of Prince Edward Island
*Clerk of the Executive Council*

| | |
|---|---|
| Earle K. Kennedy | (1965–72) |
| Doug Boylan | (1971–2) |
| Diane Blanchard | (1988–90) |
| Keith Wornell | (1990–2) |
| Charles Campbell | (1992–3) |
| R. Allan Rankin | (1993–4) |
| Barry MacMillan | (1995–6) |
| Verna Bruce | (1996–7) |
| Lynn Ellsworth | (1997–2004) |
| W. Alexander (Sandy) Stewart | (2004–7) |
| Allan Rankin | (2007– ) |

## Government of Newfoundland and Labrador
*Clerks to the Executive Council*

| | |
|---|---|
| W.J. Carew | (1949) |
| W.J. Marshall | (1949–55) |
| James G. Channing | (1955–68) |
| Robert J. Jenkins | (1968–78) |
| D.A. Vardy | (1978–85) |
| H.M Clarke | (1985–9) |
| Halcum H Stanley | (1988–94) |
| Frederick G. Way | (1994) |
| Robert J. Jenkins | (1994–6) |
| Malcolm Rowe | (1996–9) |
| John Cummings | (1999–2000) |
| Gary Norris | (2000–1) |
| Deborah Fry | (2001–3) |
| Robert Thompson | (2003–7) |
| Gary Norris | (2007– ) |

# The Institute of Public Administration of Canada Series in Public Management and Governance